PAPERS ON THE

SCIENCE OF ADMINISTRATION

PAPERS ON THE SCIENCE OF ADMINISTRATION

BY
LUTHER GULICK, L. URWICK, JAMES D. MOONEY
HENRI FAYOL, HENRY S. DENNISON, L. J. HENDERSON
T. N. WHITEHEAD, ELTON MAYO, MARY P. FOLLETT
JOHN LEE, V. A. GRAICUNAS

Edited by
LUTHER GULICK and L. URWICK

AUGUSTUS M. KELLEY · PUBLISHERS
CLIFTON 1973

First Edition 1937

Second Edition 1947

(*New York*: Institute of Public Administration, 1947)

REPRINTED 1969 & 1972 BY

AUGUSTUS M. KELLEY · PUBLISHERS

REPRINTS OF ECONOMIC CLASSICS

CLIFTON NEW JERSEY 07012

Gulick, Luther Halsey, 1892–   *ed.*
  Papers on the science of administration, by Luther Gulick
[and others] Edited by Luther Gulick and L. Urwick.
New York, A. M. Kelley, 1969.
    195 p. illus. 28 cm. (Reprints of economic classics)
    First published in 1937.
    Bibliographical footnotes.
    CONTENTS.—Notes on the theory of organization, by L. Gulick.—
Organization as a technical problem, by L. Urwick.—The principles
of organization, by J. D. Mooney.—The administrative theory in the
state, by H. Fayol.—The function of administration, with special
reference to the work of Henri Fayol, by L. Urwick.—The need for
the development of political science engineering, by H .S. Dennison.—
The effects of social environment, by L. J. Henderson, T. N. Whitehead and E. Mayo.—The process of control, by M. P. Follett.—The
pros and cons of functionalization, by J. Lee.—Relationship in organization, by V. A. Graicunas.—Science, values, and public administration, by L. Gulick.

    1. Organization. 2. Public administration—Addresses, essays, lec-
tures.   I. Urwick, Lyndall Fownes, 1891–   joint ed. II. Title.

JF1351.G8 1969   658   68–55727
ISBN 0-678-00512-5   MARC
Library of Congress   [10-2]

PRINTED IN THE UNITED STATES OF AMERICA
by SENTRY PRESS, NEW YORK, N. Y. 10013

FOREWORD

The papers brought together in this collection are essays by men scientifically interested in the phenomena of administration. Most of these writers did their thinking independently, in some cases without any acquaintance with the others, or with their writings. The striking similarity and harmony of the analyses, nomenclature, and hypotheses, frequently set forth as principles, is thus doubly significant.

Few of these papers have been published or publicly circulated in such a way as to make them accessible to practical administrators, scholars, or students. The immediate occasion for this publication is the fact that no copies of the essential papers in this collection could be found in any library in Washington at the time when the President's Committee on Administrative Management required these documents for the use of members of its research staff.

In considering the proper content of this volume and in securing the permission of the authors, or of their executors and heirs, for publication, it was only natural to draw into the enterprise as associate editor L. Urwick. His contributions speak for themselves.

It is the hope of the editors that the availability of these papers will advance the analysis of administration, assist in the development of a standard nomenclature, encourage others to criticize the hypotheses with regard to administration herein set forth and to advance their own concepts fearlessly, and to point the way to areas greatly in need of exploration. If those who are concerned scientifically with the phenomena of getting things done through co-operative human endeavor will proceed along these lines, we may expect in time to construct a valid and accepted theory of administration.

This collection does not include anything from the writings of F. A. Cleveland, Charles A. Beard, and A. E. Buck, whose works are well known, unless it is in my own papers which grow directly from long years of association with them; nor from W. F. Willoughby, Leonard D. White, Marshall Dimock or John Gaus, all of whom have recently published books or essays dealing with administration, in a form easily accessible to all.

We are indebted to the authors, and to their heirs and agents, for permitting this publication of their pioneer works without expectation of royalty or reward, and to Miss Sarah Greer for the excellent translation of Henri Fayol's paper, The Administrative Theory in the State, which has not heretofore appeared in English.

Administrators, scholars and students of the logic of administration who find this collection of value, must render their chief thanks to Miss Greer, who from her vantage point as librarian of the Institute of Public Administration, insisted that this collection was necessary, and who put back of the project that tireless pressure and devotion which is necessary to the accomplishment of any worthwhile purpose.

L. G.

New York City, June, 1937

CONTENTS

I

NOTES ON THE THEORY OF ORGANIZATION

WITH SPECIAL REFERENCE TO
GOVERNMENT IN THE UNITED STATES

By

LUTHER GULICK

Director, Institute of Public Administration
Eaton Professor of Municipal Science and Administration
Columbia University

A MEMORANDUM PREPARED AS A MEMBER OF THE
PRESIDENT'S COMMITTEE ON ADMINISTRATIVE MANAGEMENT
DECEMBER, 1936

Revised June, 1937

NOTES ON THE THEORY OF ORGANIZATION

Every large-scale or complicated enterprise requires many men to carry it forward. Wherever many men are thus working together the best results are secured when there is a division of work among these men. The theory of organization, therefore, has to do with the structure of co-ordination imposed upon the work-division units of an enterprise. Hence it is not possible to determine how an activity is to be organized without, at the same time, considering how the work in question is to be divided. Work division is the foundation of organization; indeed, the reason for organization.

1. THE DIVISION OF WORK

It is appropriate at the outset of this discussion to consider the reasons for and the effect of the division of work. It is sufficient for our purpose to note the following factors.

Why Divide Work?

Because men differ in nature, capacity and skill, and gain greatly in dexterity by specialization;

Because the same man cannot be at two places at the same time;

Because one man cannot do two things at the same time;

Because the range of knowledge and skill is so great that a man cannot within his life-span know more than a small fraction of it. In other words, it is a question of human nature, time, and space.

In a shoe factory it would be possible to have 1,000 men each assigned to making complete pairs of shoes. Each man would cut his leather, stamp in the eyelets, sew up the tops, sew on the bottoms, nail on the heels, put in the laces, and pack each pair in a box. It might take two days to do the job. One thousand men would make 500 pairs of shoes a day. It would also be possible to divide the work among these same men, using the identical hand methods, in an entirely different way. One group of men would be assigned to cut the leather, another to putting in the eyelets, another to stitching up the tops, another to sewing on the soles, another to nailing on the heels, another to inserting the laces and packing the pairs of shoes. We know from common sense and experience that there are two great gains in this latter process: first, it makes possible the better utilization of the varying skills and aptitudes of the different workmen, and encourages the development of specialization; and second, it eliminates the time that is lost when a workman turns from a knife, to a punch, to a needle and awl, to a hammer, and moves from table to bench, to anvil, to stool. Without any pressure on the workers, they could probably turn out twice as many shoes in a single day. There would be additional economies, because inserting laces and packing could be assigned to unskilled and low-paid workers. Moreover, in the cutting of the leather there would be less spoilage because the less skillful pattern cutters would all be eliminated and assigned to other work. It would also be possible to cut a dozen shoe tops at the same time from the same pattern with little additional effort. All of these advances would follow, without the introduction of new labor saving machinery.

The introduction of machinery accentuates the division of work. Even such a simple thing as a saw, a typewriter, or a transit requires increased specialization, and serves to divide workers into those who can and those who cannot use the particular instrument effectively. Division of work on the basis of the tools and machines used in work rests no doubt in part on aptitude, but primarily upon the development and maintenance of skill through continued manipulation.

Specialized skills are developed not alone in connection with machines and tools. They evolve naturally from the materials handled, like wood, or cattle, or paint, or cement. They arise similarly in activities which center in a complicated series of inter-related concepts, principles, and techniques. These are most clearly recognized in the professions, particularly those based on the application of scientific knowledge, as in engineering, medicine, and chemistry. They are none the less equally present in law, ministry, teaching, accountancy, navigation, aviation, and other fields.

The nature of these subdivisions is essentially pragmatic, in spite of the fact that there is an element of logic underlying them. They are therefore subject to a gradual evolution with the advance of science, the invention of new machines, the progress of technology and the change of the social system. In the last analysis, however, they appear to be based upon differences in individual human beings. But it is not to be concluded that the apparent stability of "human nature," whatever that may be, limits the probable development of specialization. The situation is quite the reverse. As each field of knowledge and work is advanced, constituting a continually larger and more complicated nexus of related principles, practices and skills, any individual will be less and less able to encompass it and maintain intimate knowledge and facility over the entire area, and there will thus arise a more minute specialization because knowledge and skill advance while man stands still. Division of work and inte-grated organization are the bootstraps by which mankind lifts itself in the process of civilization.

The Limits of Division

There are three clear limitations beyond which the division of work cannot to advantage go. The first is practical and arises from the volume of work involved in man-hours. Nothing is gained by subdividing work if that further subdivision results in setting up a task which requires less than the full time of one man. This is too obvi-ous to need demonstration. The only exception arises where space interferes, and in such cases the part-time expert must fill in his spare time at other tasks, so that as a matter of fact a new combination is introduced.

The second limitation arises from technology and custom at a given time and place. In some areas nothing would be gained by separating undertaking from the cus-tody and cleaning of churches, because by custom the sexton is the undertaker; in build-ing construction it is extraordinarily difficult to re-divide certain aspects of electrical and plumbing work and to combine them in a more effective way, because of the juris-dictional conflicts of craft unions; and it is clearly impracticable to establish a division of cost accounting in a field in which no technique of costing has yet been developed.

This second limitation is obviously elastic. It may be changed by invention and by education. If this were not the fact, we should face a static division of labor. It should be noted, however, that a marked change has two dangers. It greatly restricts the labor market from which workers may be drawn and greatly lessens the opportunities open to those who are trained for the particular specialization.

The third limitation is that the subdivision of work must not pass beyond physical division into organic division. It might seem far more efficient to have the front half of the cow in the pasture grazing and the rear half in the barn being milked all of the time, but this organic division would fail. Similarly there is no gain from splitting a single movement or gesture like licking an envelope, or tearing apart a series of intimately and intricately related activities.

It may be said that there is in this an element of reasoning in a circle; that the test here applied as to whether an activity is organic or not is whether it is divisible or not — which is what we set out to define. This charge is true. It must be a pragmatic test. Does the division work out? Is something vital destroyed and lost? Does it bleed?

The Whole and the Parts

It is axiomatic that the whole is equal to the sum of its parts. But in dividing up any "whole," one must be certain that every part, including unseen elements and relationships, is accounted for. The marble sand to which the Venus de Milo may be reduced by a vandal does not equal the statue, though every last grain be preserved; nor is a thrush just so much feathers, bones, flesh and blood; nor a typewriter merely so much steel, glass, paint and rubber. Similarly a piece of work to be done cannot be subdivided into the obvious component parts without great danger that the central design, the operating relationships, the imprisoned idea, will be lost.

A simple illustration will make this clear. One man can build a house. He can lay the foundation, cut the beams and boards, make the window frames and doors, lay the floors, raise the roof, plaster the walls, fit in the heating and water systems, install the electric wiring, hang the paper, and paint the structure. But if he did, most of the work would be done by hands unskilled in the work; much material would be spoiled, and the work would require many months of his time. On the other hand, the whole job of building the house might be divided among a group of men. One man could do the foundation, build the chimney, and plaster the walls; another could erect the frame, cut the timbers and the boards, raise the roof, and do all the carpentry; another all the plumbing; another all the paper hanging and painting; another all the electric wiring. But this would not make a house unless someone — an architect — made a plan for the house, so that each skilled worker could know what to do and when to do it.

When one man builds a house alone he plans as he works; he decides what to do first and what next, that is, he "co-ordinates the work." When many men work together to build a house this part of the work, the co-ordinating, must not be lost sight of.

In the "division of the work" among the various skilled specialists, a specialist in planning and co-ordination must be sought as well. Otherwise, a great deal of time may be lost, workers may get in each other's way, material may not be on hand when needed, things may be done in the wrong order, and there may even be a difference of opinion as to where the various doors and windows are to go. It is self-evident that the more the work is subdivided, the greater is the danger of confusion, and the greater is the need of overall supervision and co-ordination. Co-ordination is not something that develops by accident. It must be won by intelligent, vigorous, persistent and organized effort.

2. THE CO-ORDINATION OF WORK

If subdivision of work is inescapable, co-ordination becomes mandatory. There is, however, no one way to co-ordination. Experience shows that it may be achieved in two primary ways. These are:

1. By organization, that is, by interrelating the subdivisions of work by allotting them to men who are placed in a structure of authority, so that the work may be co-ordinated by orders of superiors to subordinates, reaching from the top to the bottom of the entire enterprise.

2. By the dominance of an idea, that is, the development of intelligent singleness of purpose in the minds and wills of those who are working together as a group, so that each worker will of his own accord fit his task into the whole with skill and enthusiasm.

These two principles of co-ordination are not mutually exclusive, in fact, no enterprise is really effective without the extensive utilization of both.

Size and time are the great limiting factors in the development of co-ordination. In a small project, the problem is not difficult; the structure of authority is simple, and the central purpose is real to every worker. In a large complicated enterprise, the organization becomes involved, the lines of authority tangled, and there is danger that the workers will forget that there is any central purpose, and so devote their best energies only to their own individual advancement and advantage.

The interrelated elements of time and habit are extraordinarily important in co-ordination. Man is a creature of habit. When an enterprise is built up gradually from small beginnings the staff can be "broken in" step by step. And when difficulties develop, they can be ironed out, and the new method followed from that point on as a matter of habit, with the knowledge that that particular difficulty will not develop again. Routines may even be mastered by drill as they are in the army. When, however, a large new enterprise must be set up or altered overnight, then the real difficulties of co-ordination make their appearance. The factor of habit, which is thus an important foundation of co-ordination when time is available, becomes a serious handicap when time is not available, that is, when change rules. The question of co-ordination therefore must be approached with different emphasis in small and in large enterprises; in simple and in complex situations; in stable and in new or changing organizations.

Co-ordination Through Organization

Organization as a way of co-ordination requires the establishment of a system of authority whereby the central purpose or objective of an enterprise is translated into reality through the combined efforts of many specialists, each working in his own field at a particular time and place.

It is clear from long experience in human affairs that such a structure of authority requires not only many men at work in many places at selected times, but also a single directing executive authority.[1] The problem of organization thus becomes the problem of building up between the executive at the center and the subdivisions of work on the periphery an effective network of communication and control.

The following outline may serve further to define the problem:

I. First Step: Define the job to be done, such as the furnishing of pure water to all of the people and industries within a given area at the lowest possible cost;

II. Second Step: Provide a director to see that the objective is realized;

III. Third Step: Determine the nature and number of individualized and specialized work units into which the job will have to be divided. As has been seen above, this subdivision depends partly upon the size of the job (no ultimate subdivision can generally be so small as to require less than the full time of one worker) and upon the status of technological and social development at a given time;

IV. Fourth Step: Establish and perfect the structure of authority between the director and the ultimate work subdivisions.

It is this fourth step which is the central concern of the theory of organization. It is the function of this organization (IV) to enable the director (II) to co-ordinate and energize all of the sub-divisions of work (III) so that the major objective (I) may be achieved efficiently.

The Span of Control

In this undertaking, we are confronted at the start by the inexorable limits of human nature. Just as the hand of man can span only a limited number of notes on the piano, so the mind and will of man can span but a limited number of immediate managerial contacts. The problem has been discussed brilliantly by Graicunas in his paper included in this collection. The limit of control is partly a matter of the limits of knowledge, but even more is it a matter of the limits of time and of energy. As a result the executive of any enterprise can personally direct only a few persons. He must depend upon these to direct others, and upon them in turn to direct still others, until the last man in the organization is reached.

This condition placed upon all human organization by the limits of the span of control obviously differs in different kinds of work and in organizations of different sizes. Where the work is of a routine, repetitive, measurable and homogeneous character, one man can perhaps direct several score workers. This is particularly true when the workers are all in a single room. Where the work is diversified, qualitative, and particularly when the workers are scattered, one man can supervise only a few. This diversification, dispersion, and non-measurability is of course most evident at the

---

[1] I.e., when *organization is the basis of co-ordination*. Wherever the central executive authority is composed of several who exercise their functions jointly by majority vote, as on a board, this is from the standpoint of organization still a "single authority"; where the central executive is in reality composed of several men acting freely and independently, then organization cannot be said to be the basis of co-ordination; it is rather the dominance of an idea and falls under the second principle stated above.

very top of any organization. It follows that the limitations imposed by the span of control are most evident at the top of an organization, directly under the executive himself.

But when we seek to determine how many immediate subordinates the director of an enterprise can effectively supervise, we enter a realm of experience which has not been brought under sufficient scientific study to furnish a final answer. Sir Ian Hamilton says, "The nearer we approach the supreme head of the whole organization, the more we ought to work towards groups of three; the closer we get to the foot of the whole organization (the Infantry of the Line), the more we work towards groups of six." [2]

The British Machinery of Government Committee of 1918 arrived at the conclusion that "The Cabinet should be small in number — preferably ten or, at most, twelve." [3]

Henri Fayol said "[In France] a minister has twenty assistants, where the Administrative Theory says that a manager at the head of a big undertaking should not have more than five or six." [4]

Graham Wallas expressed the opinion that the Cabinet should not be increased "beyond the number of ten or twelve at which organized oral discussion is most efficient." [5]

Léon Blum recommended for France a Prime Minister with a technical cabinet modelled after the British War Cabinet, which was composed of five members. [6]

It is not difficult to understand why there is this divergence of statement among authorities who are agreed on the fundamentals. It arises in part from the differences in the capacities and work habits of individual executives observed, and in part from the non-comparable character of the work covered. It would seem that insufficient attention has been devoted to three factors, first, the element of diversification of function; second, the element of time; and third, the element of space. A chief of public works can deal effectively with more direct subordinates than can the general of the army, because all of his immediate subordinates in the department of public works will be in the general field of engineering, while in the army there will be many different elements, such as communications, chemistry, aviation, ordnance, motorized service, engineering, supply, transportation, etc., each with its own technology. The element of time is also of great significance as has been indicated above. In a stable organization the chief executive can deal with more immediate subordinates than in a new or changing organization. Similarly, space influences the span of control. An organization located in one building can be supervised through more immediate subordinates than can the same organization if scattered in several cities. When scattered there is not only need for more supervision, and therefore more supervisory personnel, but also for a fewer number of contacts with the chief executive because of

---

[2] Sir Ian Hamilton, "The Soul and Body of an Army." Arnold, London, 1921, p. 230.

[3] Great Britain. Ministry of Reconstruction. Report of the Machinery of Government Committee. H. M. Stationery Office, London, 1918, p. 5.

[4] Henri Fayol, "The Administrative Theory in the State." Address before the Second International Congress of Administrative Science at Brussels, September 13, 1923. Paper IV in this collection.

[5] Graham Wallas, "The Great Society." Macmillan, London and New York, 1919, p. 264.

[6] Léon Blum, "La Réforme Gouvernementale." Grasset, Paris, 1918. Reprinted in 1936, p. 59.

the increased difficulty faced by the chief executive in learning sufficient details about a far-flung organization to do an intelligent job. The failure to attach sufficient importance to these variables has served to limit the scientific validity of the statements which have been made that one man can supervise but three, or five, or eight, or twelve immediate subordinates.

These considerations do not, however, dispose of the problem. They indicate rather the need for further research. But without further research we may conclude that the chief executive of an organization can deal with only a few immediate subordinates; that this number is determined not only by the nature of the work, but also by the nature of the executive; and that the number of immediate subordinates in a large, diversified and dispersed organization must be even less than in a homogeneous and unified organization to achieve the same measure of co-ordination.

One Master

From the earliest times it has been recognized that nothing but confusion arises under multiple command. "A man cannot serve two masters" was adduced as a theological argument because it was already accepted as a principle of human relation in everyday life. In administration this is known as the principle of "unity of command." [7] The principle may be stated as follows: A workman subject to orders from several superiors will be confused, inefficient, and irresponsible; a workman subject to orders from but one superior may be methodical, efficient, and responsible. Unity of command thus refers to those who are commanded, not to those who issue the commands. [8]

The significance of this principle in the process of co-ordination and organization must not be lost sight of. In building a structure of co-ordination, it is often tempting to set up more than one boss for a man who is doing work which has more than one relationship. Even as great a philosopher of management as Taylor fell into this error in setting up separate foremen to deal with machinery, with materials, with speed, etc., each with the power of giving orders directly to the individual workman. [9] The rigid adherence to the principle of unity of command may have its absurdities; these are, however, unimportant in comparison with the certainty of confusion, inefficiency and irresponsibility which arise from the violation of the principle.

Technical Efficiency

There are many aspects of the problem of securing technical efficiency. Most of these do not concern us here directly. They have been treated extensively by such authorities as Taylor, Dennison, and Kimball, and their implications for general organization by Fayol, Urwick, Mooney, and Reiley. There is, however, one efficiency concept which concerns us deeply in approaching the theory of organization. It is the principle of homogeneity.

It has been observed by authorities in many fields that the efficiency of a group working together is directly related to the homogeneity of the work they are perform-

---

[7] Henri Fayol, "Industrial and General Administration." English translation by J. A. Coubrough. International Management Association, Geneva, 1930.

[8] Fayol terms the latter "unity of direction."

[9] Frederick Winslow Taylor, "Shop Management." Harper and Brothers, New York and London, 1911, p. 99.

ing, of the processes they are utilizing, and of the purposes which actuate them. From top to bottom, the group must be unified. It must work together.

It follows from this (1) that any organizational structure which brings together in a single unit work divisions which are non-homogeneous in work, in technology, or in purpose will encounter the danger of friction and inefficiency; and (2) that a unit based on a given specialization cannot be given technical direction by a layman.

In the realm of government it is not difficult to find many illustrations of the unsatisfactory results of non-homogeneous administrative combinations. It is generally agreed that agricultural development and education cannot be administered by the same men who enforce pest and disease control, because the success of the former rests upon friendly co-operation and trust of the farmers, while the latter engenders resentment and suspicion. Similarly, activities like drug control established in protection of the consumer do not find appropriate homes in departments dominated by the interests of the producer. In the larger cities and in states it has been found that hospitals cannot be so well administered by the health department directly as they can be when set up independently in a separate department, or at least in a bureau with extensive autonomy, and it is generally agreed that public welfare administration and police administration require separation, as do public health administration and welfare administration, though both of these combinations may be found in successful operation under special conditions. No one would think of combining water supply and public education, or tax administration and public recreation. In every one of these cases, it will be seen that there is some element either of work to be done, or of the technology used, or of the end sought which is non-homogeneous.

Another phase of the combination of incompatible functions in the same office may be found in the common American practice of appointing unqualified laymen and politicians to technical positions or to give technical direction to highly specialized services. As Dr. Frank J. Goodnow pointed out a generation ago, we are faced here by two heterogeneous functions, "politics" and "administration," the combination of which cannot be undertaken within the structure of the administration without producing inefficiency.

Caveamus Expertum

At this point a word of caution is necessary. The application of the principle of homogeneity has its pitfalls. Every highly trained technician, particularly in the learned professions, has a profound sense of omniscience and a great desire for complete independence in the service of society. When employed by government he knows exactly what the people need better than they do themselves, and he knows how to render this service. He tends to be utterly oblivious of all other needs, because, after all, is not his particular technology the road to salvation? Any restraint applied to him is "limitation of freedom," and any criticism "springs from ignorance and jealousy." Every budget increase he secures is "in the public interest," while every increase secured elsewhere is "a sheer waste." His efforts and maneuvers to expand are "public education" and "civic organization," while similar efforts by others are "propaganda" and "politics."

Another trait of the expert is his tendency to assume knowledge and authority in fields in which he has no competence. In this particular, educators, lawyers, priests, admirals, doctors, scientists, engineers, accountants, merchants and bankers are all the same — having achieved technical competence or "success" in one field, they come to think this competence is a general quality detachable from the field and inherent in themselves. They step without embarrassment into other areas. They do not remember that the robes of authority of one kingdom confer no sovereignty in another; but that there they are merely a masquerade.

The expert knows his "stuff." Society needs him, and must have him more and more as man's technical knowledge becomes more and more extensive. But history shows us that the common man is a better judge of his own needs in the long run than any cult of experts. Kings and ruling classes, priests and prophets, soldiers and lawyers, when permitted to rule rather than serve mankind, have in the end done more to check the advance of human welfare than they have to advance it. The true place of the expert is, as A.E. said so well, "on tap, not on top." The essential validity of democracy rests upon this philosophy, for democracy is a way of government in which the common man is the final judge of what is good for him.

Efficiency is one of the things that is good for him because it makes life richer and safer. That efficiency is to be secured more and more through the use of technical specialists. These specialists have no right to ask for, and must not be given freedom from supervisory control, but in establishing that control, a government which ignores the conditions of efficiency cannot expect to achieve efficiency.

3. ORGANIZATIONAL PATTERNS

Organization Up or Down?

One of the great sources of confusion in the discussion of the theory of organization is that some authorities work and think primarily from the top down, while others work and think from the bottom up. This is perfectly natural because some authorities are interested primarily in the executive and in the problems of central management, while others are interested primarily in individual services and activities. Those who work from the top down regard the organization as a system of subdividing the enterprise under the chief executive, while those who work from the bottom up, look upon organization as a system of combining the individual units of work into aggregates which are in turn subordinated to the chief executive. It may be argued that either approach leads to a consideration of the entire problem, so that it is of no great significance which way the organization is viewed. Certainly it makes this very important practical difference: those who work from the top down must guard themselves from the danger of sacrificing the effectiveness of the individual services in their zeal to achieve a model structure at the top, while those who start from the bottom, must guard themselves from the danger of thwarting co-ordination in their eagerness to develop effective individual services.

In any practical situation the problem of organization must be approached from both top and bottom. This is particularly true in the reorganization of a going concern. May it not be that this practical necessity is likewise the sound process theoretically? In that case one would develop the plan of an organization or reorganization both from the top downward and from the bottom upward, and would reconcile the two at the center. In planning the first subdivisions under the chief executive, the principle of the limitation of the span of control must apply; in building up the first aggregates of specialized functions, the principle of homogeneity must apply. If any enterprise has such an array of functions that the first subdivisions from the top down do not readily meet the first aggregations from the bottom up, then additional divisions and additional aggregates must be introduced, but at each further step there must be a less and less rigorous adherence to the two conflicting principles until their juncture is effected.

An interesting illustration of this problem was encountered in the plans for the reorganization of the City of New York. The Charter Commission of 1934 approached the problem with the determination to cut down the number of departments and separate activities from some 60 to a manageable number. It was equally convinced after conferences with officials from the various city departments that the number could not be brought below 25 without bringing together as "departments" activities which had nothing in common or were in actual conflict. This was still too many for effective supervision by the chief executive. As a solution it was suggested by the author that the charter provide for the subdividing of the executive by the appointment of three or four assistant mayors to whom the mayor might assign parts of his task of broad supervision and co-ordination. Under the plan the assistant mayors would bring all novel and important matters to the mayor for decision, and through continual intimate relationship know the temper of his mind on all matters, and thus be able to relieve him of great masses of detail without in any way injecting themselves into the determination of policy. Under such a plan one assistant mayor might be assigned to give general direction to agencies as diverse as police, parks, hospitals, and docks without violating the principle of homogeneity any more than is the case by bringing these activities under the mayor himself, which is after all a paramount necessity under a democratically controlled government. This is not a violation of the principle of homogeneity *provided* the assistant mayors keep out of the technology of the services and devote themselves to the broad aspects of administration and co-ordination, as would the mayor himself. The assistants were conceived of as parts of the mayoralty, not as parts of the service departments. That is, they represented not the apex of a structure built from the bottom up, but rather the base of a structure extended from the top down, the object of which was to multiply by four the points of effective contact between the executive and the service departments.[10]

Organizing the Executive

The effect of the suggestion presented above is to organize and institutionalize the executive function as such so that it may be more adequate in a complicated situation. This is in reality not a new idea. We do not, for example, expect the chief executive to write his own letters. We give him a private secretary, who is part of his office and assists him to do this part of his job. This secretary is not a part of any department, he

---

[10] This recommendation was also presented to the Thatcher Charter Commission of 1935, to which the author was a consultant. A first step in this direction was taken in Sec. 9, Chap. I of the new charter which provides for a deputy mayor, and for such other assistance as may be provided by ordinance.

is a subdivision of the executive himself. In just this way, though on a different plane, other phases of the job of the chief executive may be organized.

Before doing this, however, it is necessary to have a clear picture of the job itself. This brings us directly to the question, "What is the work of the chief executive? What does he do?"

The answer is POSDCORB.

POSDCORB is, of course, a made-up word designed to call attention to the various functional elements of the work of a chief executive because "administration" and "management" have lost all specific content.[11] POSDCORB is made up of the initials and stands for the following activities:

> Planning, that is working out in broad outline the things that need to be done and the methods for doing them to accomplish the purpose set for the enterprise;
>
> Organizing, that is the establishment of the formal structure of authority through which work subdivisions are arranged, defined and co-ordinated for the defined objective;
>
> Staffing, that is the whole personnel function of bringing in and training the staff and maintaining favorable conditions of work;
>
> Directing, that is the continuous task of making decisions and embodying them in specific and general orders and instructions and serving as the leader of the enterprise;
>
> Co-ordinating, that is the all important duty of interrelating the various parts of the work;
>
> Reporting, that is keeping those to whom the executive is responsible informed as to what is going on, which thus includes keeping himself and his subordinates informed through records, research and inspection;
>
> Budgeting, with all that goes with budgeting in the form of fiscal planning, accounting and control.

This statement of the work of a chief executive is adapted from the functional analysis elaborated by Henri Fayol in his "Industrial and General Administration." It is believed that those who know administration intimately will find in this analysis a valid and helpful pattern, into which can be fitted each of the major activities and duties of any chief executive.

If these seven elements may be accepted as the major duties of the chief executive, it follows that they *may* be separately organized as subdivisions of the executive. The need for such subdivision depends entirely on the size and complexity of the enterprise. In the largest enterprises, particularly where the chief executive is as a matter of fact unable to do the work that is thrown upon him, it may be presumed that one or more parts of POSDCORB should be suborganized.

It is interesting to note that this has been recognized in many of our larger governmental units, though there has been until recently no very clear philosophy lying back

---

[11] See Minutes of the Princeton Conference on Training for the Public Service, 1935, p. 35. See also criticism of this analysis in Lewis Meriam, "Public Service and Special Training," University of Chicago Press, 1936, pp. 1, 2, 10 and 15, where this functional analysis is misinterpreted as a statement of qualifications for appointment.

of the arrangements which have been made. For example, in the federal government at the present time one may identify the separate institutionalization of:

Planning, under the National Resources Committee, though as yet rudimentary in development;

Staffing, under the Civil Service Commission, though it has missed its constructive rôle;

Reporting, under the National Emergency Council and the Central Statistics Board, in elementary form.

Budgeting, under the Budget Bureau;

Each of these agencies is as a matter of fact now serving as a managerial arm of the chief executive, particularly budgeting and planning. It will be observed that directing, co-ordinating and organizing are not institutionalized, but remain undifferentiated and unimplemented in the hands of the President. In view of the fact that he is swamped now, it would seem desirable to take out the organizing function, turning that over to the efficiency research division of the Budget Bureau, and then to increase the immediate personal staff of the White House with five or six high grade personal assistants to the President, along the line planned for the City of New York, to make it possible for him to deal adequately with the directing and co-ordinating functions.[12] What is most needed is a group of able and informed men who will see that the President has before him all relevant facts and that all appropriate clearance is secured before decisions are made and that a decision once made is known to those who are involved.

In view of the fact that the job of the President as Chief Executive is POSDCORB, institutionalization must not be allowed to take any one of these functions out of his office. They are and must remain parts of him. This was recognized when the Budget Bureau was set up in 1921, though it is only in the past three years that the office has actually functioned as an arm of the Chief Executive. The Civil Service Commission was similarly set up directly under the President, but the fact that it has an unwieldy triple head and has been interested primarily in the negative aspects of personnel has prevented its true development. Each one of these managerial establishments should be a part of the executive office. Their budgets should be brought together, and as far as possible they should be in the White House itself. It should be as natural and easy for the President to turn to the chairman of the planning board, or to the civil service commissioner when confronted by problems in their fields as it is now to call in the budget director before deciding a matter of finance.

A further illuminating illustration of the subdivision of the executive function is found in the Tennessee Valley Authority. The executive head of the authority is a board of three. The members of the board are also individually directors of various sections of the work. There is no general manager. Organizing, staffing, reporting, and budgeting are all separately institutionalized under the board, which deals with planning itself. Directing is in part handled by the board and in part by its individual members. To preserve some measure of co-ordination, the board has appointed a co-ordinator as

---

[12] As recommended by the President to Congress on January 12, 1937, in accordance with the program of the President's Committee on Administrative Management.

one of its chief officers. The results of this type of organization will be watched with interest by students of administration.[13]

Aggregating the Work Units

In building the organization from the bottom up we are confronted by the task of analyzing everything that has to be done and determining in what grouping it can be placed without violating the principle of homogeneity. This is not a simple matter, either practically or theoretically. It will be found that each worker in each position must be characterized by:

1. The major *purpose* he is serving, such as furnishing water, controlling crime, or conducting education;
2. The *process* he is using, such as engineering, medicine, carpentry, stenography, statistics, accounting;
3. The *persons or things* dealt with or served, such as immigrants, veterans, Indians, forests, mines, parks, orphans, farmers, automobiles, or the poor;
4. The *place* where he renders his service, such as Hawaii, Boston, Washington, the Dust Bowl, Alabama, or Central High School.

Where two men are doing exactly the same work in the same way for the same people at the same place, then the specifications of their jobs will be the same under 1, 2, 3, and 4. All such workers may be easily combined in a single aggregate and supervised together. Their work is homogeneous. But when any of the four items differ, then there must be a selection among the items to determine which shall be given precedence in determining what is and what is not homogeneous and therefore combinable.

A few illustrations may serve to point the problem. Within the City of New York, what shall be done with the doctor who spends all of his time in the public schools examining and attending to children in the Bronx? Shall we (1) say that he is primarily working for the school system, and therefore place him under the department of education? (2) say that he is a medical man, and that we will have all physicians in the department of health? (3) say that he is working with children, and that he should therefore be in a youth administration? or (4) say that he is working in the Bronx and must therefore be attached to the Bronx borough president's office? Whichever answer we give will ignore one or the other of the four elements characterizing his work. The same problem arises with the lawyer serving the street construction gang on damage cases in Brooklyn, the engineer who is working for the department of health in Richmond, and the accountant examining vouchers and records in Queens for the district attorney.

Departments Vertical and Horizontal

The nature of the interrelation between departments organized on the basis of *purpose* and those organized on the basis of *process* may be illustrated best by considering the former as vertical departments, and the latter as horizontal departments. This idea is presented pictorially in Chart I. In this chart four sample city departments are presented vertically, each broken down into its obvious specialized activities and

---

[13] Organization altered by the establishment of the office of General Manager after this was written.

workers. Each one of these is conceived of as a department set up to perform an important service, and fully equipped with all of the staff which it needs for the accomplishment of the major purpose involved. For example, the department of health, as here outlined, is established to guard and improve the health of all of the people of a given city. In this work it will need not only doctors, bacteriologists, nurses, and inspectors, but also lawyers, engineers, janitors, repair men, architects, clerks, statisticians, and budget, accounting, purchasing, and personnel staffs. The same is true of each of the other departments listed. In each case, it will be seen, there is (1) a central core of management which must be equipped with enthusiasm, experience, ability, knowledge of the purpose to be accomplished, and general acquaintance with the technologies used; (2) a group of workers peculiar to the department (such as fire fighters in the fire department, and school teachers in the department of education); and (3) a considerable number of highly important skilled or professional workers who are common to all, or to several departments.

These latter workers, because they are common to all or to several departments, and because they are engaged in the same sort of work group by group, may be brought together in appropriate departments. These are the "process" departments, and are shown on the accompanying chart as the several horizontal units. Turning the page on its side to look at this horizontal network, it will be noted that each department is made up of (1) a central core of management which must be equipped with enthusiasm, experience, ability, broad understanding of the general purposes of the government and its various services, and extensive knowledge of the technology involved; (2) a group of workers peculiar to the department, but with the same basic training as the remainder of the department (such as the staff engaged in tax administration in the department of finance); and (3) a group of skilled and professional workers working in other departments on assignment (like a lawyer assigned by the corporation counsel to the department of education), or performing services required to complete the job of another department (like park patrol, when handled by the police department).

Geographical division, that is departmentalization on the basis of place, presents an analogous alternative plan of organization. This too may be illustrated by a diagram, as is done in Chart II. Here again, the vertical departments, four in number, represent the great service departments, organized to perform a city-wide task. Instead of showing their technical work subdivision as on the previous chart, attention is here directed to their regional offices. It is assumed that each of the departments in this illustration maintains local offices within the same areas because of the natural divisions of the city. Such a situation is found in some of the largest cities because sections of the city are sharply defined by rivers, by parks, or by other clear demarcations. If each of the regional offices were split off from the vertical departments in question and joined with the other local offices in the same area, then new departments would appear, as is shown here by the horizontal network. Under this plan, there would be in each area a regional office which contained within itself health, education, police, recreation, and other services under a co-ordinating head. This co-ordinating head would be a regional assistant mayor. It would be his job to see that all of the city services touching the people within his area fitted together and made sense, and that any

CHART I

PURPOSE AND PROCESS SUBDIVISIONS IN ORGANIZATION

	HEALTH DEPARTMENT	EDUCATION DEPARTMENT	POLICE DEPARTMENT	PARK DEPARTMENT	
	Director Assistant Directors	Superintendent Assistant Superintendents	Chief Assistant Chiefs	Commissioner Assistant Commissioners	
CLERICAL AND SECRETARIAL SERVICE — Director	Private secretaries Stenographers File clerks Clerks Messengers	Private secretaries Stenographers File clerks Clerks Messengers	Private secretaries Stenographers File clerks Clerks Messengers	Private secretaries Stenographers File clerks Clerks Messengers	
FINANCE DEPARTMENT — Director	Budget officer Accountants Purchasing officer Statisticians	Budget officer Accountants Purchasing officer Statisticians	Budget officer Accountants Purchasing officer Statisticians	Budget officer Accountants Purchasing officer Statisticians	Other finance activities including tax administration, controlling accounts, etc.
	Personnel manager Lawyer	Personnel manager Lawyer	Personnel manager Lawyer	Personnel manager Lawyer	
ENGINEERING DEPARTMENT — Director	Engineers Architects Repair force Janitors	Engineers Architects Repair force Janitors	 Repair force Janitors	Engineers Architects Landscape staff Repair force Janitors	
	Physicians Dentists Nurses Psychologists	Physicians Dentists Nurses Psychologists	Physicians Psychologists		
	Bacteriologists Inspectors	Laboratory assistants Gardeners Classroom teachers Special teachers Librarians Recreation leaders Playground supervisors Traffic supervisor	Crime laboratory staff Police school staff Uniformed force Detective force Traffic force Jail staff Mounted force	Plant laboratory staff Gardeners Recreation leaders Playground supervisors Park police Traffic force Zoo staff Veterinarian	
	Switchboard operator	Switchboard operator	Veterinarian Communications staff	Switchboard operator	
MOTORIZED SERVICE — Supt.	Motorized service	Motorized service	Motorized service	Motorized service	

Vertical network — Purpose departments
Horizontal network — Process departments

CHART II

GEOGRAPHICAL SUBDIVISIONS IN ORGANIZATION

HEALTH DEPARTMENT	EDUCATION DEPARTMENT	POLICE DEPARTMENT	PARK DEPARTMENT
Director	Director	Director	Director
Assistant Director	Assistant Director	Assistant Director	Assistant Director
Headquarters Staff	Headquarters Staff	Headquarters Staff	Headquarters Staff
Technical Staff	Technical Staff	Technical Staff	Technical Staff
Downtown Regional Office	Downtown Regional Office	Downtown Regional Office	Downtown Regional Office
North Side Regional Office	North Side Regional Office	North Side Regional Office	North Side Regional Office
South Side Regional Office	South Side Regional Office	South Side Regional Office	South Side Regional Office
West Side Regional Office	West Side Regional Office	West Side Regional Office	West Side Regional Office

Director Staff
Director Staff
Director Staff
Director Staff

Vertical network — Purpose departments
Horizontal network — Regional departments

CHART III
FABRIC OF ORGANIZATIONAL INTERRELATIONS

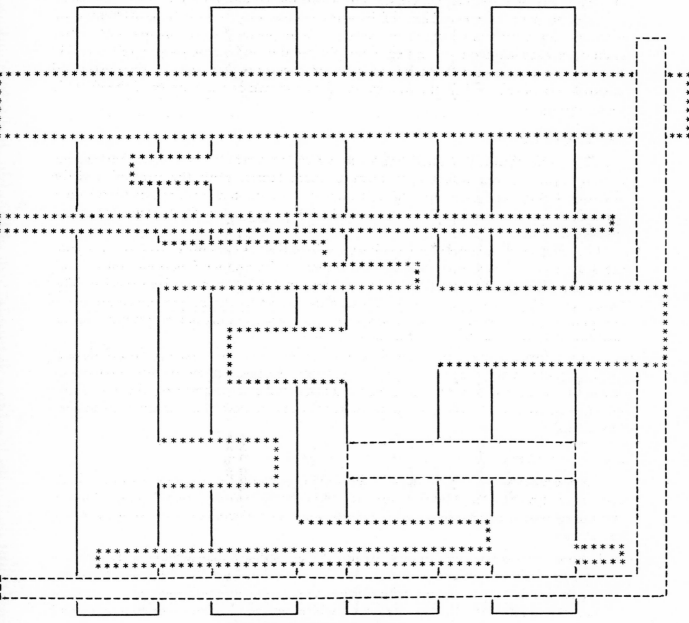

Solid network — Purpose departments
Star network — Process departments
Dash network — Regional departments

new problem was given prompt attention. If the problem proved to be local, he would see that it was dealt with by one of his own little departments, but if it proved to be city-wide in scope, then he would see that it was passed along for city-wide attention.

No diagram is presented here of departments organized on the basis of clientele or *matériel*, the former are similar in nature to the purpose departments, unless the clientele is geographically restricted in which case they follow the pattern of Chart II. The *materiel* departments are more akin to the process departments in the horizontal network of Chart I, in fact the motorized service shown at the bottom of the chart is such a grouping.

The Tangled Fabric

The effort is made in Chart III to show how departments established on various principles are woven together to form a single fabric. Both the vertical and the horizontal networks shown in Charts I and II are repeated. This might better have been done in three dimensions,[14] but it will suffice to portray the complexity of the problem involved.

In Chart III no special nomenclature is included as the entire structure is hypothetical. The top Star bar may be considered as the finance functions; the second, statistical services; the third, medical services; and the last, motorized service. The Dash network, inserted merely for illustration, might be the public information and complaint offices, serving not only several of the service departments, but also the tax assessment bureau of the department of finance.

It is a further function of this chart to show how certain departments are in part vertical and in part horizontal. This is true, for example, of the health department where that department is set up with a reasonably full staff to perform all of the public health functions, and then does some work for other departments through its professional staff.

Practice and Theory

These charts serve to bring out the major questions and considerations which arise in the practice and theory of organization. It may not be amiss therefore to note certain of them in this connection, though they are referred to more systematically elsewhere.

1. Is there any advantage in placing specialized services like private secretaries or filing in the Star network? In a very small organization, yes; in a large organization, no. In a small organization, where there is not a full-time job each day, and more than a full-time job on some days for each secretary, it is better to have a central secretarial pool than to have a private secretary for each man. In a large organization, the reverse is true, and there is great loss from failure to accumulate specialized knowledge and experience. The grouping of all stenographers, moreover, adds little or nothing to co-ordination.

2. The engineers are another matter. Engineering is highly specialized within itself, different engineers dealing with design, construction, operation, hydraulics, elec-

---

[14] Cf. "State Organization Model" and "Jungle Gym" by Henry Toll, 1934.

tricity, sanitation, cement, highways, bridges, steel, etc. Only a very large volume and scope of engineering service can possibly afford to have even a modest array of specialized talent of this sort. Therefore the small department is doomed to the employment of a staff, which though expert in one line will be relatively inexpert in some other. When all of the engineering work of the city is brought together in a single department, this danger is greatly reduced. Hence, engineering should be brought together except where departments are so large that they can by themselves afford a sufficient volume of work to use the most efficient specialization which the current technology makes possible.

The establishment of horizontal technical process departments such as engineering, statistics, or motorized service, along with departments set up vertically on the basis of major purpose does introduce a tendency to the co-ordination of these phases of their work, and by a sort of inductance, to a greater co-ordination of other phases of their work as well.

3. The major arms of co-ordination are found, however, in the horizontal services which handle planning, budget, and personnel. In this context the budget includes not alone the making of fiscal plans, but also their execution, together with the research, accounting, inspection and informational services which are involved. The major reason for bringing these services together in the Star network is not increased efficiency through specialization, but rather the development of tools of co-ordination.

4. From the standpoint of co-ordination it would seem that the heads of departments should visualize and understand the network in which they belong, so that they may proceed intelligently and energetically not only to carry out the work under their direction, but to see that that part of their work which falls within the overlapping purpose, or process, or regional area of another department may be fitted together harmoniously. Such an approach may serve to dispel the feeling of exclusive ownership and jealousy so common in government departments.

5. The chief executive, by the same token, should understand the network of the organization and should make a special endeavor to watch the areas of overlap and friction, and should hold the co-ordinating elements of the red network not only in his own hands, but in proper check so that they may not interfere with the accomplishment of the major purposes of the government.

With these illustrations and comments in mind we may now turn to the consideration of the advantages and disadvantages which may be expected with the application of one or another of the principles of departmentalization. Unfortunately we must rest our discussion primarily on limited observation and common sense, because little scientific research has been carried on in this field of administration.

Organization by Major Purpose

Organization by major purpose, such as water supply, crime control, or education, serves to bring together in a single large department all of those who are at work endeavoring to render a particular service. Under such a policy, the department of education will contain not only teachers and school administrators, but also architects, engineers, chauffeurs, auto mechanics, electricians, carpenters, janitors, gardeners, nurses, doctors, lawyers, and accountants. Everything that has to do with the schools would be included, extending perhaps even to the control of traffic about school properties. Similarly the department of water supply would include not only engineers and maintenance gangs, but also planners, statisticians, lawyers, architects, accountants, meter readers, bacteriologists, and public health experts.

The advantages of this type of organization are three: first, it makes more certain the accomplishment of any given broad purpose or project by bringing the whole job under a single director with immediate control of all the experts, agencies and services which are required in the performance of the work. No one can interfere. The director does not have to wait for others, nor negotiate for their help and co-operation; nor appeal to the chief executive to untangle a conflict. He can devote all his energies to getting on with the job.

Second, from the standpoint of self-government, organization by purpose seems to conform best to the objectives of government as they are recognized and understood by the public. The public sees the end result, and cannot understand the methodology. It can therefore express its approval or disapproval with less confusion and more effectiveness regarding major purposes than it can regarding the processes.

Third, it apparently serves as the best basis for eliciting the energies and loyalties of the personnel and for giving a focus and central drive to the whole activity, because purpose is understandable by the entire personnel down to the last clerk and inspector.

The statement of these strong points of organization by major purpose points the way to its dangers. These are to be found, first, in the impossibility of cleanly dividing all of the work of any government into a few such major purposes which do not overlap extensively. For example, education overlaps immediately with health and with recreation, as does public works with law enforcement. The strong internal co-ordination and drive tends to precipitate extensive and serious external conflict and confusion, just as there is more danger of accident with a high powered motor car. This is apparent particularly in the development of a reasonable city plan, or in arriving at a consistent policy throughout the departments for the maintenance of properties, or in handling legal matters, or arranging similar work and salary conditions. The lawyers, engineers, accountants, doctors of different departments will all have their own ideas as to how similar matters are to be dealt with.

Second, there is danger that an organization erected on the basis of purpose will fail to make use of the most up-to-date technical devices and specialists because the dominance of purpose generally tends to obscure the element of process, and because there may not be enough work of a given technical sort to permit efficient subdivision.

Third, there is also danger in such an organization that subordinate parts of the work will be unduly suppressed or lost sight of because of the singleness of purpose, enthusiasm and drive of the head of the department. For example, medical work with children when established under the department of education as a division is likely to receive less encouragement than it would if independently established in the health department, because after all the department of education is primarily interested in schools and has its own great needs and problems.

Fourth, a department established on the basis of purpose falls easily into the habit of overcentralization, and thus fails to fit its service effectively to the people. Or if it does decentralize its services, as do the fire department, the police department, the health department and the department of education of New York City, the representatives of these departments in the field do not always make the best use of each other's assistance and co-operation, and when any difficulty does arise, it is such a long way to the top where co-ordination can be worked out, that it is easier to get along without it.

Fifth, an organization fully equipped from top to bottom with all of the direct and collateral services required for the accomplishment of its central purpose, without the need of any assistance from other departments, drifts very easily into an attitude and position of complete independence from all other activities and even from democratic control itself.

Organization by Major Process

Organization by major process, such as engineering, teaching, the law, or medicine, tends to bring together in a single department all of those who are at work making use of a given special skill or technology, or are members of a given profession. Under such a policy the department of law would comprise all of the lawyers and law clerks, including those who are devoting their time to school matters, or water supply suits, or drafting ordinances. The department of engineering and public works would have all the engineers, including those concerned with planning, design, construction, maintenance and other phases of engineering work, wherever that work was found. This would include the work in the parks, on the streets, in the schools, and in connection with water, sewer, waste and other services. The department of health would include all of the doctors, nurses, and bacteriologists, and would not only carry on the general public health work, but would do the medical and nursing work for the schools, the water department, the department of social welfare, etc., as has been outlined above.

In every one of these cases it will be observed that the basis of organization is the bringing together in a single office or department of all the workers who are using some particular kind of skill, knowledge, machinery, or profession. This principle of organization has the following advantages:

First, it guarantees the maximum utilization of up-to-date technical skill and by bringing together in a single office a large amount of each kind of work (technologically measured), makes it possible in each case to make use of the most effective divisions of work and specialization.

Second, it makes possible also the economies of the maximum use of labor saving machinery and mass production. These economies arise not from the total mass of the work to be performed, not from the fact that the work performed serves the same general purpose but from the fact that the work is performed with the same machine, with the same technique, with the same motions. For example, economy in printing comes from skill in typesetting, printing, and binding and the use of modern equipment. It makes no difference to the printer whether he is printing a pamphlet for the schools, a report for the police department, or a form for the comptroller. Unit costs, efficiency in the doing of the job, rest upon the process, not the purpose.[15]

---

[15] Of course overall efficiency by the same token rests on the purpose, not the process. For example, a report may be printed at a phenomenally low cost, but if the pamphlet has no purpose, the whole thing is a waste of effort.

Third, organization by process encourages co-ordination in all of the technical and skilled work of the enterprise, because all of those engaged in any field are brought together under the same supervision, instead of being scattered in several departments) as is the case when organization is based upon some other principle.

Fourth, it furnishes an excellent approach to the development of central co-ordination and control when certain of the services such as budgeting, accounting, purchasing, and planning are set up on a process basis and used as instruments of integration even where other activities are set up on some other basis.

Fifth, organization by process is best adapted to the development of career service, and the stimulation of professional standards and pride. A career ladder can be erected very much more easily in a department which is from top to bottom engineers, or doctors, or statisticians, or clerks, than it can in a department which is partly engineers, partly doctors, partly statisticians, partly clerks. In the vertical departments,[16] the rungs of a professional ladder are a flying trapeze requiring the employee in his upward course to swing from department to department. This cannot be accomplished "with the greatest of ease."

These are the major advantages of organization on the basis of process. There are, of course, offsetting difficulties. As in the case of any other principle of organization, it is impossible to aggregate all of the work of the government on such a basis alone. It is not difficult to do so for engineering and medicine and teaching, but it becomes impossible when we reach typing and clerical work. It cannot furnish a satisfactory basis for doing the whole job in any large or complicated enterprise.

In the second place, there is always the danger that organization by process will hinder the accomplishment of major purposes, because the process departments may be more interested in *how* things are done than in *what* is accomplished. For example, a housing department which must clear the slums, build new low cost tenements and manage them, and inspect existing housing and approve new building plans, may find it difficult to make rapid progress if it must draw its legal help from the corporation counsel, its architects from the department of engineering, its enforcement officers from the police department, and its plans from the planning commission, particularly if one or more of these departments regards public housing as a nuisance and passing fad. There are also accountants who think that the only reason for the running of a government is the keeping of the books!

Third, experience seems to indicate that a department built around a given profession or skill tends to show a greater degree of arrogance and unwillingness to accept democratic control. This is perhaps a natural outgrowth of the insolence of professionalism to which reference has already been made.

Fourth, organization by process is perhaps less favorable to the development of a separate administrative service, because it tends to bring rather narrow professional specialists to the top of each department, men who are thereby disqualified for transfer to administrative posts in other fields.

And finally, the necessity of effective co-ordination is greatly increased. Purpose departments must be co-ordinated so that they will not conflict but will work shoulder to shoulder. But whether they do, or do not, the individual major purposes will be ac-

---

[16] See Chart I.

complished to a considerable extent and a failure in any service is limited in its effect to that service. Process departments must be co-ordinated not only to prevent conflict, but also to guarantee positive co-operation. They work hand in hand. They must also time their work so that it will fit together, a factor of lesser significance in the purpose departments. A failure in one process affects the whole enterprise, and a failure to co-ordinate one process division, may destroy the effectiveness of all of the work that is being done.

While organization by process thus puts great efficiency within our reach, this efficiency cannot be realized unless the compensating structure of co-ordination is developed.

2) Organization by Clientele or Matériel

(Organization on the basis of the persons served) or dealt with, or (on the basis of the things dealt with, tends to bring together in a single department, regardless of the purpose of the service, or the techniques used, all of those who are working with a given group or a given set of things) Examples are the veterans' administration which deals with all of the problems of the veteran, be they in health, in hospitals, in insurance, in welfare, or in education; and the immigration bureau which deals with immigrants at all points, including legal, financial, and medical services. Departmentalization on the basis of *matériel* is more common in private business than in public. Department stores, for example, have separate departments for furniture, hardware, drugs, jewelry, shoes, etc., and have separate buyers and sales forces for each. In many communities the school is in reality such a service, as it concentrates most of the community services touching children in school, including medical inspection, corrective treatment, free lunches and recreation, and certain phases of juvenile crime. The Forest Service is another organization based on *matériel* — in this case, trees.

(The great advantage of this type of organization is the simplification and co-ordination of the service of government in its contact with the consumer. He does not encounter first one and then another representative, each of whom does or demands something different or even something contradictory) At the international border one may be met by an immigration inspector who is interested in one's nationality and residence, by a customs inspector who is interested in goods brought in, by an agricultural inspector interested in certain pests, by a game warden interested in guns and rods, etc. In New York City, at one time, each tenement was subject to separate inspection at periodic intervals by men interested in slums, crime, fire escapes, plumbing, fire hazards, and electric wiring. Many cases have been reported of conflicting orders being issued to individual property owners under such a system.

(A second advantage is found in the increasing skill which attends the handling over and over of the same material.

A third gain arises from the elimination of duplicate travel, particularly in dealing with widely separated or sparsely distributed work.

—(The disadvantages of an organization which brings together all of the contacts with a given individual or thing are:

First, it tends to sacrifice the efficiency of specialization, because it must after all perform several otherwise specialized functions through the same organization or even at times through the same agent. For example, if the effort is made to combine all building inspections in the field, the same man must examine plumbing, wiring, living conditions and fire escapes. Or, at the international border, the same man must know and enforce the immigration law, the customs laws, the hunting laws, and the crop pest laws, and must possess the required special knowledge in the various technical fields involved. Or, in the veterans' administration the same director must supervise and direct specialists in medicine, institutional administration, insurance, and vocational education and rehabilitation.

It is to be noted that this difficulty has been overcome in certain notable instances by the creation of a new specialist profession to deal with the specific combination of functions brought together in a given service. The best illustration is the United States Forest Service. This can be done only where there is a large volume of work and an opportunity for a career within the service itself.

A second difficulty is found in the impossibility of applying the principle of division by persons served to all of the work of a government, without encountering extensive conflict and duplication. It is not difficult to pick out special groups like the aged, the youth, the criminal, the veteran, the real estate owner, etc., but when all is said and done there remains a great number of the ordinary citizens that does not fall into *any single* grouping. Each individual will appear in various groups at various times, and in the general group known as "the public" the rest of the time. And it is clearly impossible to organize a special department for the public, with all of the heterogeneous elements which this would entail from the standpoint of dissimilar technologies and conflicting objectives. It must be remembered also that even such departments as seem to be organized on the basis of persons served do not as a matter of fact cover all of the services rendered to or government contacts with a class of individuals. Taking even the most expanded school systems where the schools really are youth departments, it will be found that general quarantine is enforced by the health authorities, that children benefit also by police traffic and crime prevention work, that they drink water furnished by the water department, and milk protected by the division of foods, and live in homes supervised by the housing authority, and are protected by the fire department.

A third difficulty arises from the danger of dominance by favor-seeking pressure groups. Departments set up by clientele seldom escape political dominance by those groups, and are generally found to be special pleaders for those groups, at times in opposition to the general interest of society as a whole. This is in part due to the fact that the organization itself is often brought into being through the action of a pressure group and its demand for a special agency to serve it, but it is also continued through the efforts of the agency once established to marshal and maintain a group in its support. It follows that agencies so set up as to maintain or develop their own pressure backing are peculiarly difficult of democratic control and tend not to fit into a coordinated social policy.

Organization by Place

Organization on the basis of the place at which the service is performed brings together all of those who work in a limited area regardless of the service they are performing or of the techniques they represent. This is the general practice in territorial or colonial governments. Even where the home government has separate departments interested in health, education, law enforcement, natural resources, labor relations, and commercial development, it will be found that these departments have no direct representatives within a given territory or colony, but that there is a single representative of the home government there, under whom there are organized separate divisions to deal with health, education, law enforcement, natural resources, etc. In other words all or most of the representatives of the home government in the area are brought together in a single local agency, in place of serving as the far distant field representatives of the various central departments.

It is not only in colonial government that this plan is utilized. It is found also in greater or lesser degree in many of the regular departments of all large governmental units. In some of the largest city police systems the city is divided into precincts, and most of the police activities within a given area are under the complete direction of a precinct officer through whom all communication to and from headquarters must go. A similar situation is found in the postal system. Though the Washington office contains divisions in charge of mail delivery, stamp sale, postal savings, money orders, parcel post and other services, these services do not each maintain independent local offices. A single local office is maintained with a postmaster in charge, under whom there are separate divisions for performing these particular services and for reporting the results of their work to the several supervisory and control divisions at headquarters. The Treasury Department, on the other hand, though it has customs officers, income tax examiners, bank examiners, narcotic officers, secret service, and others in the field representing various administrative divisions of the Treasury in Washington, does not establish a general local director of these field services, but supervises each in turn directly from Washington, or through some regional office which has no organic relationship with any one of the other services.

The most extreme cases of subdivision of the work of government are found in the American states where the state has not only sub-divided itself into geographic areas for the performance of certain types of governmental service, but has actually turned over to these geographic areas a large measure of the right to determine how the local service shall be conducted. This is known as "home rule," and is found in all kinds of local government, particularly in the cities. It is common in the conduct of schools, the management of the police, the enforcement of justice, and the maintenance of the courts, all of which are legally "state functions." It is also the general basis of operation for poor relief, local highways, water supply, waste removal, property tax administration, and health administration. Where these functions are turned over to cities, villages, towns, or counties, they are in reality sub-organized on a geographical basis. It is significant that in France, Napoleon called his major geographical subdivisions *Départements*. From the standpoint of the theory of organization, this is a thoroughly accurate designation.

It should be noted that every department in every government of any size must be broken down geographically. In no other way can it reach the people who are to be served or who are to be controlled. In the government of the United States, only 20 per cent of the employees are located in Washington, and thousands of this number are

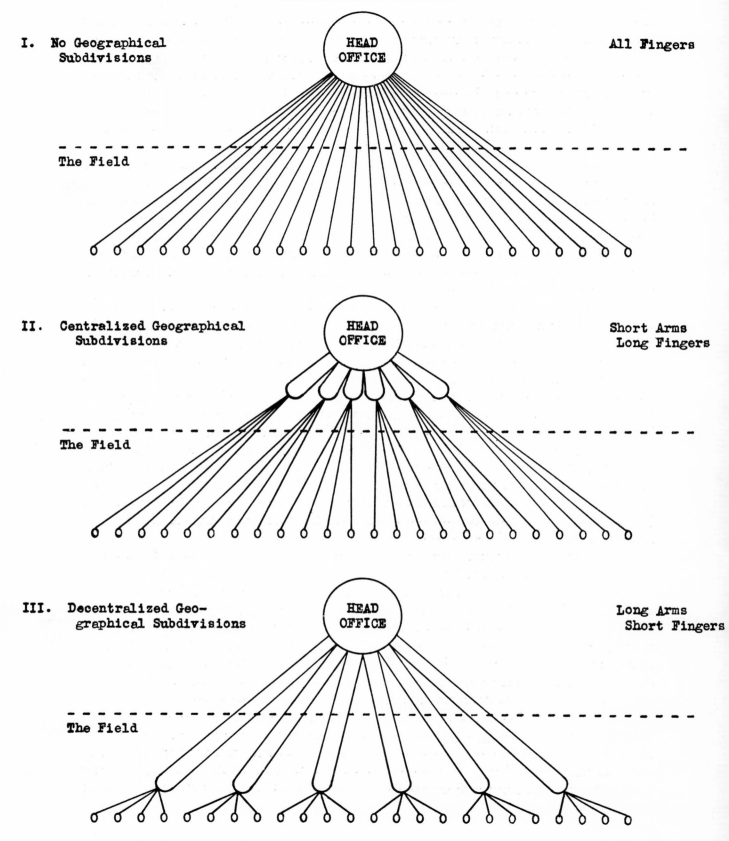

CHART IV
GEOGRAPHICAL SUBDIVISIONS

I. No Geographical Subdivisions

HEAD OFFICE

All Fingers

The Field

II. Centralized Geographical Subdivisions

HEAD OFFICE

Short Arms
Long Fingers

The Field

III. Decentralized Geographical Subdivisions

HEAD OFFICE

Long Arms
Short Fingers

The Field

actually in the field. Eighty per cent are regularly assigned to offices or work scattered throughout the country. They carry the government to the people and to the soil. The same is true of state governments and of city governments. Only a small part of the force actually works in the state capitol or the city hall. The real work of government is done out among the people in the various sections of the state or city. In the supervision of these forces it is often necessary to establish some form of regional organization, if for no other reason than to save the time of the supervisory officers who cannot be in two places at once. It is thus generally a question as to how high up in the organization geographical subdivision shall be introduced. Obviously this may be done at the very top, as the first division of the work under the chief executive of an enterprise, or it may be introduced far down the line after the major divisions have been set up by purpose, by process, or by clientele. The former may be termed *primary* geographical subdivision and the latter *secondary*, *tertiary*, or *subordinate* geographical subdivision. A department or major activity, like the Tennessee Valley Authority, which is set up on the basis of geographical boundaries is in fact a primary geographical subdivision of the government.

It is important to note also that geographical subdivisions of an office may be within the central office or they may be located away from the central office in the field, that is, they may be centralized or decentralized. In the first case the central office would itself have an "Eastern Division," a "Southern Division," a "Western Division," etc., each with an extensive staff at headquarters. In the United States Department of State, the Division of Latin American Affairs and the Division of Near Eastern Affairs, to mention but two, are illustrations of this system of organization. The alternative is the establishment of the regional suboffices in the field, far removed from headquarters. Under this system the "Eastern Division" would have an office within the Eastern area, and would have its staff located there. An illustration of this is found in the Tennessee Valley Authority and in the plans for the seven power authorities suggested by Senator Norris and endorsed by the President in his Message of June 3, 1937. It is, with certain modifications, the underlying plan of the Federal Reserve System and of the Farm Credit Administration.

The essential difference between these types of geographical division of work may be illustrated best by Chart IV.

These diagrams are oversimplified for purposes of illustration. They do not, for example, distinguish between the purpose and the process activities, nor do they deal with the structure in the field for the co-ordination of the various fingers.[17] Then, too, the whole chart is spread out to gain separation of the lines, whereas the true picture is more like a piano duet in which the treble of one player overlaps the base clef of the other, and in which the score is far from distinct, and "swing" is the rule!

The advantages of departmentalization on the basis of geographical areas, that is on the basis of superior geographical subdivision, are fairly obvious in practice. They consist first of the greater ease of co-ordination of services rendered and controls exercised within a given area; second, of the greater tendency to adapt the total program to the needs of the areas served, not alone because of the discretion resting within the divisions, but also because the needs and differences of the areas will be

---

[17] See page 36.

more vigorously represented at headquarters in the general consideration of broad policy; and third, of the greater ease with which co-operative relations may be established with subordinate governmental units, which are of necessity first of all geographically defined units. Decentralization of geographical divisions strengthens these tendencies, and serves, moreover, to reduce travel costs, short circuit adjustment problems, cut red tape, and speed up all joint activities and administrative decisions. It increases not only the awareness of the officials to local needs and to the interrelation of service and planning problems, but develops a new sensitivity to the process of democratic control through intimate association of the officials with the people served.

With decentralized subdivision a large amount of discretion must be delegated to the men in charge of field offices; in fact, they must be men of ability equal to if not superior to those who would be selected to head centralized departments of similar scope.

The difficulties of primary geographic subdivision are also not far to seek. They consist of the increased difficulty of maintaining a uniform nation-wide, state-wide, or city-wide policy; the danger of too narrow and short-sighted management; and the increased difficulty of making full use of technical services and the highest specialization because of the division of the work into limited blocks. Decentralization tends to enhance these difficulties by reason of physical isolation. It introduces other factors as well, such as higher costs for supervisory personnel, the general hesitancy of central administrative heads to delegate sufficient real power, the lesser prestige of localized officials, and the increased tendency of such a system to come under the control of localized logrolling pressure groups. Political parties under our system of representation are based upon geographical areas. An administrative system also set up by areas is peculiarly subject to spoliation by politicians as long as we have the spoils system.

Whenever the concept of geographic areas is introduced into the structure of organization, either as a primary or as a subordinate plan of division of work, there is always the further practical problem of delineating appropriate boundaries. This is particularly difficult when it is planned to deal with several activities widely differing in their nature and technology. There is always the danger that the tasks to be dealt with do not follow compact geographic boundaries and that the administrative separation introduced by the geographic division will complicate rather than simplify the work.

–Line and Staff –

The army has contributed much to the theory of organization. Not the least of these contributions has been the concept of line and staff. The implications of this idea for other than military organizations have been discussed brilliantly by Urwick, by Frederick A. Cleveland, and by Mooney and Reiley.[18] In view of the clarity of these expositions it is astonishing that so many who discuss administration fail to understand what a staff is and what function it performs in the organization.

---

[18] L. Urwick, "Organization as a Technical Problem," Paper II of this collection; Frederick A. Cleveland, "Expert Staff Aids to Management," Industrial Service and Equipment Co., Boston, 1918; James D. Mooney and Alan C. Reiley, "Onward Industry!" Harper and Brothers, New York, 1931.

When the work of government is subjected to (the dichotomy of "line" and "staff," there are included in staff all of those persons who devote their time exclusively to the knowing, thinking and planning functions, and in the line all of the remainder who are, thus, chiefly concerned with the doing functions.) The overhead directing authority of the staff group, usually a board or committee, is the "general staff."

(Obviously those in the line are also thinking and planning, and making suggestions to superior officers. They cannot operate otherwise. But this does not make them staff officers. Those also in the staff are *doing* something; they do not merely sit and twiddle their thumbs. But they do not organize others, they do not direct or appoint personnel, they do not issue commands, they do not take responsibility for the job. Everything they suggest is referred up, not down, and is carried out, if at all, on the responsibility and under the direction of a line officer.)

The important point of confusion in considering line and staff has arisen in speaking of the budget director, the purchasing agent, the controller, the public relations secretary, as "staff" officers. On the basis of the definition it is clear that they are all line officers. They have important duties of direction and control. When administrative responsibility and power are added to any staff function, that function thereby becomes immediately and completely a line function. There is no middle ground.

The chief value of the line and staff classification is to point to the need (1) of developing an independent planning agency as an aid to the chief executive, and (2) of refusing to inject any element of administrative authority and control into such an agency.

The necessity for central purchase, for personnel administration, for budgeting and for fiscal control rests on other considerations and not on the philosophy of the general staff.)

4. Interrelation of Systems of Departmentalization

Students of administration have long sought a single principle of effective departmentalization just as alchemists sought the philosophers' stone.[19] But they have sought in vain. There is apparently no one most effective system of departmentalism.

(Each of the four basic systems of organization is intimately related with the other three, because in any enterprise all four elements are present in the doing of the work and are embodied in every individual workman. Each member of the enterprise is working for some major purpose, uses some process, deals with some persons, and serves or works at some place.)

(If an organization is erected about any one of these four characteristics of work, it becomes immediately necessary to recognize the other characteristics in constructing the secondary and tertiary divisions of the work. For example, a government which is first divided on the basis of place will, in each geographical department, find it necessary to divide by purpose, by process, by clientele, or even again by place; and one

[19] Charles A. Beard, "The Administration and Politics of Tokyo." Macmillan, New York, 1923, Ch. 3; A. E. Buck, "Administrative Consolidation in State Governments," 5th ed. National Municipal League, New York, 1930; Great Britain, Ministry of Reconstruction, Report of the Machinery of Government Committee. H. M. Stationery Office, London, 1918; Luther Gulick, "Principles of Administration," *National Municipal Review*, vol. 14, July, 1925, pp. 400–403; W. F. Willoughby, "Principles of Public Administration." Johns Hopkins Press, Baltimore, 1927, Part I, Ch. 5.

divided in the first instance by purpose, may well be divided next by process and then by place. While the first or primary division of any enterprise is of very great significance, it must none the less be said that there is no one most effective pattern for determining the priority and order for the introduction of these interdependent principles. It will depend in any case upon the results which are desired at a given time and place.

An organization is a living and dynamic entity. Each activity is born, has its periods of experimental development, of vigorous and stable activity, and, in some cases, of decline. A principle of organization appropriate at one stage may not be appropriate at all during a succeeding stage, particularly in view of the different elements of strength and of weakness which we have seen to exist in the various systems of departmentalization. In any government various parts of its work will always stand at different stages of their life cycle. It will therefore be found that not all of the activities of any government may be appropriately departmentalized neatly on the basis of a single universal plan. Time is an essential element in the formula.

Another variable is technological development. The invention of machines, the advance of applied science, the rise of new specializations and professions, changes in society and in the way men work and move in their private life must be continually reflected in the work of government, and therefore in the structure of government. Medieval governments made use of warriors, priests, artists, builders, and tax gatherers; they had no place for sanitary engineers, chemists, entomologists, pneumatic drill operators and typists. Before you organize a statistical division there must be statistical machinery and statistical science, but as soon as there are such machinery and science, any large organization which fails to recognize the fact in its organization may greatly lessen its utilization of the newly available tools and skills.

A further variable influencing the structure of any enterprise is its size, measured not so much by the amount of work done as by the number of men at work and their geographical dispersion. A drug store is an excellent illustration of the problem encountered. It must have a prescription department with a licensed pharmacist, no matter how small it is, because of the technological requirements involved. But it does not need to have a separate medicine and supply department, refreshment department, book department, toy department, sporting goods department, cigar department, and delivery department, each with a trained manager, buyer and sales force, unless it is a big store. In the small store, the pharmacist may even be the manager, the soda jerker, and the book dispenser. If the business is big enough, it may be desirable to have more than one store in order to reach the customers, thus introducing geographical subdivision. Similarly, in government the nature of the organization must be adapted not only to the technological requirements but also to the size of the undertaking and the dispersion of its work.

Measurements and Organization

We must not fail to recognize the importance of the techniques of administration upon what is possible and what is not possible in the organization of large-scale enterprise. How far could men go in the organization of business without double-entry bookkeeping and the balance sheet? How far could they go without the invention of the corporation? What has been the influence upon the practicable size and structure of business of such things as the telephone, the elevator, the adding and computing machines, or the conveyor belt? It is not difficult, looking into the past, to note these individual inventions and to trace their influence upon the structure of organization. Just as changes in production and distribution have altered the work requirements of every enterprise, so these inventions and technological advances in administration have altered the process of central co-ordination, direction and control.

If we turn to the future, we are thus compelled to see that systems of organization which we now find to be necessary to produce specific results may become completely archaic and unnecessary with the invention of new administrative machines and techniques. Of very great importance, for example, is the effort now being made to find "measurements of administration" in many fields.[20] Though little advance has been made as yet, the high perfection to which automatic and machine accounting has been brought, offers real promise. If, for example, effective units of highway work are worked out by the experts, these, with the aid of rapid machine statistics, can give an executive effective control over a farflung decentralized organization of a character which he could not handle under existing technologies. If to this is added the new developments of communication, with two-way radio, and even television, we may find that we are confronted with entirely new possibilities in the field of organization.[21]

Structure and Co-ordination

The major purpose of organization is co-ordination, as has been pointed out above. It should therefore be noted that each of the four principles of departmentalization plays a different rôle in co-ordination. In each case the highest degree of co-ordination takes place within the departments set up, and the greatest lack of co-ordination and danger of friction occurs between the departments, or at the points where they overlap.

If all of the departments are set up on the basis of purpose, then the task of the chief executive in the field of co-ordination will be to see that the major purposes are not in conflict and that the various processes which are used are consistent, and that the government as it touches classes of citizens or reaches areas of the community is appropriate, rational, and effective. He will not have to concern himself with co-ordination within the departments, as each department head will look after this.

If all of the departments are set up on the basis of process, the work methods will be well standardized on professional lines, and the chief executive will have to see that these are co-ordinated and timed to produce the results and render the services for which the government exists, and that the service rendered actually fits the needs of the persons or areas served.

---

[20] A. E. Buck, "Measuring the Results of Government," *National Municipal Review*, vol. 13, March, 1924, pp. 152–157; Luther Gulick, "Wanted: A Measuring Stick for School Systems," *National Municipal Review*, vol. 18, January, 1929, pp. 3–5; Clarence E. Ridley, "Measuring Municipal Government," Municipal Administration Service, New York, 1927. See also articles in *Public Management*, 1937, by Clarence E. Ridley and H. A. Simon; John J. Theobald, "An Economic Analysis of Highway Administration in the State of New York," pages 140–192, and 657–679 of the Report of the New York State Commission for the Revision of the Tax Laws, 1935.

[21] An excellent illustration of this is already upon us in police administration, where motorized service and two-way radio have made precinct organization and small town set-ups of doubtful value.

If place be the basis of departmentalization, that is, if the services be decentralized, then the task of the chief executive is not to see that the activities are co-ordinated locally and fit the locality, but to see that each of these services makes use of the standard techniques and that the work in each area is part of a general program and policy.

If the work of the government be departmentalized in part on the basis of purpose, in part on the basis of process, in part on the basis of clientele, and in part on the basis of place, it will be seen that the problems of co-ordination and smooth operation are multiplied and that the task of the executive is increased. Moreover, the nature of his work is altered. In an organization in which all of the major divisions follow one philosophy, the executive himself must furnish the interdepartmental co-ordination and see that things do not fall between two stools. In an organization built on two or more bases of departmentalization, the executive may use, for example, the process departments as a routine means of co-ordinating the purpose departments. None the less the task of the executive is extraordinarily complicated. There is also great danger in such an organization that one department may fail to aid or actually proceed to obstruct another department. When departments cross each other at right angles, the danger of collision is far greater and far more serious than when their contacts are along parallel lines at their respective outer limits.

The Holding Company Idea

A large enterprise engaged in many complicated activities which do not require extensive or intimate co-ordination may need only the loosest type of central co-ordinating authority. Under such conditions, each activity may be set up, on a purpose basis, as virtually independent, and the central structure of authority may be nothing more than a holding company. In practice various industrial holding companies, particularly in the power field, require little or no co-ordination whatsoever. They have no operating services in common, and seem to have few interrelations except in finance. It has been suggested that the larger governmental units are in a comparable position, and that they may well be looked upon not as single enterprises like the Ford Motor Company, but rather as if they were each holding companies like the American Telephone and Telegraph Company, or General Motors. From this point of view, the government of the United States would be the parent company, and each department would be an independent subsidiary. While the parent company would give certain central services and require conformity to certain central plans and policies, each subsidiary, that is each department, would be given extensive freedom to carry on as it saw fit, and the President at the center of the parent company would not pretend to do more than prevent conflict and competition.

This point of view is helpful to the student of administration in that it brings out two important factors:

1. It makes clear the important difference between the operating functions and departments, such as agriculture, war, and labor, and the co-ordinating and central services, such as the budget, planning, and personnel. In the holding company analogy, the former would be subsidiaries, while the latter would be functions of the parent company; and

2. It directs attention to the kind of service to which the central agencies, including

the President and the Cabinet, should limit themselves in any case. If the co-ordinating agencies of the government would look upon themselves as holding company officials and staff, they would devote their energies to the larger problems of co-ordination, and would leave to the departments and their staffs the internal problems of operation.

While this attitude toward the respective functions of the operating and the co-ordinating services of the government may be valuable for certain purposes, it cannot be accepted as the sound theoretical foundation for the consideration of the federal government, or of any of the governments of the states or larger cities. It is not a satisfactory analogy for four important reasons:

1. There is but one board of directors in the governmental set-up, and a single avenue of democratic responsibility;
2. The interrelations between the various departments are many and intimate, requiring extensive and continuous co-ordination;
3. In government there must be highly developed uniform standards and methods, particularly in finance and personnel; and
4. There is in government no simple, final measure of successful operation of subsidiaries like the profit and loss statement in business. Supervisory relations must be intimate and complete, not distant and limited.

In the actual operation of the larger American governmental units we are, as a matter of fact, confronted at the same time by too much activity by the co-ordinating authorities, and by too little co-ordination. This anomalous situation seems to come about because of the lack of understanding both by experts and by laymen of the true function of the chief executive; because of the lack of proper managerial staffs attached to the chief executive; and because of the tendency of legislative bodies to step over the line into administration and to meddle with appointments. It must be recognized that the chief executive of any enterprise has but a limited amount of time and energy at his command. These he can use either in participating in detail in the administration of a few activities, or in dealing broadly with the policies and problems of many activities. If the task of the executive is first of all co-ordination, it would seem that the latter is his true function. But in any large enterprise, the executive cannot perform this function intelligently or skillfully unless he has adequate assistance. Where he is denied such assistance, he must act either tardily or ruthlessly, and an executive who recoils from either course is immediately drawn down into the minutiae of administration and fails to perform his main job.

In public administration the holding company concept is helpful if it is used to emphasize the need of broad co-ordination and the methods of achieving it. It must be recognized, however, that government is actually not a holding company at all.

Other Means of Interdepartmental Co-ordination

In the discussion thus far it has been assumed that the normal method of interdepartmental co-ordination is hierarchical in its operation. That is, if trouble develops between a field representative (X) of one department and the field representative (A) of another department, that the solution will be found by carrying the matter up the line from inferior to superior until the complaint of Mr. X and the complaint of Mr. A finally reach their common superior, be he mayor, governor or President. In actual practice, there are also other means of interdepartmental co-ordination which must be regarded as part of the organization as such. Among these must be included planning boards and committees, interdepartmental committees, co-ordinators, and officially arranged regional meetings, etc. These are all organizational devices for bringing about the co-ordination of the work of government. Co-ordination of this type is essential. It greatly lessens the military stiffness and red tape of the strictly hierarchical structure. It greatly increases the consultative process in administration. It must be recognized, however, that it is to be used only to deal with abnormal situations and where matters of policy are involved, as in planning. The organization itself should be set up so that it can dispose of the routine work without such devices, because these devices are too dilatory, irresponsible and time-consuming for normal administration. Wherever an organization needs continual resort to special co-ordinating devices in the discharge of its regular work, this is proof that the organization is bad. These special agencies of co-ordination draw their sanction from the hierarchical structure and should receive the particular attention of the executive authority. They should not be set up and forgotten, ignored, or permitted to assume an independent status.

The establishment of special regional co-ordinators to bring about co-operation in a given region between the local representatives of several central agencies presents special difficulties. There are three chief plans which have been tried. One is the device of propinquity, the juxtaposition of offices in the same building or city, and reliance on ordinary daily contact. Another is the establishment of a loose committee, or "conference," meeting locally from time to time to discuss local problems of co-ordination, under a local chairman who is actually nothing but a presiding officer and formulator

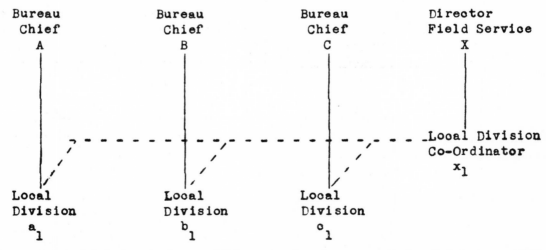

of agenda. A third plan is the establishment of such groups under the chairmanship of a regional co-ordinator designated by and responsible to a central office of co-ordination of field service. When this is attempted, to whom should the head of the field service be subordinate? For example, in the accompanying diagram to whom should X report? Certainly not to A, or to B, or to C. The central director of a co-ordination field service must be on a par with the central directors of the services which are being co-ordinated in the field, or possibly even on a higher plane.

In the devices of co-ordination, one must recognize also joint service contracts and coincident personnel appointments. Independent agencies may be pulled together in operation through such use of the same staff or service. There are many illustrations of the former, especially in engineering services. The county agent who is at the same time a county, a state, and a federal official is an example of the latter.

A great obstacle in the way of all of these plans of co-ordination is found in the danger of introducing confusion in direction through the violation of the principle of unity of command, and also in the difference in the level of authority of those who are brought together in any interdepartmental or intergovernmental co-ordinating arrangement. The representatives of the Department of Agriculture, for example, may have a large measure of responsibility and power, and may therefore be in a position to work out an adjustment of program through conference and to agree to a new line of conduct, but the representatives of the Army, coming from an entirely different kind of an organization, are sure to be in a position where they cannot make any adjustments without passing the decision back to headquarters.

– 5. Co-ordination by Ideas –

Any large and complicated enterprise would be incapable of effective operation if reliance for co-ordination were placed in organization alone. Organization is necessary; in a large enterprise it is essential, but it does not take the place of a dominant central idea as the foundation of action and self-co-ordination in the daily operation of all of the parts of the enterprise. Accordingly, the most difficult task of the chief executive is not command, it is leadership, that is, the development of the desire and will to work together for a purpose in the minds of those who are associated in any activity.

Human beings are compounded of cogitation and emotion and do not function well when treated as though they were merely cogs in motion. Their capacity for great and productive labor, creative co-operative work, and loyal self-sacrifice knows no limits provided the whole man, body-mind-and-spirit, is thrown into the program.

Implications –

After all that has been written about morale in war and in work, the psychology of group effort, and the art of leadership, it is not necessary to elaborate this point here. It is appropriate, however, to note the following specific elements which bear directly upon the problem of co-ordination:

1. Personnel administration becomes of extraordinary significance, not merely from the standpoint of finding qualified appointees for the various positions, but even more from the standpoint of assisting in the selection of individuals and in the maintenance of conditions which will serve to create a foundation of loyalty and enthusiasm.

   The new drive for career government service and for in-service training derives its significance not so much from the fact that better persons will enter the service when the chance for promotion is held out to them, but from the fact that a career service is a growing and learning service, one that believes in the work and in the future of the enterprise.

2. Even where the structure of the organization is arranged to produce co-ordination by authority, and certainly in those realms in which the structure as such is wanting, the effort should be made to develop the driving ideas by co-operative effort and compromise so that there may be an understanding of the program, a sense of participation in its formulation, and enthusiasm in its realization.

3. Proper reporting on the results of the work of the departments and of the government as a whole to the public and to the controlling legislative body, and public appreciation of good service rendered by public employees is essential, not merely as a part of the process of democratic control, but also as a means to the development of service morale.

4. As a matter of public policy the government should encourage the development of professional associations among the employees of the government, in recognition of the fact that such associations can assist powerfully in the development of standards and ideals. In situations where it is natural, office and shop committees should be built up.

5. A developing organization must be continually engaged in research bearing upon the major technical and policy problems encountered, and upon the efficiency of the processes of work. In both types of research, but particularly in the latter, members of the staff at every level should be led to participate in the inquiries and in the development of solutions.

6. There is need for a national system of honor awards which may be conspicuously conferred upon men and women who render distinguished and faithful, though not necessarily highly advertised public service.

7. The structure of any organization must reflect not only the logic of the work to be done, but also the special aptitudes of the particular human beings who are brought together in the organization to carry through a particular project. It is the men and not the organization chart that do the work.

Dominant Ideals -

(The power of an idea to serve as the foundation of co-ordination is so great that one may observe many examples of co-ordination even in the absence of any single leader or of any framework of authority. The best illustration is perhaps a nation at war. Every element steps into line and swings into high gear "to help win the war." The co-ordination is enthusiastic and complete, within the limits of knowledge of course. In an old stable community, small enough for each person to know the other, even competing businesses generally work along together in harmony. The town board, the school board, the park commission, the overseer of the poor, though answerable to no single executive, manage to get along with each other and each to fit his part of the work into that of the others to arrive at a sensible result for the whole picture. Men of intelligence and good will find little difficulty in working together for a given purpose even without an organization. They do not need to be held in line or driven to do a specific task in a specific way at a specific time. They carry on because of their inner compulsion, and may in the end accomplish a far better result for that very reason.

Hire and Fire

Closely akin to these considerations is the place of discipline in the technique of co-ordination. In most American thinking on management it has been assumed that the power to hire and fire must of necessity follow the hierarchical lines of the organization. Even students of administration have assumed that a chart of any organization may be drawn in terms either of the lines of appointment or in terms of the duties performed, because it was thought that the two are coincident, or should be. American business men have shared the same view. In their labor relations they take the traditional position that no man can run a business unless he has the free and unlimited power to hire and fire. It is the cornerstone of their thinking.

From the standpoint of modern management, however, competent observers have come to see that this approach is neither justified by the facts nor conducive to effective results. In practical situations employers do not as a matter of fact have the power to fire, even when they have the legal right. There are public relations, and increasingly there are labor unions. Frequently employers do not have the unlimited power to appoint. Here again there are standards, public relations, and closed shops. An individual minor executive in a large corporation generally has his employees selected for him. He is not free either to hire or to fire. These limitations of the right to hire and fire are destined, it is clear, to become more and more restrictive.

It becomes increasingly clear, therefore, that the task of the administrator must be accomplished less and less by coercion and discipline and more and more by persuasion. In other words, management of the future must look more to leadership and less to authority as the primary means of co-ordination.

These undoubted facts of experience are re-emphasized here not for the purpose of arguing that the consideration of the philosophy of organization is after all a "fools' contest," but rather to insist that the more important and the more difficult part of co-ordination is to be sought not through systems of authority, but through ideas and persuasion, and to make clear the point that the absurdities of the hierarchical system of authority are made sweet and reasonable through unity of purpose. It may well be that the system of organization, the structure of authority, is primarily important in co-ordination because it makes it easy to deal with the routine affairs, and thereby lessens the strain placed upon leadership, so that it can thus devote itself more fully to the supreme task of developing consent, participation, loyalty, enthusiasm, and creative devotion.

6. CO-ORDINATION AND CHANGE

The Limits of Co-ordination

Are there limits to co-ordination? Is mankind capable of undertaking activities which though interrelated are beyond man's power of systematic co-ordination?

In the field of big business, economists and lawyers have raised this question, and have asked whether some of the larger corporations were not already too large for effective operation. Certainly in government, we face what often seem superhuman tasks because of their size and complexity. And not too encouraging are such efforts as we have seen in Italy, Germany, and Russia, where government is co-ordinating not only the social controls but also production and distribution. In a lesser degree, and with greater reliance upon voluntary action within a broad framework of regulation, England, France and the United States are also striving for the same ends, with greater and greater imposition of public controls. There are apparently no limits to the effort mankind is prepared to make to render life more secure and more abundant through socially enforced co-ordination. If there are limits to man's power of co-ordination, it would be well to recognize their nature now rather than at some future time.

Considerable light is thrown upon this question by the techniques which have been worked out in the authoritarian states. In every case we find: the abolition of representative government; the extinguishment of local government, including home rule; the transfer of all policy determination as well as execution to a single executive, the legislative assembly becoming a channel for manufacturing consent; the erection of an immense bureaucratic machine responsible also for the control of conduct and of economic life; the determination of production programs and quotas; the establishment of a factional party in supreme control and subject to no discipline but its own; the rise of a single powerful leader; the disappearance of compromise as a basis of action; the stringent control and use of press, radio, schools, universities, public assembly, and all private associations to condition the whole nation, particularly the rising generation; the intensification of separatist nationalism and race consciousness; the fabrication of national scapegoats; the stimulation of great mass diversions, particularly in sport and expeditions; the extinction of criticism and difference of opinion; and the termination of free inquiry.

It will be observed that there are two great efforts in this whole program, first to make the government all powerful in every important sphere of life so that it may have the facilities and authority for the co-ordination of all of life; and second, to create absolute and universal consent and enthusiastic adherence to the program of the state. The attention which is devoted to this latter objective by the authoritarian states is a powerful testimonial to the power of ideas in co-ordinating the activities of humanity.

It is clear also from the observation of these experiments, in which direction the limitations of co-ordination lie. The difficulties arise from:

1. The uncertainty of the future, not only as to natural phenomena like rain and crops, but even more as to the behavior of individuals and of peoples;
2. The lack of knowledge, experience, wisdom and character among leaders and their confused and conflicting ideals and objectives;
3. The lack of administrative skill and technique;
4. The vast number of variables involved and the incompleteness of human knowledge, particularly with regard to man and life;
5. The lack of orderly methods of developing, considering, perfecting and adopting new ideas and programs.

It may also be noted that the authoritarian states are in trouble internationally. Some regard this as intentional, as part of the diversion and scapegoat technique, while others think that it is more or less inevitable because of the very co-ordination of the economic activities of the individual nations in question. If this latter explanation is correct, then we may regard the increased friction at the periphery experienced by co-ordinated states as a further illustration of the general principle noted above.[22]

It is a striking fact that the authoritarian states have thus far found little difficulty in regimenting the thinking and conduct of the masses of the population. This is the least of their troubles. The upper and middle classes and the educated are no exception to the rule. It is of course too early to accept the dominion of opinion that has been established as a long-time phenomenon, and there have been those who have before this predicted its early collapse. It must be recorded, however, that there is no indication of this breakdown as yet. It is difficult to see how such a collapse can come except through a failure of the administration or of the economic policies of the government. In other words, the weak link in the chain is not the securing of popular support; it is rather in the field of policy and execution. It is at this point that the lack of a systematic method for bringing in new ideas, the corrective of free criticism, and the common man's appraisal of the end results may prove disastrous. Certainly a state which attempts the extraordinarily difficult task of co-ordinating most of life will need these sources of regeneration and correction even more than a state which undertakes a more limited responsibility.

If this analysis is sound, the limits of co-ordination are to be found in lack of knowledge and lack of administrative skill. It would therefore be sound policy (1) to advance knowledge through research in public affairs, and administration both through research and through the adoption of improved techniques. It would seem also desirable (2) to advance the area of attempted co-ordination in sectors and experimentally so that the necessary skill may be gained through trial and error. This would mean a deliberate advance in a wave motion, with periods of pause and consolidation after each forward move.

If this course of action is adopted there is no need of accepting the view that there are fixed limits of co-ordination beyond which mankind can never go. It is also probable that the area of co-ordination will always be less extensive than all of life because the ability of mankind to co-ordinate, though continually advancing, can never overtake the creative capacity of individuals to invent new fields of activity and knowledge.

The Accretion of Functions

In view of the fact that organization must conform to the functions performed, attention must be given to the process by which new functions are assumed by governmental units. There have been few studies of functional accretion, and in none of these studies has the effort been made to analyze the sequence of events sufficiently to arrive at a philosophy of growth.[23]

Certain hypotheses may be stated, however, on the basis of the studies already made, such as:

---

[22] Pp. 21–22.

[23] William Anderson, "American City Government," Henry Holt, New York, 1925, Chapter XVI, *Municipal Functions;* New York State, Joint Legislative Committee on Taxation and Retrenchment, "A Study of the Growth of the Functions and Expenditures of the State Government," J. B. Lyon, Albany, 1926 (Legislative document, 1926, no. 28); Lent D. Upson, "The Growth of a City Government; an Enumeration of Detroit's Municipal Activities," Detroit Bureau of Governmental Research, 1931; Sidney Webb and Beatrice Webb, "Statutory Authorities for Special Purposes; with a Summary of the Development of Local Government Structure," Longmans, Green, London, 1922, Vol. IV of their *English Local Government.*

1. Strikingly new activities are generally developed outside of the government by private groups and organizations before they are taken over and made a part of the normal service of government;
2. This is particularly the case in highly decentralized governments, and in those which do not have a highly developed and professionalized civil service;
3. In their initiation most governmental services are established on an autonomous or semi-autonomous basis, both as to authority and finance and are subsequently integrated as to authority and finance with the other activities of government and deprived of this preliminary autonomy in spite of their resistance to this change;
4. Important activities also arise first as special services within a given department, and are then made general and set up on an independent footing;
5. The majority of the services of government have been undertaken under the stress of war or of economic depression, and not as advances in periods of prosperity;
6. Few new services are undertaken after a consideration of their relations to other services or of their ultimate costs or benefits;
7. Private associations, pressure groups, paid secretaries and vigorous new officers of civic groups play an important part in bringing government to undertake new services. Highly organized communities often "advance their government" more rapidly than unorganized communities which may stand in greater need;
8. A single dominant and original individual either in the community or in the public service may be more influential in the development of new government activities than any environmental factor;
9. The general stream of culture among a people and the universal desire to "keep up with the Joneses" are fundamental factors in the adaptation of governmental activities;
10. Once an activity is taken over by government it is rarely if ever abandoned.

There have of course been important recessions of the scope of government. These should be studied also. The most sweeping of the past three centuries on this continent are the separation of church and state and the withdrawal of the state from intimate and unquestioned control of economic life. The former was not so much a restriction of the functions of the state as of the power of the church. Similarly, the latter may be considered not so much a limitation of the function of government as a step in the limitation of the power of small entrenched economic groups. When a city charter was no longer the charter of a private corporation, and its extensive economic powers [24] were passing from "the corporation" to the hands of elected officials, the unhorsed economic groups inevitably desired *laissez faire* and the separation of business and government in much the same way that the church withdrew in the face of the advance of the democratic dogma. In both cases there is the appearance of the retraction of the sphere of government. In reality, however, it would seem that the significant element is the change in the "ownership" of the government. But in any case these retractions need examination.

Another type of abandonment of governmental activities takes place with de-

---

[24] E.g., to grant freedoms, to operate docks and transportation, to regulate all business, to license and control all trades and professions, to regulate commerce, and to manage important monopolies, such as "all trade with the Indians."

mobilization at the end of a war. It will be found, however, that this is primarily a process of shrinkage, not of amputation, and that a great many new services are left behind when the flood recedes. Here again there are important recent exceptions, as when the United States government ceased running the railroads after the World War.

In planning for the demobilization of emergency activities, the question arises as to whether this may be better worked out when the agency to be liquidated is largely independent, or when the agency is a subordinate division of a larger department, the remainder of which is permanent. Also, how does the type of organization (i.e. purpose, process, clientele, place) influence the demobilization? Though little material has been collected bearing directly on these questions, it would seem that dependent activities, especially those organized on the basis of purpose, are the most readily terminated, though it depends, of course, on the nature of the continuing obligation involved. After all, demobilization must be carried out by the overhead, and may be better done when that overhead itself is not directly involved.

In view of the growth processes of governmental functions, those who are concerned with the mechanics of organization will fail to develop a satisfactory theory of organization unless they regard their basic problem as dynamic. In considering the organization of government we deal not alone with living men, but with an organism which has its own life.

The Evolution of Government

To what extent is this organism subject to the Darwinian laws of survival? It was a basic theory of classical economists that business enterprises survive only in so far as they adapt themselves to the changing economic environment, and that only the fittest survive, fitness being measured in terms of prices and profits. Whatever the truth of that hypothesis, mankind has determined not to try it out. At one end business has upset the free competitive test by monopolies and cartels, and at the other end the public has refused to let itself be pushed around freely by such combinations or to let business enterprises go to the wall in any wholesale fashion, when a whole system cannot meet the economic judgment day.

When we turn to governmental organizations we find even less "survival of the fittest." Governmental organizations seem to be extraordinarily immune to evolutionary changes. Next to the church, they are in all civilizations the most vigorous embodiments of immortality.[25] A governmental unit is by nature a monopoly, and is thus not subject to the purifying influence of competition. It does not have a profit and loss record; its balance sheet is buoyed up by "good will"; its product is priceless and often imponderable; its deficits are met from taxes, loans and hope. Under these conditions a governmental unit can continue for many years after its utility has passed, or its form of organization or program have become obsolete.

---

[25] The church has, of course, great advantage over the state in that the church deals with the inner spiritual life, and does not often come into direct physical conflict with those embattled forces which arise in the world of iron, coal, oil, labor, boundaries, colonies, wages, land, security, and airplanes. When the church does speak on these topics, it generally leaves the battle to other organizations, principally to the state. Under such conditions it is the state and not the church which runs the risk of extinction. A good illustration is the comparative mortality of the church and the state south of the Mason-Dixon line in 1865.

Mankind is extraordinarily docile and tolerant. Though men are born with the "unalienable Right"

> "to alter or abolish their Government and to institute new Government, laying its foundation on such principles and organizing its powers in such form, as to them shall seem most likely to effect their Safety and Happiness . . . all experience hath shown that mankind are more disposed to suffer, while evils are sufferable, than to right themselves by abolishing the forms to which they are accustomed."

While the immortality of governmental institutions thus reflects the natural conservatism of mankind and the tremendous force of inertia in human institutions, it shows also the ultimate elasticity of governmental institutions. Governments generally mend their ways and their policies so that they may survive. This is particularly true in a democracy. A democracy is characterized by the fact that there is built into the structure of the government a systematic method of introducing changes in program and method as the result of the broad movements of public opinion. As a result democratic constitutions should be more elastic, more subject to evolution, and therefore more immortal than other constitutions.

The struggle for survival in government thus becomes not so much a fight to the death, a test to destruction, but an endless process of adaptation to changed conditions and ideas. In this sense, governmental institutions are in continual evolution. But the process of evolution of human institutions is quite different from the process of evolution of living organisms.

The process of adaptation falls partly in the field of politics and partly in the field of administration. The two are so closely related, however, that the political aspects cannot be ignored completely even here, where we are concerned only with administrative organization. A glance at the present world situation makes it clear that the modern state faces as never before the need of rapid and radical adaptation to changed conditions. Governments which cannot make the necessary evolutionary changes will not survive. It becomes necessary, therefore, in the structure of the organization to make more elaborate provision for those agencies of management which concern themselves with the processes of adaptation.

What are these agencies? Are they not:

First, those which have to do with political life and leadership;

Second, those which have to do with getting new work promptly undertaken and efficiently done; and

Third, those which have to do with the careful observation of results?

This is not the place to discuss the first item, politics. From the standpoint of organization, however, it does seem that insufficient attention has been given to political life and leadership. Except in England, with its long tradition of collegiate executive responsibility, the political life of the nations of the world seems to be drifting into the hands of a single strong leader, and the currents of political life to be more and more confined by dikes within a narrow channel. While this may be the short cut to effective and immediate adaptation of the program and organization of the state, human experience seems to indicate that this structure of political life will have precisely the opposite result in the long run. If there is any truth in this observation, it would seem of extraordinary importance to take steps to expand the structure of political leadership and free the currents of political life. There must be leadership with increased scope for action, but every step toward increased power must be matched with a step toward increased accountability.

Instead of superseding or destroying legislative bodies, consultative institutions, and independent examination and audit because they stand in the way of quick changes in governmental programs, has not the time come to strengthen these organizations especially as agencies for the effective examination and criticism of policies which have been put into operation and thus as agencies for the more orderly consideration of new policies for the future?

In the field of organization the needs are clear. In periods of change, government must strengthen those agencies which deal with administrative management, that is, with co-ordination, with planning, with personnel, with fiscal control, and with research. These services constitute the brain and will of any enterprise. It is they that need development when we pass from a regime of habit to one demanding new thinking and new acting.

II

ORGANIZATION
AS A TECHNICAL PROBLEM

By

L. URWICK, O.B.E., M.C., M.A.

Chairman, Urwick Orr and Partners, Ltd.
Consulting Industrial Engineers

formerly
Director of the International Management Institute
Geneva

BASED ON A PAPER READ TO THE DEPARTMENT OF INDUSTRIAL CO-
OPERATION OF THE BRITISH ASSOCIATION FOR THE
ADVANCEMENT OF SCIENCE, LEICESTER
SEPTEMBER 7, 1933

ORGANIZATION AS A TECHNICAL PROBLEM

1. Need for a Technique of Organization

It is the general thesis of this paper that there are principles which can be arrived at inductively from the study of human experience of organization, which should govern arrangements for human association of any kind. These principles can be studied as a technical question, irrespective of the purpose of the enterprise, the personnel composing it, or any constitutional, political or social theory underlying its creation. They are concerned with the method of subdividing and allocating to individuals all the various activities, duties and responsibilities essential to the purpose contemplated, the correlation of these activities and the continuous control of the work of individuals so as to secure the most economical and the most effective realization of the purpose.

In existing world conditions, the practical importance of this subject can scarcely be exaggerated. In every aspect of its common life humanity is registering failures and enormously costly failures in its capacity for purposeful association. The majority of all nations earnestly desire peace: the machinery of peace works haltingly and ineffectively. In country after country liberty of speech and of person are lost, because democratic institutions fail to devise an administrative structure adapted to the speed and complexity of social evolution. The world's productive equipment is manifestly capable of yielding vastly increased quantities of goods and services: millions starve because the financing and distribution of this plenty are not organized. A machine technology points to the obvious economies of large-scale units of business control: amalgamations founder because there is widespread ignorance as to the methods of managing these aggregations.

2. Co-ordination

In 1931, under the title "Onward Industry,"[1] Messrs. James D. Mooney and Alan C. Reiley published a full-length book examining the comparative principles of organization as displayed historically in governmental, ecclesiastical, military and business structures. The general outline of their concepts is shown in *Figure I*. Their book constitutes the first serious attempt to deal with the subject comparatively and synoptically.

For the purpose of this paper it is sufficient to note their insistence on the importance of co-ordination:

> "This term expresses the principles of organization *in toto;* nothing less. This does not mean that there are no subordinated principles; it simply means that all the others are contained in this one of co-ordination. The others are simply the principles through which co-ordination operates, and thus becomes effective."[2]

Co-ordination operates in two different senses. If the total of the activities involved in any enterprise are represented as a square plane, the various groups of activ-

---

[1] James D. Mooney and Alan C. Reiley, "Onward Industry." Harper & Brothers, New York and London, 1931.
[2] *Ibid.*, p. 19.

THE PRINCIPLES OF ORGANIZATION

LOGICAL SCHEME DEVELOPED BY J.D.MOONEY & A.C.REILEY

"Comparatively speaking industrial organization has no history. ... Efficient forms of organization can be evolved only out of the hard school of human experience, and modern industry, because of the lack of this historical background, must seek for the principles it seeks to apply in other and older forms of human association."

ORGANIZATION
"is the form of every human association for the attainment of a common purpose."

PRINCIPLE
"In the practical sense the word principle may be applied to any underlying cause of more or less correlated facts in any particular field of investigation. The word principle as applied to organization is used by us strictly in this meaning."

	1. PRINCIPLE	2. PROCESS	3. EFFECT
1. THE COORDINATIVE PRINCIPLE	**AUTHORITY, OR COORDINATION PER SE**	**PROCESSIVE COORDINATION**	**EFFECTIVE COORDINATION**
"Organization begins when people, even if they be only two or more, combine their efforts for a given purpose. A simple illustration is two people combining their strength to lift a more a weighty object. The efforts of these two lifters must be coordinated. If first one lifted and then the other, there would be no unity of action, and hence no true organization of effort. .. Coordination expresses the principles of organization 'in toto'. . . . There are always two objectives of organization, the internal and the external. The latter may be anything according to the active purpose or interest which calls the group together, but the internal objectives of organization are coordinative, always."	"As coordination is the all-inclusive principle of organization, it must have its own principle and foundation in Authority, or the supreme coordinating power. Always in every organization, this supreme coordinating authority must rest somewhere, else there would be no directive for any truly coordinated effort."	"Coordination operates through the scalar process of leadership, with its delegation of duties."	"to effectuate a complete perpendicular functional correlation, which becomes likewise horizontal through organized staff contacts."
2. THE SCALAR PROCESS	**LEADERSHIP**	**DELEGATION**	**FUNCTIONAL DEFINITION**
"It is essential to the very idea and concept of organization that there must be a process, formal in character. A simple illustration is... The supreme coordinating authority operates throughout the whole structure of the organized body. This process is not an abstraction: it is a tangible reality observable in every form of organization. ... The Scalar Process is the same form in organization which is sometimes called hierarchical. ... It means the graduation of duties, not according to differentiated functions, for this involves another and different principle of organization, but simply according to degrees of authority and corresponding responsibility."	"Leadership is the form which authority assumes when it enters into process. . . . The supreme coordinating authority must be anterior to leadership in logical order, for it is this coordinating force which makes the organization. Leadership on the other hand always presupposes the organization. There can be no leadership without something to lead."	"Delegation means the conferring of a certain specified authority by a higher authority. . . . Delegation always means the conferring of authority of some kind and can never mean anything else. . . . Even the foreman of a section gang delegates an authority to his men to do certain things, which carries with it the responsibility for doing what is thus authorized. . . . When an organization outgrows the possibility of universal face-to-face leadership there must ensue that feature of organization which we may call sub-delegation. The leader no longer delegates an authority to do certain specific things, but he begins to delegate an authority similar to his own, in other words he delegates the right of delegation itself."	"Functional definition is antecedent to all actual functions because it is the form in organization that assigns all functions. . . . We have defined the scalar principle as the processive form and the functional principle as the effective form of organized coordination. It is evident therefore that there must be in this scalar process some ultimate form that produces the functional effect. . . . This form is functional definition which is the end, the aim and the finality of the entire scalar process. . . . The scalar chain may be a long one with its successive links . . . but always there is the last link, where authority ceases to delegate authority over others and simply delegates or assigns specific functions."
3. THE FUNCTIONAL EFFECT	**DETERMINATIVE FUNCTIONALISM**	**APPLICATIVE FUNCTIONALISM**	**INTERPRETATIVE FUNCTIONALISM**
"By the term functionalism, considered as a principle of organization, we mean the differentiation or distinction between kind of duties. . . . The scalar differentiation refers simply to degrees or gradations of authority, implicit in the very existence of a separate department, there may be certain general functions, appearing in some form in many departments, which in turn may require organized supervision and correlation. This we have cross-functionalism. . . . The organized supervision of any function of this character itself becomes departmental. . . . Cross departmentalism is an extended application of the principle of horizontal correlation."	"In every organization there must be some function that decides or determines the objective & the procedure necessary to its attainment ... may be called the determinative ... in secular government always known as the legislative."	"another that moves through this procedure to the attainment of this purpose .... the applicative or the executive"	"and a third that makes interpretative decisions in accordance with those rules or laws of procedure that have been determined .... the interpretative or judicial."

THE STAFF PHASE OF FUNCTIONALISM

"The fact that functions may not be separated in any way destroy their identity as functions. ... The ideal of organized efficiency is not the complete segregation, but the integrated correlation of the three primary functions as such. ... The organizer must identify these functional principles as they appear in every job and make them the basis of his correlation. ... The duty of the manager is to correlate the people who perform these functions. .. Management however represents the scalar principle ... perpendicular correlation.... the horizontal correlation requires other contacts. ...The dissemination of understanding .. of the common purpose, of the relation of individuals to that purpose & to each other.. (leads to) the staff phase of functionalism, the service of advice or counsel as distinguished from the function of authority or command. This service has three phases:"

THE INFORMATIVE

"refers to those things authority should know in framing its decisions.... Always there are too many things to think about..for the unaided capacity of one leader to think about..for the unaided capacity of one leader to compass. .... It is imperative that these problems should come to him predigested."

THE ADVISORY

"refers to the actual counsel, based on such information. ...Though all decisions must remain with the directing head... (he needs) all the thought and all the research that organized staff service can bestow on them. .... No advance in human knowledge will ever exclude the leader's need for the counsel of elemental human wisdom, & especially of collective wisdom, in the making of all important decisions."

THE SUPERVISORY

"refers to both of the preceding phases as applied to all the details of execution. Through this phase the informative & advisory features become operative through-out an entire organization...There are two prime necessities in an efficient staff service which may be termed coordination & infiltration....Those down the line to whom is delegated the carrying out of orders need the information that is requisite in a truly intelligent execution."

FIGURE I. THE PRINCIPLES OF ORGANIZATION

(As developed by J. D. Mooney and A. C. Reiley)

ities will be found to be divided both by vertical and by horizontal lines drawn up and down and across the square. The work of individuals is always divided by vertical lines into different tasks. Such subdivision is usually either "serial" — the responsibilities follow each other in process, "unitary" — the responsibilities are defined by areas or objects, or "functional" — the responsibilities are distinguished by kinds or subjects. But where any large numbers are concerned, work must also be divided up by horizontal lines into different *levels of authority and responsibility.* This grouping into levels is the special thesis of this paper. The adjustment of the resulting authorities and responsibilities to each other and their continuous correlation constitute one of the main tasks of leadership in any enterprise.

3. THE SCALAR PROCESS

The evolution of ideas on this question has been comparatively simple. Originally almost all undertakings were organized on what has been called the "line" or, incorrectly, the "military," principle. Emphasis was placed on the importance of what Mooney and Reiley have described as the "scalar process" [3] —

> "The supreme co-ordinating authority must rest somewhere and in some form in every organization. . . . It is equally essential to the very idea and concept of organization that there must be a process, formal in character, through which this co-ordinating authority operates from the top throughout the entire structure of the organized body."

The considerations which appeared of greatest importance were that there should be clear lines of authority running from the top into every corner of the undertaking and that the responsibility of subordinates exercising delegated authority should be precisely defined. Since, in all cases, concrete objects, physical boundaries or the limits of some well-known technical process, offer the simplest and readiest means of definition, the unitary or serial methods were almost universally adopted in subdividing and grouping activities into tasks. Division into levels followed the method, A supervises B-C-D and E; B supervises P-Q-R and S; P supervises W-X-Y and Z and so on, the supervisor at each level being totally responsible for every aspect of his subordinates' work.

4. SPECIALIZATION

Modifications of this arrangement have occurred throughout human history. Wherever human knowledge and skill have been specialized, for instance in the case of the law, somehow and somewhere that specialized authority has had to be integrated with overall authority and responsibility. But, since the introduction of power-driven machinery and the great advances in applied scientific knowledge of the nineteenth century, the amount and complexity of specialized skill required in connection with every kind of human enterprise have vastly increased.

The first formal recognition of the consequence of this tendency for previous ideas about organization came from F. W. Taylor. Imbued as he was with the necessity of basing industrial management upon exact measurement and specialized knowledge, he was impressed with the impossibility of discovering subordinates who could exercise overall responsibility with maximum effectiveness in respect of all its aspects. In

---

[3] James D. Mooney and Alan C. Reiley, *op. cit.*

this connection he developed two of his well-known principles of management. The first was the separation of planning from performance —

> "All possible brain work should be removed from the shop and centered in the planning department."

The second was the substitution for the older type of organization of what he called "functional" management.

> "Functional Management consists in so dividing the work of management that each man from the assistant superintendent down shall have as few functions as possible to perform." [4]

By a "function" Taylor meant a particular kind of work, a subject.

Under these principles as Taylor operated them each worker was managed by four foremen in the shop specialized in certain aspects of his task. The task itself was set by four further specialists working in the planning department. This part of his general management practice has been applied less, and with less success where attempted, than any other feature of his work. It must be recognized, however, that his ideas on the subject rendered an immense service. In the first place the removal of much of the routine of management from detailed personal control to the operation of system eliminated an important source of friction from industrial life. In the second place his insistence on the need for specializing the work allotted to individuals in order to command exact and scientific knowledge made possible immense advances in the art of management. On the other hand his mis-description of the older type of management as "military," has discouraged students of organization from turning to the one field where the need for co-ordination is overwhelming and in which experience in the control of large numbers is centuries old. Taylor's experiments were chiefly concerned with a single department — usually a machine shop. And even in such cases co-ordination was secured through a Superintendent in charge of the shop as a whole, and an Assistant Superintendent who looked after the Planning Room. But, when his conception of a division of responsibilities by function is carried higher up the line of control in any large enterprise difficulty is encountered immediately. The "scalar process" is weakened. Co-ordination lapses or is secured only by exceptional efforts.

> "When a considerable amount of staff organization is introduced . . . this tends naturally to weaken the disciplinary effects of line control; and where staff organization is used to any marked degree special care must be used to supply co-ordinative influences to compensate for this weakness." [5]

5. THE SPAN OF CONTROL

For this, there is a quite definite reason. Students of administration have long recognized that, in practice, no human brain should attempt to supervise directly more than five, or at the most, six other individuals whose work is interrelated. Mr. A. V. Graicunas of Paris has shown why this is so. An individual who is co-ordinating the work of others whose duties interconnect must take into account in his decisions, not only the reactions of each person concerned as an individual, but also his reactions

---

[4] Cf. F. W. Taylor, "Shop Management," pp. 98 and 99.

[5] Dexter S. Kimball, "Principles of Industrial Organization," p. 63. "Staff" as used in this quotation implies a man or department specialized in a particular function.

THE SPAN OF CONTROL — GRAICUNAS' THEORY.

If Tom supervises two persons, Dick and Harry, he can speak to each of them individually or he can speak to them as a pair.

Thus, even in this extremely simple unit of organization, Tom must hold four to six relationships within his span of attention:

Direct Single Relationships.
Tom to Dick and Tom to Harry 2

Direct Group Relationships.
Tom to Dick with Harry and Tom to Harry with Dick 2

Cross Relationships.
Harry with Dick and Dick with Harry 2

Total Relationships 6

The effect of these distinctions as brought out in the accompanying tables and chart, should be read as follows:

n — number of persons supervised;
a — number of direct single relationships;
b — number of cross relationships;
c — number of direct group relationships;
d — $a+b$;
e — $a+c$;
f — $a+b+c$,

computed on the maximum basis as indicated above. In the second table b', c', d', e', and f', indicate similar figures computed on the minimum basis.

DIRECT AND CROSS RELATIONSHIPS

Table I Computed on Maximum Basis

relationship		formulae	1	2	3	4	5	6	7	8	9	10	11	12
direct single	$a =$	n	1	2	3	4	5	6	7	8	9	10	11	12
cross	$b =$	$n(n-1)$	0	2	6	12	20	30	42	56	72	90	110	132
direct group	$c =$	$n\left(\frac{2^n}{2}-1\right)$	0	2	9	28	75	186	441	1016	2295	5110	11253	24564
total direct single and cross	$d =$	$a+b = n^2$	1	4	9	16	25	36	49	64	81	100	121	144
total direct	$e =$	$a+c$	1	4	12	32	80	192	448	1024	2304	5120	11264	24576
total direct and cross	$f =$	$a+b+c = n\left(\frac{2^n}{2}+n-1\right)$	1	6	18	44	100	222	490	1080	2376	5210	11374	24708

Table II Computed on Minimum Basis

relationship		formulae	1	2	3	4	5	6	7	8	9	10	11	12
direct single	$a =$	n	1	2	3	4	5	6	7	8	9	10	11	12
cross	$b' =$	$\frac{n}{2}(n-1)$	0	1	3	6	10	15	21	28	36	45	55	66
direct group	$c' =$	2^n-n-1	0	1	4	11	26	57	120	247	502	1013	2036	4083
total direct single and cross	$d' =$	$a+b'$	1	3	6	10	15	21	28	36	45	55	66	78
total direct	$e' =$	$a+c'$	1	3	7	15	31	63	127	255	511	1023	2047	4095
total direct and cross	$f' =$	$a+b'+c' = \frac{n}{2}(n-1)+2^n-(n-1)-1$	1	4	10	21	41	78	148	283	547	1068	2102	4161

Illustrations of Direct and Cross Relationships

a — direct single relationship (Tom — Dick — Harry)

b — cross relationship (Tom, Dick, Harry)

c — direct group relationship (Tom, Dick-Harry, Harry-Dick)

Chart of Direct and Cross Relationships

$a = n$
$b = n(n-1)$
$c = n\left(\frac{2^n}{2}-1\right)$
$f = n\left(\frac{2^n}{2}+n-1\right)$

Curves: f = total direct plus cross relationships; c = direct group relationships; b = cross relationships; a = direct single relationships

Axes: Number of Relationships (0–500); Number of Subordinates (0–7)

Note: Sharp rise in curve beyond four subordinates denotes rapid increase in complexity of relationships

CHART SHOWING DIRECT GROUP RELATIONSHIPS

Number of members per group

1 Subordinate
- 1: A

2 Subordinates
- 1: A B
- 2: AB

3 Subordinates
- 1: A B C
- 2: AB AC BC
- 3: ABC

4 Subordinates
- 1: A B C D
- 2: AB AC AD BC BD CD
- 3: ABC ABD ACD BCD
- 4: ABCD

5 Subordinates
- 1: A B C D E
- 2: AB AC AD AE BC BD BE CD CE DE
- 3: ABC ABD ABE ACD ACE ADE BCD BCE BDE CDE
- 4: ABCD ABCE ABDE ACDE BCDE
- 5: ABCDE

6 Subordinates
- 1: A B C D E F
- 2: AB AC AD AE AF BC BD BE BF CD CE CF DE DF EF
- 3: ABC ABD ABE ABF ACD ACE ACF ADE ADF AEF BCD BCE BCF BDE BDF BEF CDE CDF CEF DEF
- 4: ABCD ABCE ABCF ABDE ABDF ABEF ACDE ACDF ACEF ADEF BCDE BCDF BCEF BDEF CDEF
- 5: ABCDE ABCDF ABCEF ABDEF ACDEF BCDEF
- 6: ABCDEF

7 Subordinates
- 1: A B C D E F G
- 2: AB AC AD AE AF AG BC BD BE BF BG CD CE CF CG DE DF DG EF EG FG
- 3: ABC ABD ABE ABF ABG ACD ACE ACF ACG ADE ADF ADG AEF AEG AFG BCD BCE BCF BCG BDE BDF BDG BEF BEG BFG CDE CDF CDG CEF CEG CFG DEF DEG DFG EFG
- 4: ABCD ABCE ABCF ABCG ABDE ABDF ABDG ABEF ABEG ABFG ACDE ACDF ACDG ACEF ACEG ACFG ADEF ADEG ADFG AEFG BCDE BCDF BCDG BCEF BCEG BCFG BDEF BDEG BDFG BEFG CDEF CDEG CDFG CEFG DEFG
- 5: ABCDE ABCDF ABCDG ABCEF ABCEG ABCFG ABDEF ABDEG ABDFG ABEFG ACDEF ACDEG ACDFG ACEFG ADEFG BCDEF BCDEG BCDFG BCEFG BDEFG CDEFG
- 6: ABCDEF ABCDEG ABCDFG ABCEFG ABDEFG ACDEFG BCDEFG
- 7: ABCDEFG

Note that for four subordinates it is quite easy to grasp and remember every combination of groups, but that from five on, this is no longer possible, because the various groups become a maze of confusion.

FIGURE II. THE SPAN OF CONTROL—GRAICUNAS' THEORY

as a member of any possible grouping of persons which may arise during the course of the work.

The psychological conception of "the span of attention" places strict limits on the number of separate factors which the human mind can grasp simultaneously. It has its administrative counterpart in what may be described as *"the span of control."* A supervisor with five subordinates reporting directly to him, who adds a sixth, increases his available human resources by 20 per cent. But he adds approximately 100 per cent to the complexity and difficulty of his task of co-ordination. The number of relationships which he must consider increases not by arithmetical but by geometrical progression. The operation of this principle is shown graphically in *Figure II.* [6]

Neglect of the limitations imposed by "the span of control" creates insoluble problems in co-ordination. Two examples are given in *Figures III and IV*.

The first shows the organization of the Secretariat of the League of Nations proposed by a Committee which reported in 1930. Arrangements are made for no less than 15 independent officials to report direct to the Secretary-General. When it is remembered that, in addition to this administrative task, he has also to maintain personally, political and diplomatic relations with the individuals composing the heterogeneous and constantly changing delegations of more than fifty states, members of the League, some of the breakdowns in the machinery of peace, call for little further explanation. The organization is totally inadequate to the complexity of the task.

The second shows in outline the administrative organization of the British Government. In the Cabinet alone the Prime Minister has to co-ordinate the work of 17 ministers. There are as many or more departments not represented in the Cabinet. The provision of a number of separate departments dealing with functional questions in relation to Scotland only is an interesting example of the persistence of local sentiment and traditional arrangements, despite altered circumstances and a great increase in the complexity of government. Such mechanisms cannot apply the scientific knowledge which is available to the task of administration.

Specialization is essential. Without it men cannot be found capable of placing at the service of any undertaking the most recent and approved methods in relation to each of its activities. On the other hand, if it is to be effective, specialization must be to some degree authoritative. This consideration inevitably complicates the work of co-ordination. In a business enterprise, for instance, a chief executive with a pure departmental organization who wishes to market a new product, X, will simply tell the manager of the department responsible for that class of product to go and make X and sell it. But a chief executive with a highly specialized organization must bring all kinds of officials together to plan out the part that each has to play in producing and selling X. Plans having been made, he must supervise each separate specialist to secure that his work coincides in time, space, quantity and quality with the work of others. Moreover, conflicts between specialists of different kinds or between specialists and general managers are difficult to avoid.

> "The great difficulty lies in getting the members of the Staff Departments and those of the Line Departments to co-operate." [7]

---

[6] For a fuller exposition of Mr. Graicunas' theory, vide his paper in this collection, entitled "Relationship in Organization," pp. 181–187.

[7] Paul M. Atkins, "Factory Management," p. 39. Here again "staff" is used of a department specialized in a particular function.

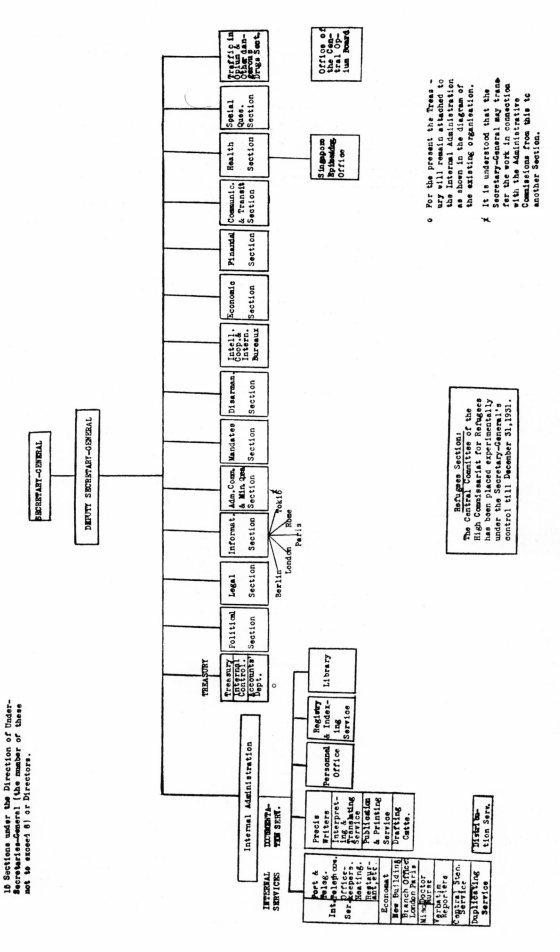

FIGURE III. FUTURE ORGANIZATION OF THE SECRETARIAT OF THE LEAGUE OF NATIONS

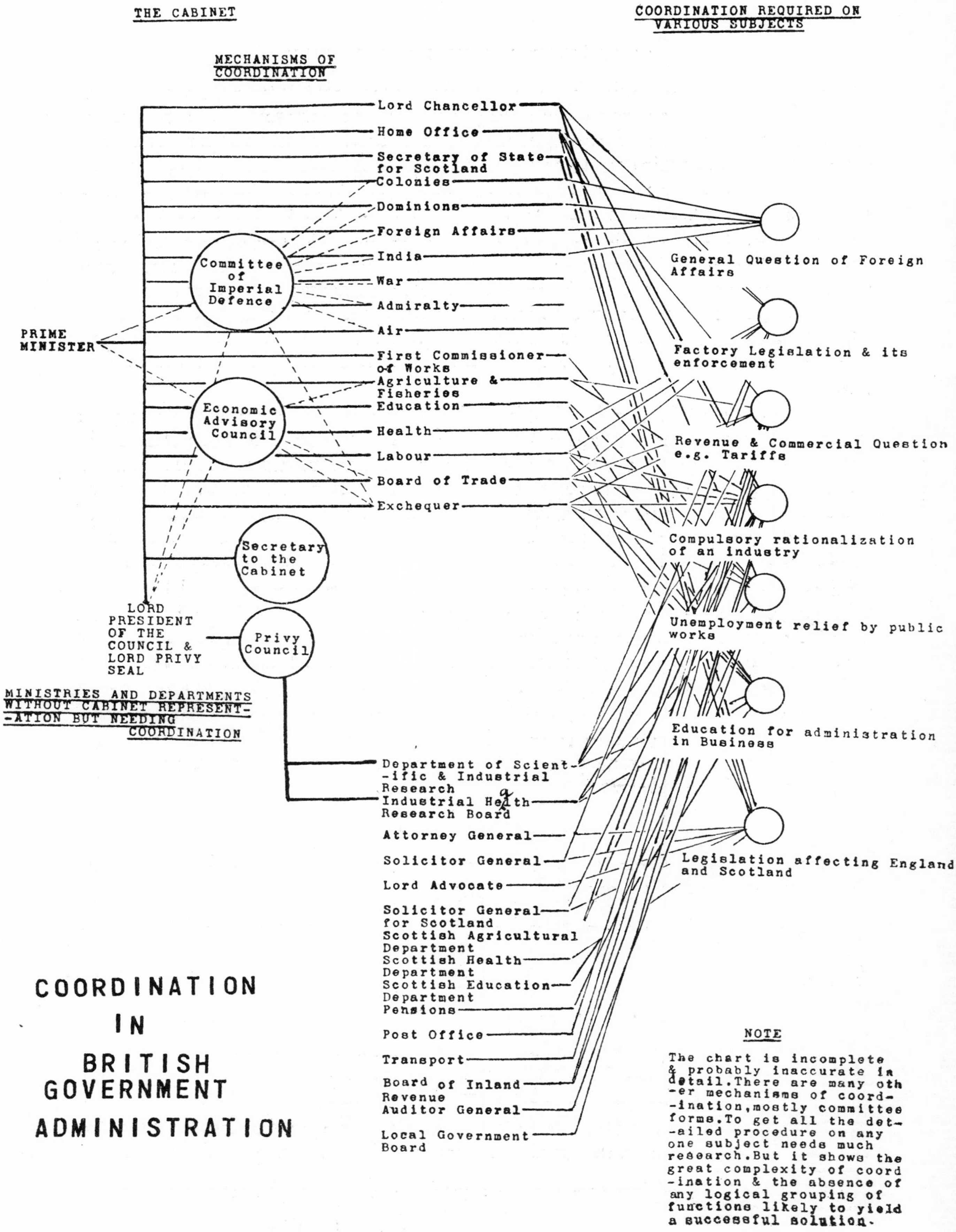

THE CABINET
COORDINATION REQUIRED ON VARIOUS SUBJECTS
MECHANISMS OF COORDINATION
Lord Chancellor
Home Office
Secretary of State for Scotland
Colonies
Dominions
Foreign Affairs
India
War
Admiralty
Air
First Commissioner of Works
Agriculture & Fisheries
Education
Health
Labour
Board of Trade
Exchequer
Committee of Imperial Defence
Economic Advisory Council
Secretary to the Cabinet
PRIME MINISTER
LORD PRESIDENT OF THE COUNCIL & LORD PRIVY SEAL
Privy Council
MINISTRIES AND DEPARTMENTS WITHOUT CABINET REPRESENT-ATION BUT NEEDING COORDINATION
Department of Scient-ific & Industrial Research
Industrial Health Research Board
Attorney General
Solicitor General
Lord Advocate
Solicitor General for Scotland
Scottish Agricultural Department
Scottish Health Department
Scottish Education Department
Pensions
Post Office
Transport
Board of Inland Revenue
Auditor General
Local Government Board
General Question of Foreign Affairs
Factory Legislation & its enforcement
Revenue & Commercial Question e.g. Tariffs
Compulsory rationalization of an industry
Unemployment relief by public works
Education for administration in Business
Legislation affecting England and Scotland
COORDINATION IN BRITISH GOVERNMENT ADMINISTRATION
NOTE
The chart is incomplete & probably inaccurate in detail. There are many oth-er mechanisms of coord-ination, mostly committee forms. To get all the det-ailed procedure on any one subject needs much research. But it shows the great complexity of coord-ination & the absence of any logical grouping of functions likely to yield a successful solution.

FIGURE IV. CO-ORDINATION IN BRITISH GOVERNMENT ADMINISTRATION

In every undertaking the "scalar principle" must be observed or authority breaks down. If the subdivision of the authority of the leading officials is on "functional" lines, this subdivision recurs throughout the enterprise. Decisions multiply which call for a correlation of different "functional" views, a correlation which can only be authoritative if made by the chief executive himself. At the same time there must be subordinate co-ordinating points. A planning room in New York cannot manage a factory in San Francisco. But when this is admitted the chief executive finds himself with immediate subordinates both on a "functional" and on a "unitary" basis. There is a tendency for their number to exceed his "span of control." If he groups "functions" the same difficulty of cross-correlation occurs at lower levels of the organization. The dilemma is a real one. In a large organization the complex of different principles which demand consideration in the structure of authority and responsibility may be most serious.

An example of the problem is offered by the British postal organization. Under the Postmaster General, a political appointment, the Director of the Post Office is the chief of a very large staff. Obviously some form of area delegation of the work of co-ordinating Post Office services and activities is indicated. On the other hand, the work calls for specialized supervision in certain important respects, notably finance, engineering and personnel. But in the minds of the public who control the Post Office through Parliament, it is the various different services — mails, telegraphs and telephones — which are the focus of attention. Parliamentary questions are apt to take the form of "Who is responsible for the telephones?"

There are thus three different requirements which should be met, and must all to some degree be met, in delegating authority — area co-ordination, control of special functions and responsibility for different services. How is the Director of the Post Office to secure that his work is properly supervised and co-ordinated in each of these respects, without infringing the principle of "the span of control"? Yet that principle is absolute. In so far as the chief of any enterprise departs from it, he renders his control weaker and less effective.

6. "Line and Staff"

The solution so far adopted in practice is known as the "Line and Staff" system of organization. It is admittedly a compromise.

> "The line and staff type of organization is a combination of the best features of both the line and functional types"[8]

or again

> "Line and staff organization combines features of both the line and functional types."[9]

Precise statement of what is meant by the term is lacking. A form of organization may be described with reference to the functions allotted to the various positions or with reference to the relations between different positions.

On the first point writers on business administration give divergent opinions. Thus "staff" positions or departments have been variously described as those which

---

[8] N. B. Cornell, "Industrial Organization and Management.'   [9] L. P. Alford, "Management's Handbook."

a. "deal with one particular phase of business." [10]

b. "give expert advice to the line officers. The primary functional divisions are Sales, Engineering, Manufacturing and Finance." [11]

c. "are in charge of a single staff function or certain similar or supplementary functions." [12]

d. are engaged in "the business of analyzing, testing, comparing, recording, making researches, co-ordinating information and advising." [13]

e. "furnish the means of developing standards and plans for which a regular line position leaves no time." [14]

f. "give special types of services." [15]

g. are "responsible for investigations, study and designing. . . . Routine executive direction of performance usually requires the rapid shifting of attention from one immediate problem to another, leaving little time either for reverie or for continuous concentrated attention to a single idea." [16]

The dominating idea is that of specialization — Taylor's conception. Any function which is specialized may apparently become a "staff" function.

On the second point there is a greater measure of agreement. The majority of writers emphasize that the relation of the staff to other departments is advisory.

a. "The essential feature of the staff organization is that it is purely consultative and advisory." [17]

b. "Fundamentally the staff departments are advisory in their character." [18]

c. "The staff man usually serves in an advisory capacity to a line executive. He frequently has no authority." [19]

But on the other hand

d. "The line supervisor . . . is responsible for seeing that the recommendations and instructions of the staff experts are carried out." [20]

e. "In theory, a staff department has complete authority in its particular field in so far as policies and methods are concerned." [21]

In a few business concerns which have paid close attention to organization the relationships between "staff" and line officials have been defined closely. Messrs. Mooney and Reiley have perceived that the "staff" function has not only informational and advisory phases, but a supervisory phase which includes the services of inspection. As might be expected, the General Motors Export Company of which Mr. Mooney is President has definite and acceptable ideas on this point.

"A line officer exercises authority over all of the body of organization lying beneath him on the chart, whereas the influence exerted by a staff officer outside of his immediate department is, so far as it is authoritative, an authority of ideas. The staff officers are, in their functional capacities, responsible advisers to their respective line superiors, and advisers also to the corresponding staff officers in the subordinate organization strata, but any direct line instructions they may wish to see promulgated may be promulgated only back through

[10] B. H. Lansburgh, "Industrial Management."

[11] Dexter S. Kimball, "Principles of Industrial Organization."

[12] W. B. Cornell, "Industrial Organization and Management."

[13] H. S. Dennison, "Organization Engineering."   [14] O. Sheldon, "The Philosophy of Management."

[15] Paul M. Atkins, "Factory Management."   [16] H. P. Dutton, "Principles of Organization."

[17] O. Sheldon, op. cit.   [18] Paul M. Atkins, op. cit.   [19] H. P. Dutton, op. cit.   [20] W. B. Cornell, op. cit.

[21] R. C. Davis, "Factory Organization and Management."

their line of contact with their superiors and down thence to the line officers in the next subordinate stratum. . . . If the expression descriptive of a staff officer's authority — an 'authority of ideas' — means anything at all, it means that the staff executives' plans and recommendations are entitled to the respect and consideration of the line executive. A very definite burden is, therefore, put upon the line executive who sees fit to disregard or to reject the counsel and help of his staff associates. . . . Four cardinal principles . . . enter into a proper understanding of the relationship between line and staff. . . .

1. Line and staff are jointly responsible for performance.
2. A staff officer discharges his responsibility by furnishing information and advice which he makes available to the line officer unselfishly and without thought of personal credit for the results accomplished.
3. Although staff executives are charged with responsibilities that have to do with internal administrative phases of the work in their own departments, this does not give them direct authority over the line forces in subordinate organization strata, nor does it relieve their line superiors of the basic responsibility for the results of their work.
4. The line recognizes the purpose and value of the staff and makes full use of its advice and assistance. In order that the line may properly do so, the staff must create for itself an authority of ideas, and must, by competence and tact, obtain and justify the line's confidence." [22]

7. Emphasis on Relationship

Indeed, hitherto, the major emphasis in business organization has been placed on this question of relationships. There is a natural resistance among subordinates in all undertakings to any new form of specialization. Officials, as human beings, resent and obstruct any suggestion that functions which they are performing and authority which they are exercising should be transferred to another. An historic and very amusing example is found in Lytton Strachey's account of the difficulties raised by doctors of the Royal Army Medical Corps when Florence Nightingale first suggested the specialization, and, last horror, the feminization, of the function of nursing. When that very determined lady insisted on unpacking shirts for wounded men who were freezing, before a Board of Audit had sat on these supplies — a procedure which usually occupied three weeks — the Purveyor stood helplessly by "wringing his hands in departmental agony." [23]

Leaders are apprehensive of any weakening among subordinates of the sense of full responsibility and hence of discipline. They recognize that if responsibility is not direct, the "scalar process" will break down. As the work of subordinates becomes more specialized it is apparent that, in the absence of any adequate solution of the problem of co-ordination, the overall control of the chief will be less effective.

In consequence almost every discussion and every experiment concerned with the introduction of new specialist supervision, centers round the relationships with the existing line officials, the safeguarding of their authority and the protection of the direct chain of responsibility. Business has become more concerned in determining what specialized officials are *not* to do, than in studying what they *should* do. It does not define a man's functions and responsibilities in an organization to tell him that they are "purely consultative and advisory." It merely throws upon him the responsibility of securing executive action, without giving him the necessary authority.

---

[22] Cf. "Organization and Operating Principles," E. W. Smith, Handbook of Business Administration, pp. 1474–1488.
[23] Cf. Lytton Strachey. "Eminent Victorians."

Inevitably there has been tacit evasion of the more important question as to what should be the duties and functions of officials in a "staff" position. This has added to the confusion of thought on the whole subject. There is reason to suspect that the compromise does not integrate the two principles. The necessity for specialized authority is accepted in theory. But the difficulties which it raises in practice in relation to co-ordination are concealed in verbiage. It is said that the specialists have no authority or only "an authority of ideas." In effect such phrases imply a surrender of specialized control.

8. EFFECT ON CO-ORDINATION

More important, if the various functions and relationships assigned to "staff" officials in books on industrial management are a correct description of practice, they carry the implication that such officials cannot, by the very nature of their work and position relieve their chiefs of any of the increased burden of co-ordination which is the central theme of this paper. It is impossible to contend that an official is diminishing his chief's co-ordinating task:

1. If he is specializing in the work of some function previously performed by subordinates in the normal "line" organization. He is merely adding one to the number of individuals whose views the chief has to consider, and the geometric progression of the number of direct subordinates whom his work affects, to the relationships his chief must take into consideration.

2. If he is a specialist himself in some particular function. The main task of co-ordination on the intellectual side is to synthesize the views of various specialists and to iron out the bias which specialization inevitably produces. If an official is himself a specialist he merely adds to the number of opinions which his chief must analyze and correlate in his own mind. Moreover, co-ordination is essentially a question of relationships. As has been pointed out, "specialization tends so to narrow the executive's appreciation and knowledge of relationships as to make it impossible for him effectively to create and to maintain those relationships for which he is responsible."

3. If he combines staff and "line" functions, other than the immediate control of such few subordinates as are necessary for investigation and record in connection with his own proper work. If he is responsible for any of the main functions of the undertaking, an executive bias is added to the intellectual bias mentioned in 2. In addition this form of arrangement violates both Taylor's main principles. The official has not "as few functions as possible to perform." His position does not segregate "planning from performance," a feature emphasized by a number of writers as the fundamental characteristic of the "staff" concept.

4. If his relationship to his chief or to this chief's principal subordinates, is "purely advisory." Co-ordination is essentially an executive function. No part of the executive burden of co-ordination is removed from a chief's shoulders by the receipt of advice, additional to that which he should seek in any event from his principal subordinates. The chief purpose of co-ordination is to secure detailed correlated action by individuals: the chief obstacles it has to overcome are differences of outlook or emphasis leading to heterogeneous initiatives. An official who is only entitled to "give ad-

vice" which may or may not be accepted, cannot relieve his chief of any part of the personal difficulties involved.

5. If his main work is investigational. A "staff" official may well undertake investigations for his chief. But, unless those investigations are synthetic, are designed to bring together various functional aspects of a particular problem, they do not contribute to the task of co-ordination. If they are concerned with a single "function" or subject, they might equally well be undertaken by an official in any other relationship. Their assignment to a member of the "staff" merely indicates that the organization is not equipped to deal with that particular function or subject.

"A staff is something to lean on." [24] A chief cannot lean on a "staff" official who is adding to, rather than decreasing, the burden of his main preoccupation.

9. The Problem of Terminology

One reason for this situation appears to be a lack of discrimination in terminology. The "staff" conception is admittedly borrowed from military life. But in military phraseology the term "staff" is used by a number of armies in two senses. The wider sense implies all specialized troops and services; the narrower sense, sometimes qualified as "general staff," implies selected officers who assist the commander in carrying out his functions of command. These two groups, the specialist troops and services and the "staff" proper, have completely different functions and relationships in army organization. Even the most authoritative students of business organization appear to have missed the full significance of this distinction.

The terms used in the United States army distinguish between "general staff officers" and "technical and administrative staff officers." It is interesting that so sympathetic an authority as Mr. H. S. Dennison actually quotes from a United States army manual which makes this distinction without, apparently, appreciating its significance from the standpoint of business practice.

> "*General staff officers* assist the commander by performing such *duties pertaining to the function of command* as may be delegated to them by regulations or given them by the commander. *Technical and administrative staff officers* assist the commander *and his general staff* in an advisory capacity in *matters pertaining to* their *special branches.*" [25]

Mr. Dennison comments:

> "Business uses the term 'functionalizing' to distinguish, though not always very clearly, the establishment of departments to give special types of service, usually advisory, to the more strictly operating departments. They correspond to what in the older Army parlance are called 'staff' departments or 'staff' officers in distinction from the 'line.' . . . The history of the evolution of army organization as it has worked itself out over many centuries is rich in suggestive material." [26]

Mooney and Reiley note that:

> "The modern military application concreted in the term 'general staff' is something to which the student of organization must give his careful attention. . . . There is a vital respect in which military staff organization is in advance of anything yet developed in the

---

[24] Edgar W. Smith, *op. cit.*

[25] "Command, Staff and Tactics," General Service Schools, Fort Leavenworth, quoted by Dennison. Italics are the author's.　　　　　[26] H. S. Dennison, "Organization Engineering," pp. 144–7.

average industrial establishment. This is in the service of transmission of line decisions to everyone concerned. . . . Although co-ordinated staff service in a form that resembles the military general staff is growing in business institutions, the office of Chief of Staff or any office under any name existing solely for the purpose of co-ordinating these functions is unknown in industrial organizations." [27]

Other writers who discuss methods of co-ordination do not mention "staff" as a means to this end.

"Of the several mechanisms that are in use to secure co-ordination of effort and executive control the most important, perhaps, are organization charts, organization records, standard procedure instructions, orders and returns, records of performance, administrative reports and committees." [28]

In the British army the distinction between staff and specialized functions is definite. Those who "assist the commander in the execution of his functions of command" are known as "staff officers" irrespective of their special branch: "General Staff" is used to describe the particular branch of staff duties concerned with operations as contrasted with the branches concerned with administration. The troops commanded and administered by the commander and his staff are divided into fighting troops and services. "Fighting troops carry out the actual operations." Their maintenance is secured by "the services" which "provide them with all their requirements in personnel, animals and military material." [29]

Both these groups are themselves considerably specialized — the fighting troops into various technical arms and the services into various administrative functions, supply and transport, equipment, medical, veterinary and so on. In practice the "line" really consists of Infantry and Artillery — the principal arms. The "staff" co-ordinates all arms and services. But the technical fighting troops — engineers, signals, machine guns etc. — are co-ordinated with the "line" almost exclusively through the staff, and the services report to the staff in accordance with regulations. The Commanders of Infantry and Artillery formations in a division are senior to, the commanders of units of the more important technical troops and services are the equals in rank of, the principal staff officers.

The duties of "the staff" are laid down with great precision.

"It must be the main object of staff organization to ensure a smooth and efficient co-ordination of effort between all portions of the force." [29]

There is a very wide distinction in character between the command of technical troops or specialized services, i.e. in business parlance, the control of specialized staff departments, and the co-ordinative duties allocated to the "staff." The principal officers of such technical troops or specialized services carry out some "staff" duties in that they act as advisers to the commander on the subjects falling within their field. But nine times out of ten he will seek such advice through the appropriate staff officer. The staff officer's relations to such specialized or technical troops and services are closely defined.

---

[27] *Op. cit.*   [28] Cf. Dexter S. Kimball, "Principles of Industrial Organization," p. 103.
[29] Quotations from British "Field Service Regulations," Vol. I, *Organization and Administration.*

"The commander's staff is responsible that his intentions are known and understood . . . is charged with the issue, both to the services at headquarters and to the subordinate commanders, of such orders and instructions as will enable co-ordinated action to be taken. . . . Staff officers alone have authority to sign on behalf of commanders. Every order and instruction issued through the staff is given by the authority of the commander and on his responsibility."

But

"the commander and his principal staff officers are responsible for decisions on technical and financial questions only when the head of a service refers such questions to them and . . . the power of interposing in questions of this nature is confined to the commander." [29]

The Staff Officer is not himself a specialist.

"The heads and representatives of services are the advisers of the staff in regard to matters connected with their services, and the staff should consult them before forming an opinion. . . . The methods to be adopted should be left to the head of a service to determine."

Moreover

"while it is necessary that the work of the staff should be distributed in accordance with the nature of the duties to be performed, . . . there is but one staff, having but one purpose. . . . It is essential for efficient staff work that officers of each branch should have a practical knowledge of the work of other branches. . . . The relationship between all officers serving on the staff must be close and cordial." [29]

The Staff Officer has virtually no "line" functions, other than the control of such subordinate staff officers and clerical staff as are required for his own special work of co-ordination. His and their duties are:

a. The collection of information for the assistance of the commander and its dissemination to his subordinates.
b. The transmission of the commander's orders and instructions.
c. The anticipation of the difficulties likely to be encountered or material required and the arrangement of all matters so as to facilitate the carrying out of the commander's plans.

Thus it may be said that, though he commands no one, he assists the commander to command everyone, that while he provides nothing but information, yet he arranges everything so that the fighting troops and services whose function it is to "execute," may be enabled to do so with the maximum of unity and the minimum of friction.

10. DIFFICULTY IN UNDERSTANDING STAFF PRINCIPLE

Civil administrators have found it difficult to understand this special relationship by which the commander retains his full responsibility and authority while delegating much of the work of administration. Co-ordination has always been associated with command, with control. It has not been regarded merely as one of the special aspects of command, but as bound up with the personality of the chief. Leaders themselves have not appreciated the possibility of delegating not only the drafting of formal arrangements, but many of the personal contacts and adjustments, necessary to secure co-ordination, while at the same time retaining full personal responsibility and authority.

---

[29] Quotations from British "Field Service Regulations," Vol. I, *Organization and Administration.*

Subordinates equally have associated the formal operation of issuing instructions with superiority of status. Where private secretaries or assistants are employed by chiefs in civil life their relations with subordinates of equal or superior status are frequently vague and easily strained. A secretary or assistant who issues instructions on his own initiative and signs them is necessarily regarded as "encroaching" on the independence or authority of officials senior to himself. The conception that the authority and responsibility remain his chief's is absent. Much of this difficulty is avoided in military life through the separation of function from status by the device of rank. Status is determined by rank and staff officers are almost invariably junior in rank to their commander's principal subordinates and the equals in rank of the chiefs of services whose work they co-ordinate. Thus it is clear that their actions are in virtue of their appointment, their functions, and involve no assertion of unjustified authority.

Any lack of courtesy, any unreasonableness in instructions, can be taken up immediately by the subordinate with the commander. The commander on his side will know, or will find out, whether the difficulty is due to the fault of the staff officer or to a failure on the part of the subordinate, perhaps unavoidable, to distinguish between a local and a general situation. On the other hand the fact that the chief is himself responsible for the staff officer's action precludes any wide possibility of pursuing an unfortunate personal relationship through such channels. The subordinate knows that unjustifiable criticism of the staff will react to his own disadvantage. The staff officer knows that failure to make the best arrangements possible in any given circumstances will probably be reported to his commander.

Failure to appreciate the proper functions of officials in a "staff" capacity or to recognize the necessity for this third type of control, distinct both from "line" and from "specialized" authority, is one of the chief obstacles to more effective co-ordination in civil administration. Co-ordination depends in large measure on personal relations, reinforcing detailed and definite provisions for securing correlation at every point where it is necessary for effective effort. The chiefs of large modern enterprises, cannot and should not have time, either to work out the details which follow from their decisions or to explain them personally. The heads of the major functions and departments of such enterprises have their own heavy executive responsibilities. Moreover, their attempts at self-co-ordination are inevitably biassed and consequently lead to much unnecessary friction. Where it is no one's business to co-ordinate, except a chief's, who has a thousand other preoccupations, it is a miracle that some unity of action is nevertheless achieved.

11. STAFF RELATIONS

In view of the importance of the subject it is suggested that some closer study of military practice in this matter is desirable.

Figure V shows in diagram the relations between a British staff officer in the field and those in immediate touch with him. He is under the "line" command of his chief. In virtue of his position he issues instructions to his chief's immediate subordinates who are his superiors in rank and to the heads of specialized services under his chief's command, who are his equals. He communicates officially through his chief and his

STAFF RELATIONS

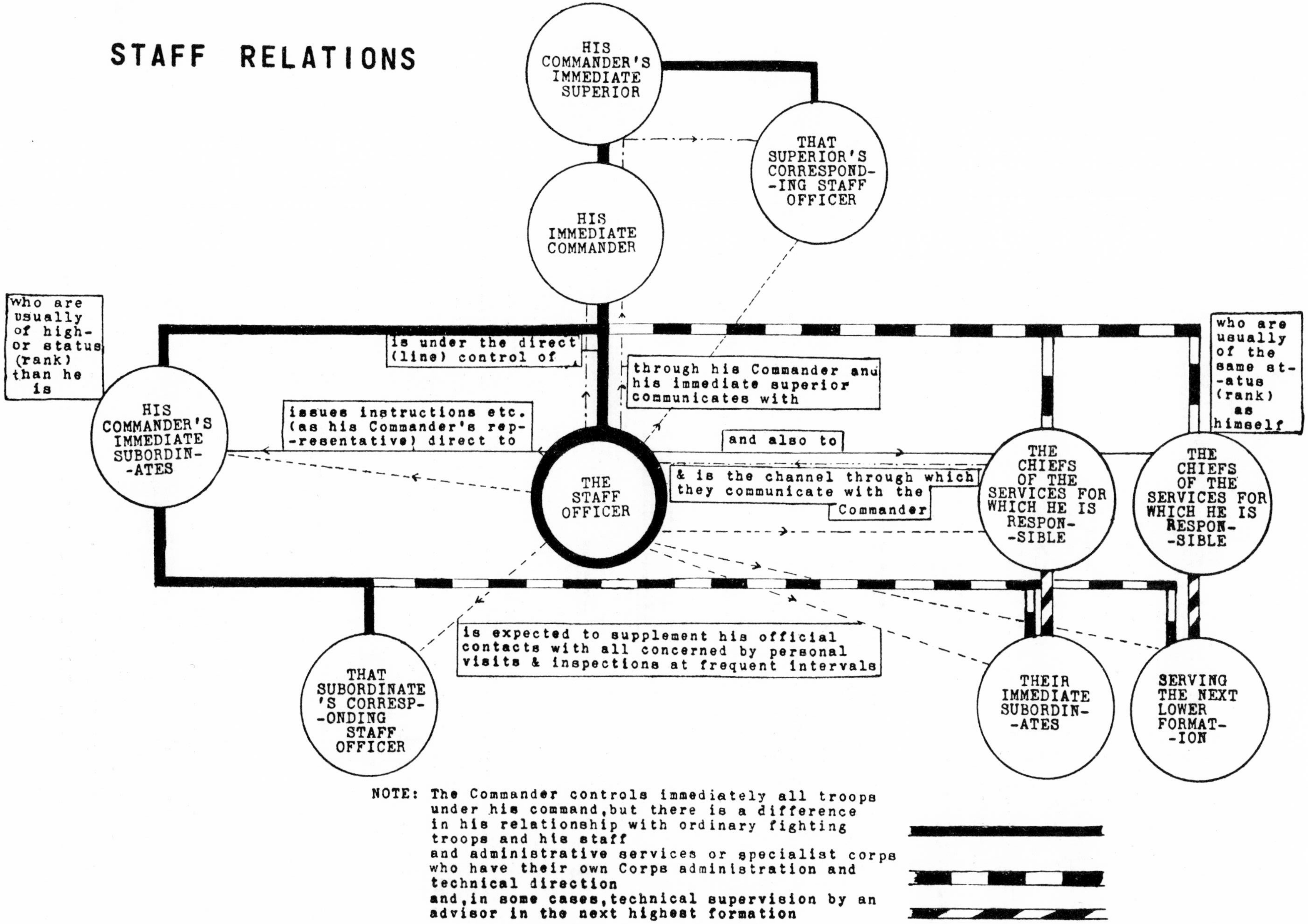

HIS COMMANDER'S IMMEDIATE SUPERIOR

HIS IMMEDIATE COMMANDER

THAT SUPERIOR'S CORRESPOND-ING STAFF OFFICER

who are usually of the same st-atus (rank) as himself

THE CHIEFS OF THE SERVICES FOR WHICH HE IS RESPON-SIBLE

THE CHIEFS OF THE SERVICES FOR WHICH HE IS RESPON-SIBLE

SERVING THE NEXT LOWER FORMAT-ION

THEIR IMMEDIATE SUBORDIN-ATES

through his Commander and his immediate superior communicates with

and also to

& is the channel through which they communicate with the Commander

is under the direct (line) control of

THE STAFF OFFICER

is expected to supplement his official contacts with all concerned by personal visits & inspection at frequent intervals

issues instructions etc. (as his Commander's rep-resentative) direct to

THAT SUBORDINATE'S CORRESP-ONDING STAFF OFFICER

HIS COMMANDER'S IMMEDIATE SUBORDIN-ATES

who are usually of high-er status (rank) than he is

NOTE: The Commander controls immediately all troops under his command, but there is a difference in his relationship with ordinary fighting troops and his staff and administrative services or specialist corps who have their own Corps administration and technical direction and, in some cases, technical supervision by an advisor in the next highest formation

FIGURE V. STAFF RELATIONS

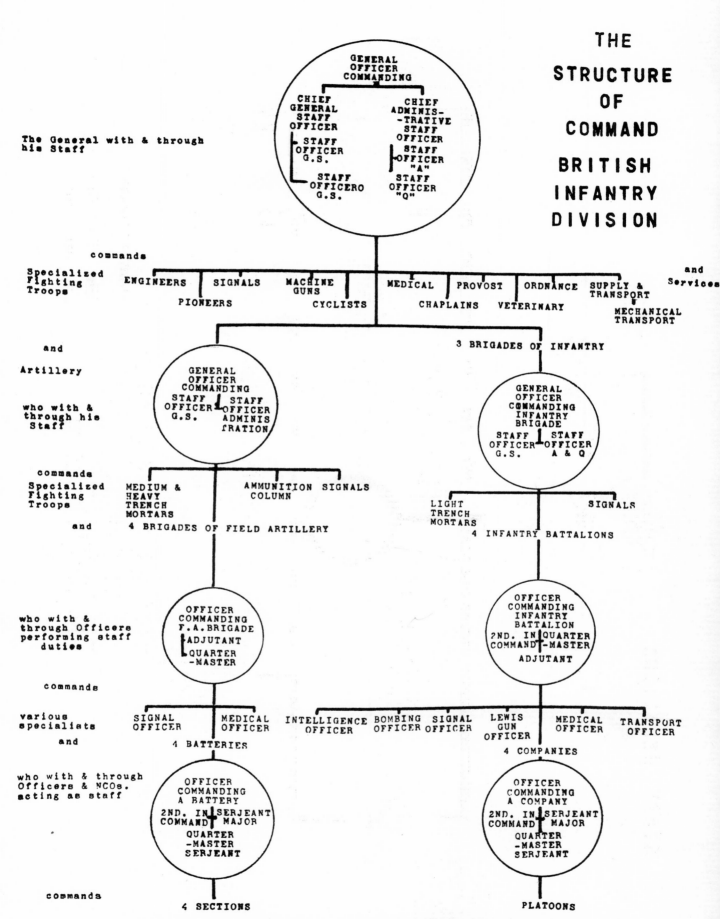

THE
STRUCTURE
OF
COMMAND

BRITISH
INFANTRY
DIVISION

The General with & through
his Staff

GENERAL
OFFICER
COMMANDING

CHIEF
GENERAL
STAFF
OFFICER

CHIEF
ADMINIS-
-TRATIVE
STAFF
OFFICER

STAFF
OFFICER
G.S.

STAFF
OFFICER
"A"

STAFF
OFFICERO
G.S.

STAFF
OFFICER
"Q"

commands

Specialized
Fighting
Troops

ENGINEERS | SIGNALS | MACHINE GUNS | MEDICAL | PROVOST | ORDNANCE | SUPPLY & TRANSPORT

PIONEERS | CYCLISTS | CHAPLAINS | VETERINARY

and
Services

MECHANICAL
TRANSPORT

and

Artillery

3 BRIGADES OF INFANTRY

who with &
through his
Staff

GENERAL
OFFICER
COMMANDING

STAFF
OFFICER
G.S.

STAFF
OFFICER
ADMINIS
TRATION

GENERAL
OFFICER
COMMANDING
INFANTRY
BRIGADE

STAFF
OFFICER
G.S.

STAFF
OFFICER
A & Q

commands
Specialized
Fighting
Troops

MEDIUM &
HEAVY
TRENCH
MORTARS

AMMUNITION
COLUMN

SIGNALS

LIGHT
TRENCH
MORTARS

SIGNALS

and

4 BRIGADES OF FIELD ARTILLERY

4 INFANTRY BATTALIONS

who with &
through Officers
performing staff
duties

OFFICER
COMMANDING
F.A.BRIGADE

ADJUTANT

QUARTER
-MASTER

OFFICER
COMMANDING
INFANTRY
BATTALION

2ND. IN
COMMAND

QUARTER
-MASTER

ADJUTANT

commands

various
specialists

and

SIGNAL
OFFICER

MEDICAL
OFFICER

INTELLIGENCE
OFFICER

BOMBING
OFFICER

SIGNAL
OFFICER

LEWIS
GUN
OFFICER

MEDICAL
OFFICER

TRANSPORT
OFFICER

who with & through
Officers & NCOs.
acting as staff

4 BATTERIES

4 COMPANIES

OFFICER
COMMANDING
A BATTERY

2ND. IN
COMMAND

SERJEANT
MAJOR

QUARTER
-MASTER
SERJEANT

OFFICER
COMMANDING
A COMPANY

2ND. IN
COMMAND

SERJEANT
MAJOR

QUARTER
-MASTER
SERJEANT

commands

4 SECTIONS

PLATOONS

FIGURE VI. THE STRUCTURE OF COMMAND — BRITISH INFANTRY DIVISION

chief's superior with that superior's staff officer of the same branch and the heads of specialist services under his command. He communicates officially through his chief's immediate subordinate with that subordinate's staff officer of the same branch. These "channels of communication" safeguard "the scalar process."

But they are supplemented by a network of personal contacts of all kinds between the staff officer and other staff officers of the same branch above and below him, the heads of specialist services above and below him, and the commanders of fighting troops whom he serves. The minute such personal contacts degenerate into personalities, anyone concerned can get back into the "official channels." But everyone concerned also knows that the official channels are slow and the necessities of war urgent. The importance of these personal contacts as supplementing and expediting official procedure is a feature which is emphasized in all staff work. If there are no officials whose specific function it is to secure such liaison, misunderstanding and friction are almost inevitable in any large organization.

Figure VI shows these relations as part of the general structure of command — "the scalar process." Each commander and his "staff" operate as a unit, the authority and responsibility remaining the commander's. Specialist or "functional" troops and services have to be commanded just as much as "line" formations and units. But, while nominally they report directly to the commander, actually all official business is transacted by his staff. He is thus safeguarded from exceeding his "span of control." The safeguard is in a sense a fiction or convention. But it works smoothly in practice and is seldom abused. Where the command of formations and units of all kinds is thus exercised by commanders and their staffs acting as a single personality, there is in effect a specialization and segregation into levels of the actual functions of command.

12. STAFF AND THE FUNCTION OF SUPPLY

Figure VII shows how "staff" officers, or officers of the line acting in a "staff" capacity, at every level of command secure the co-ordination of a particular service, that of supply.

It must be noted that supply will be one of 12 to 20 specialized services and functions for which the commander is responsible, and one of five or six major questions allotted to a subordinate staff officer of an administrative branch of the staff. But at each level of command there is such a staff officer concerned and solely concerned to secure co-ordination, both laterally between the supply specialists and the remaining troops of the formation whom they serve in respect of that function, and up and down the line of supply.

A second point of interest is the fact that the degree of specialization of those concerned with supply varies at different levels in the chain of command. At the two higher levels (in Army parlance the Corps and the Division) there are officers of a special service concerned professionally solely with transport and supply. Such a specialist of appropriate status is placed in a "line" relationship to the commander of the formation, subject to co-ordination by his "staff." But he is under the technical control of the superior officer of his service in the higher formation. The Commander of his formation, for instance, would not dream of interfering with him over questions of method or the internal economy of his own functional units. The commander's

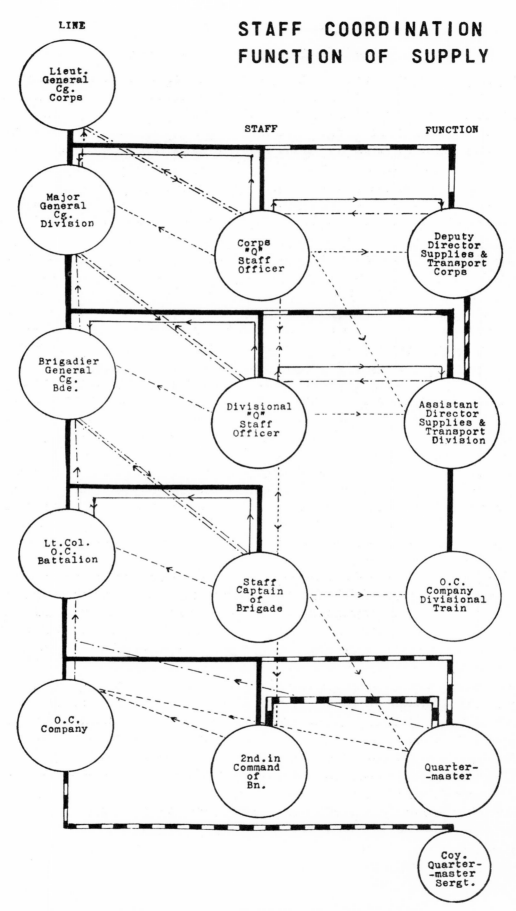

FIGURE VII. STAFF CO-ORDINATION — FUNCTION OF SUPPLY

concern would be with the results obtained in the supply of his troops. Similarly the specialist officer would look to his own service for promotion and personnel matters.

At the next level of command (the Brigade) there is no specialist supply officer in a "line" relation to the Commander. But a unit of the supply service under the "line" command of the supply service officer of the Division will be detailed to work with each Brigade — during the Great War a Horse Transport Company of the Divisional Train. The work of this unit is co-ordinated by the administrative staff officer of the Brigade who is in constant touch with its commander. Should the Brigade be "detached" from the divisional command, this supply unit automatically comes under the "line" command of the commander of the Brigade.

This difference in arrangements for control corresponds to a difference in the physical arrangements for the delivery of supplies. Supplies were loaded on the wagons of the horse transport companies of the Divisional Train under divisional control, ready packed for distribution to units, and were delivered direct to the transport of units. The Brigade commander, while remaining responsible that his troops were properly supplied, had a less intimate concern with the actual arrangements than the commanders of the higher formations.

At the next lower level (in the British army the Battalion, artillery Brigade, or other units) the question of supply is taken over from the specialist service by the unit itself. But there is still a substantial degree of specialization. The officer responsible is known as the Quartermaster. He is not a trained professional supply officer. He is usually a promoted non-commissioned officer of the unit. His duties combine the functions of two specialized services — supply (food and forage) and ordnance (equipment, clothing, etc.). But he is wholly specialized in these duties and will, in practice, devote the remainder of his career to them. He is not responsible for transport, which is commanded by a combatant officer of the battalion, specialized in this duty for a period of years after a preliminary course of instruction, but looking to return to ordinary command.

The commander of a Battalion usually delegates questions of interior economy to his Second-in-Command. The Quartermaster acts in a staff capacity to this officer, but also exercises "line" command over headquarters personnel concerned with his functions. The Quartermaster is of course expected to be conversant with all arrangements, procedure, and regulations governing questions of supply and to secure that his unit benefits from them.

At the next level of command (the Company) the supply arrangements are again specialized in the hands of a non-commissioned officer — the Company Quartermaster Sergeant. He carries out the same duties as the Quartermaster and similarly acts in a "staff" capacity to the Company Commander or to his Second-in-Command. But, like the Transport Officer, he is specialized in such duties only for a period and is in the normal line for promotion to other duties with the remaining non-commissioned officers of the Battalion.

At this point specialization of supply arrangements terminates.

13. Supply in an Industrial Undertaking

Figure VIII shows, for purposes of comparison, the Purchasing Department organization of a world-famous business enterprise with scattered producing units. It is interesting for what it omits.

It does not show how Purchasing is co-ordinated with the central control at the top. The report from which it is drawn [30] indicates that in the case of 22 important companies investigated the Chief Purchasing Officer reported

> To the President in 4.
> To the Executive Officers (presumably a committee) in 6.
> To the General Manager in 8.
> To the Treasurer in 2.
> To the Superintendent in 2.

But Purchasing is an essential function of business. If it does not report to the Principal Executive Officer how is he to secure co-ordination when purchasing activities are required for one of the functions under the control of another subordinate? When Purchasing reports to the General Manager and the Treasurer is dissatisfied with the stationery or wants 20,000 forms in a hurry, what happens? Usually the Purchasing Officer fights it out for himself. Sometimes he goes to the General Manager and he deals with the Treasurer. In any event the question reduces itself to one of argument, which means relative weight of status and personality, not control and swift executive action. If, on the other hand, Purchasing does report to the principal executive officer the latter has too many subordinates.

Secondly the chart does not show what is the relative authority of the Divisional Purchasing Agents and of the Managers of those Divisions. The text states that "Division Purchasing Agents, in addition to centralizing the purchasing functions in their own particular divisions, are authorized to place directly with vendors orders for materials only needed for their plants or orders for emergency supplies which are needed at once." But if the Division Manager disagrees with his purchasing agent as to what is an emergency, what happens? What are the limits of the technical and financial control of the General Purchasing Agent? Such difficulties are bound to arise. Who is there to foresee them, to prevent them arising, to deal with them when they occur? If the Principal Executive Officer attempts to do so, he will be over-worked in a month.

The point which the chart illustrates is a simple one. Specialization high up in the organization of a large enterprise of the control of functions which interlock in execution is bound to create throughout the undertaking innumerable interrelationships of subordinate officials with different functional points of view over problems which call for action. If the "scalar process" is clear cut the "line" officer will usually have his way and the advantages of specialization will be lost. If it is not clear cut there will be a blurring of responsibility and consequent delay or inefficiency in action.

Every one of such interrelationships is a point calling for co-ordination.

---

[30] "Functions of the Purchasing Agent." Pamphlet issued by the Policyholders Service Bureau of the Metropolitan Life Insurance Company.

AN EXAMPLE OF A PURCHASING DEPARTMENT.
_____

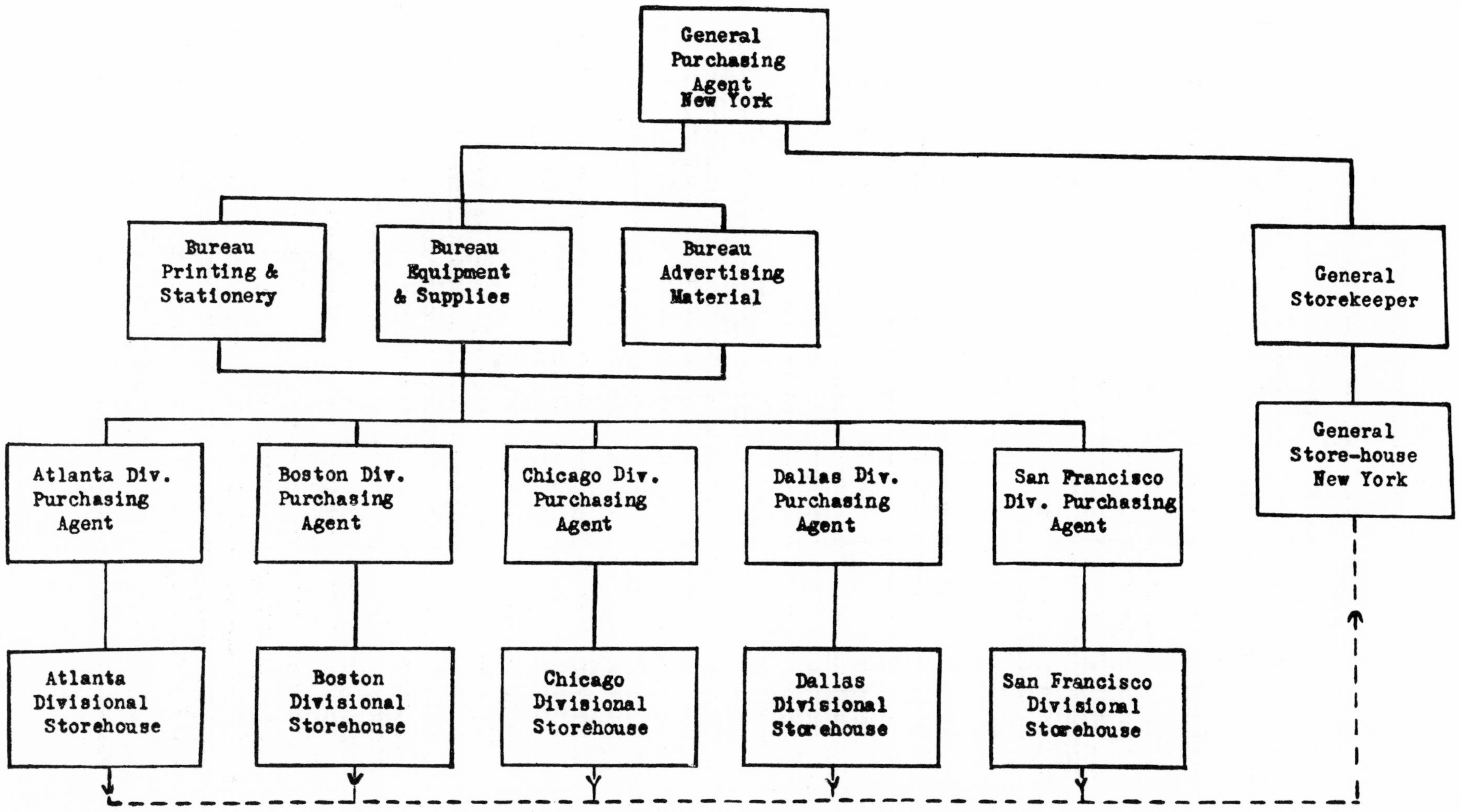

FIGURE VIII. AN EXAMPLE OF A PURCHASING DEPARTMENT

14. Staff and General Co-ordination

Turning from the analysis of a particular function to the general co-ordination of a large undertaking, *Figure IX* shows the co-ordination of all functions in a British infantry division as it was organized during the Great War. Some of the details of specialist troops and services are omitted. The same principles of organization were followed as in the case of the infantry. The points of importance are:

a. The presence at every level of command of staff officers or of officers or non-commissioned officers of the unit concerned acting in a "staff" capacity, i.e. "assisting the commander in the execution of his functions of command."

b. The fact that the "scalar process," "line" command, runs clear down from the General commanding to the private of infantry. The same is true for privates of other arms and services not shown in detail.

c. That this does not prevent a high degree of specialization or functionalization, more than a dozen functions apart from the "line" command of infantry and artillery (why not production and selling?) being provided with their own specialist departments or officials with considerable though varying degrees of technical independence.

d. That the method of organizing this specialization varies in the case of every function. The degree of professional independence (membership of a separate technical Corps with its own regulations and system of promotion) and the level to which this independence is carried down in the chain of command is adjusted to the character of the function. Each battalion has medical and ordnance personnel belonging to these services. Signal personnel of the Royal Corps of Signals are not detached below Brigades. Machine gun specialists of the Machine Gun Corps are centralized under Divisional Headquarters.

e. That, as described in connection with the previous chart, specialization is carried down below the levels at which these professional officials are employed by officers and non-commissioned officers of the unit concerned who (i) are permanently specialized on a particular function or (ii) carry out a specialized function for a period after instruction, but expect in due course to be promoted to other duties.

f. That, despite this multiplication of functions, the line command at every level is enabled to secure complete co-ordination of all activities for which it is responsible, without in any case exceeding a total of six individuals directly supervised, because, and only because, of the presence of the "staff" function.

g. As a result of the tying together of line and functional specialists by the "staff" function, every conceivable service and subject has its clear channel of communication and action from the commander of the division to the private soldier. And, at frequent intervals along those channels, are officials whose express duty is to see that they work and to take immediate and direct action if they do not.

15. General Co-ordination in an Industrial Undertaking

Again for purposes of comparison, *Figure X* illustrates the principles of organization of the General Motors Export Company.[31]

The four General Managers at headquarters are spoken of as being in a "staff" relationship to the General Manager. In fact they are specialized officers in "line" control of particular functions. In the absence of any "staff" system in the military sense the amount of specialization is necessarily limited to these four functions;

---

[31] Reproduced from "Organization and Operating Principles," Edgar W. Smith, Handbook of Business Administration, pp. 1474–1488.

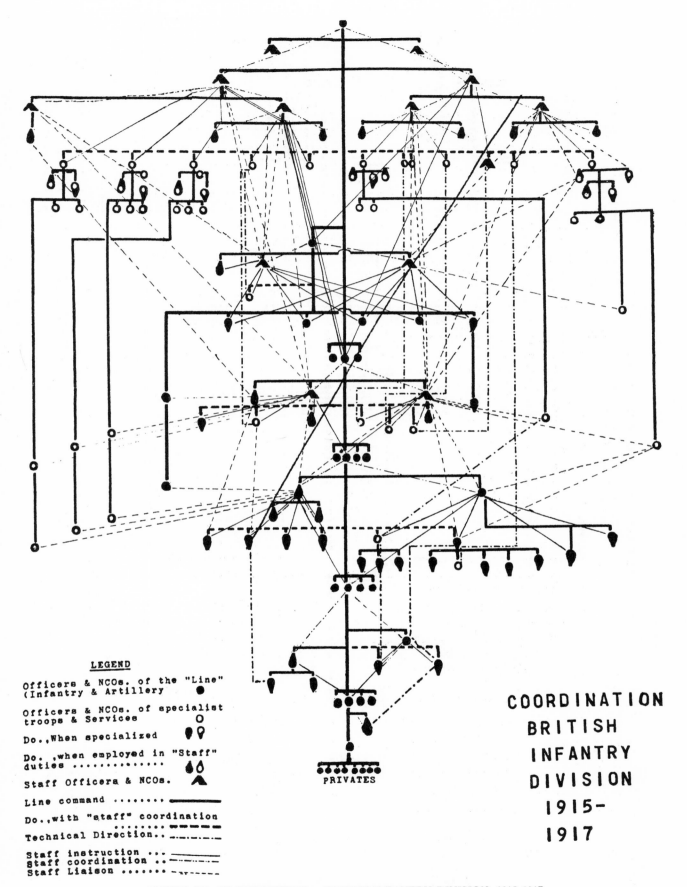

LEGEND

Officers & NCOs. of the "Line" (Infantry & Artillery	●
Officers & NCOs. of specialist troops & Services	O
Do.,When specialized	◑ Ꝩ
Do.,when employed in "Staff" duties	◣◢
Staff Officers & NCOs.	▲
Line command	▬▬▬
Do.,with "staff" coordination	▬ ▬ ▬
Technical Direction..	▬ · ▬ ·
Staff instruction · · ·	—————
Staff coordination ··	————
Staff Liaison · · · · · ·	▬ · · ▬

COORDINATION
BRITISH
INFANTRY
DIVISION
1915-
1917

PRIVATES

FIGURE IX. CO-ORDINATION — BRITISH INFANTRY DIVISION, 1915–1917

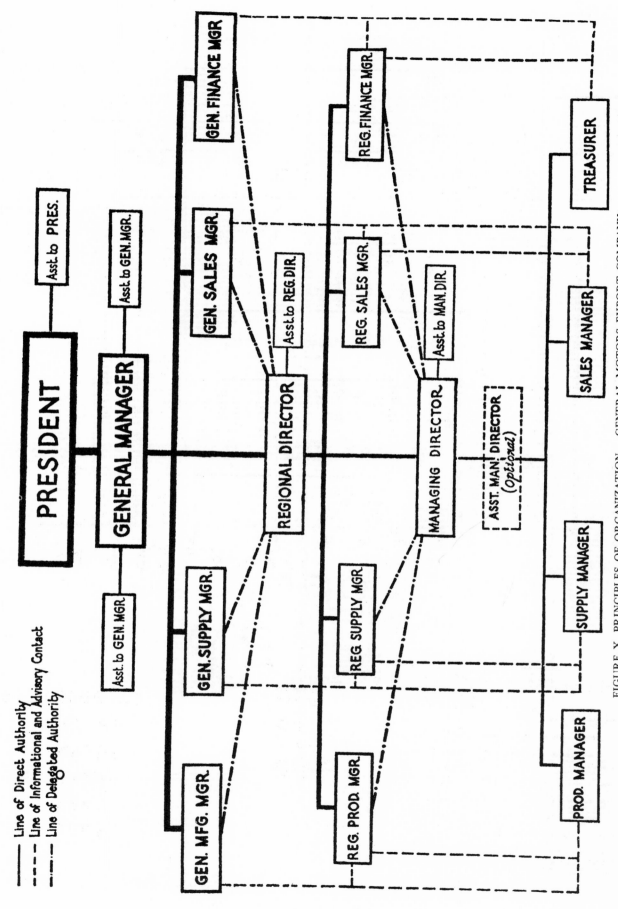

Line of Direct Authority
Line of Informational and Advisory Contact
Line of Delegated Authority

FIGURE X. PRINCIPLES OF ORGANIZATION — GENERAL MOTORS EXPORT COMPANY

otherwise the General Manager's "span of control" would be exceeded. The number of Regional Directors is not shown.

It should be added that this represents a very advanced form of business organization which has been developed with exceptional insight. But it is doubtful if the two-dimensional grouping of authority and responsibility on which it is avowedly based is sufficiently refined for the requirements of modern scientific administration. The "Line and Staff" form of organization might be renamed the "Line and Functional" form. It would then appear for the compromise which, essentially, it is. It would be replaced in due course by a "Line, Staff and Functional" form, "staff" in the military sense being introduced to effect a real integration between the other two principles.

16. THE TRUE "STAFF" CONCEPT IN BUSINESS

The only positions in civil life which at all correspond to those of "staff officers" in the Army, are Private Secretary and Executive Assistant. While there is great variety in practice and some "staff" functions inevitably gravitate to such officials, it is clear that they are seldom, if ever, used solely or in large measure to secure devolution of the actual functions of command. The degree to which "staff" are allowed to assist their chief is largely an individual question, depending on the chief's powers of delegation.

One enquiry directed to companies including the position of Executive Assistant in their organization revealed an astonishing variety of practice.[32] The Assistants in one case or another exercised direct supervision over nine different types of function or department. They acted as Secretaries or members of nine separate kinds of committee. They performed a heterogeneous collection of special duties from "a survey of the general management methods of the Company" to "assistance in connection with some special hobby or interest of the superior." Finally they performed coordinating duties or served in a liaison capacity between "their chief and various officials" — the wording implying that, where this occurred, it was a special function requiring definition in each case. There was no indication at all of any general recognition that the central purpose of officials in a true staff capacity is to assist in coordination.

The report concluded:

"the position of an Executive Assistant has come about primarily because of the multiplicity and urgency of the demands on the time of the chief executive in present-day business. It is the principal function of the assistant to help to relieve this pressure."

These words may be compared with those of the author who may be described as the father of the modern general staff theory in military organization:

"As long as armies were small, and movements, encampments and fighting formations were laid down by hard and fast regulations, the want of trained General Staff officers was less felt. The plan determined upon by the General in command usually contained the details of execution. . . . The enormous numerical strength of modern armies and the way they must be organized to meet the constantly changing requirements of war, render necessary

---

[32] "Functions of an Assistant to the President." Pamphlet issued by the Policyholders Service Bureau of the Metropolitan Life Insurance Company.

great differences in carrying out the details of military operations even under apparently similar circumstances of time and place. Consequently the higher leaders and Commanders require a regular staff of specially selected and trained officers." [33]

Today, the central point of the pressure on the chief, in business as in military life, is the additional work of co-ordination called for by the specialization rendered essential by scientific development. The assistant can only relieve pressure from this cause if his duties and his relationships with other officials are so laid down as to secure delegation of actual co-ordinating work.

17. The Staff Principle and the Span of Control

There is no question that effective control of large and complex formations such as are found in armies would be impossible without "staff" assistance. But it may be asked how does the "staff" principle reduce the commander's task of co-ordination: does it not merely add further to the number of individuals he has to consider?

It reduces it in two ways. In the first place it throws upon the staff all the *detail* of commanding. If orders are to be issued, instructions prepared, arrangements made for this or that or the other purpose the Commander has only to indicate the broad outlines of his decision — with or without preliminary conference with his principal subordinates, conference at which his principal staff officer or two principal staff officers are always present. At that point it becomes the duty of the staff to work out all the consequences in consultation with everyone concerned, to prepare orders and instructions, and to satisfy themselves that such orders and instructions can be executed.

In the second place it throws upon the staff much of the detail of controlling — of satisfying the Commander that instructions issued are in fact being carried out. This part of the work of a staff includes functions both of inspection and of co-ordination. The staff officer must satisfy himself as to the facts. If instructions are not being executed he must take steps to iron out the obstacles, whether personal or material, which are preventing the fulfilment of the Commander's intentions.

On the other hand it in no way interferes with the "scalar process," or overstrains the Commander's "span of control." The commander of a British division in the field actually supervises directly the commanders of his three Infantry Brigades, and the commander of his Artillery, — his principal subordinates, — and two chief staff officers, one for operations and one for administration, six persons in all. Six may seem a large number, but the work of the three infantry Brigades does not interrelate closely under normal conditions and they are standardized formations.

He has also under his direct command, it is true, the chief representatives of three or four other arms and of six or eight services. Each of these men can be called upon for specialized advice if required: each of them has the right to approach the commander directly upon an issue of major importance. But 99 per cent of their work is correlated by the staff. Just because this is so, and because the relationship is well understood, the commander is free to visit units and formations, to see for himself

[33] "The Duties of the General Staff," General Bronsart von Schellendorf. English translation of the Fourth Edition, London 1905, p. 4; also quoted by the late Lord Haldane of Cloan in a Memorandum announcing the formation of a General Staff for the British Army, *London Times*, September 13, 1906.

what is happening, to meet men unofficially and to weigh them up, to stimulate or to restrain them, in short to exercise the positive and vital functions of leadership.

18. THE FUNCTIONS OF ADMINISTRATION AND THE USE OF STAFF

It may be suggested that, while the special staff functions and relationships which have been described are applicable to armies where discipline is enforceable, they are not utilizable in business or other forms of civil administration. No doubt a considerable educational effort is necessary before any new concept of organization can be introduced into an environment where individuals are unaccustomed to it. But, there is no underlying reason to justify the assumption that the principle is not equally applicable, and likely to prove beneficial to, other forms of undertaking, once it is accepted and understood.

To take an example from an industrialist of wide experience, Fayol has analyzed the functions of administration, of the commander, under five heads: to plan, organize, command, co-ordinate and control.[34] But these functions, since they are an integral part of the duty of the leader, cannot in any case be separated wholly from his personality. A planning room can secure that the routine operations of manufacturing are systematically performed and that all minor obstructions or mishaps are dealt with. It cannot settle the policy of a business, forecast its probable lines of future development, or make major decisions. The responsibility for preplanning in this larger sense (Fayol's word was "prévoyance")[35] must remain with the highest authority.

Organization must depend on such preplanning. It is the provision and arrangement of the appropriate human and material resources for a given purpose. That purpose depends on the plan. Only he who is responsible for the conception and broad outlines of the plan can really decide in the last instance whether such resources are appropriate, excessive, or insufficient for the purpose. To command is to set the organization to work in accordance with the plan. Every subordinate who exercises delegated authority commands. But that authority is delegated from somewhere. Finally the function of command must lead back to the principal executive officer; the responsibility cannot be divorced from his personality.

To co-ordinate is described as "to give things and actions their proper proportions and to adapt the means to the end."[36] In other words, it is the operating side of organization. Where organization is concerned with quantities and numbers and the setting up of a structure to facilitate their unified working, co-ordination is concerned with securing that working from day to day and hour to hour; it involves constant attention to the machine in action to secure that harmony and balance are preserved in operation as well as in design and structure.

Control consists in seeing that everything is carried out in accordance with the plan which has been adopted, the organization which has been set up, and the orders which have been given. Maintaining the metaphor of the machine, it is the

---

[34] Henri Fayol, "Industrial and General Administration." English translation published by the International Management Institute, Geneva.

[35] "To foresee," as the word is used here, means both to foretell the future and to prepare for it; it includes, in fact, the idea of action, and can best be expressed by "planning." *Ibid.*, p. 35.   [36] *Ibid.*

gauges and records of performance. Just as co-ordination is the operating side of organization and depends on it, so control is in a sense the consequent of command, the constant checking up of the results of command in action. The commander cannot delegate wholly his personal responsibility for co-ordination and control, for the same reasons that he cannot delegate it in matters of organization and command.

If Fayol's analysis is examined closely it appears that his idea of planning also contains two related conceptions, one involving the "foretelling of the future" and the other the consequent action of "preparing for it." If, at the same time, investigation is given its proper place as the underlying principle in all decisions in any scientific form of administration, Fayol's arrangement of the functions of administration corresponds closely with Mooney and Reiley's "Principle, Process and Effect" in their arrangement of the principles of organization. Moreover, these functions fall into three groups corresponding to the three aspects of staff service which Mooney and Reiley distinguish, viz., the Informational, the Advisory, and the Supervisory. Thus

	PRINCIPLE	PROCESS	EFFECT
The Functions of Command	1.	2.	3.
(Fayol's analysis *in italics*)	Investigation	*Forecasting*	*Plan*
	2.	*Organization*	*Co-ordination*
	3.	*Command*	*Control*
Aspects of staff service	Informational	Advisory	Supervisory
(Mooney and Reiley)			

The principle of investigation leads to the process of "foretelling the future" and the effect of "preparing for it." But "foretelling the future" issues into process with the establishment of organization and organization in use has the effect of co-ordination. Similarly the plan enters into process through the action of command which has the effect of control. In investigation the commander needs information. In attempting to forecast or to set up his organization and secure its unified working he needs counsel. In securing that his plan is worked out in all its details, that his orders and instructions reach all concerned, and that they are carried out, he needs help in supervision.

Investigation, as in the case of the other functions of the administrator, cannot be wholly separated from his personality. Despite the insistence of the literature of business administration on the investigational aspect of "staff" functions, somewhere and somewhen the final authority, the man responsible, must take the available facts into account. However predigested they may be, it is his brain which must review them, weigh them, and base decisions upon them.

Thus, of the whole seven functions of administration, none can be entirely delegated to others. The hard core of responsibility remains. At the same time the "staff" system, as it has been described, does follow very closely Taylor's main principle that one man should as far as possible confine himself to one function.

As far as the commander is concerned, it does this by enabling him to concentrate as far as is humanly possible, upon the principal of his seven functions, namely to command. Fayol lists the main requirements of command in industry as follows:

"Any man who has to command must:
1. Have a thorough knowledge of his staff.
2. Eliminate the incompetent.
3. Have a sound knowledge of the agreements between the undertaking and its employees.
4. Set a good example.
5. Make periodical examinations of the organization, with the help of charts.
6. Collect his principal assistants in conferences, in which unity of management and effort can be arranged.
7. Not let himself be absorbed by details.
8. See that his staff possesses energy, initiative and loyalty." [37]

Of these eight requirements, 1, 2, 4 and 6 are essentially matters of face-to-face leadership. They cannot, with the possible exception of 6, be met in an office. And conferences summoned too frequently at the chief's office, take men away from the scene of action: they are less fruitful than conferences on the spot. Number 8 depends also on personal contacts. If the word staff is used in the wider industrial sense this is obvious. If it is used in the narrower army sense, there is no way of judging the work of a "staff" so accurately, as frequent personal inspection of the results in the comfort and convenience of the administered — the "line."

In army life 3 and 5 are covered by regulations and War Establishments. The leader is little concerned with them unless there are important changes. It is the staff's business to know the detail and to advise when required to do so. 7 is obviously a condition on which the successful fulfilment of 1 to 6 and 8 depends, but it is also applicable to the method of fulfilling the remaining requirements. In any event it is likely to become serious, if and when the chief has no adequate machinery for delegating the other functions of administration.

The point of importance is that the essence of the function of command is personal contact with all concerned. It is not an office job. The constant complaints in industry as to the loss of "the personal touch" mean one of two things. Either the administrator is glued to his office doing what should be "staff" duties, or he has no personality. Under the Army System of organization no general who uses his "staff" properly and has some personality has any difficulty in making it felt throughout commands larger than any at present contemplated by industry.

Since there is no practical experience of the application of the true "staff" concept to business undertakings, it is not possible to give any precise measurement of the degree to which its effective employment can relieve the chief. If, however, Fayol's analysis of the task of administration is accepted, it is possible to indicate how far each of the tasks under each of the administrative functions, would, on the basis of military experience, normally be carried by Staff Officers.

19. The Staff Concept and Functionalization

It is also possible to test the validity of the "staff" concept for business undertakings, by comparing military practice in the matter with the principles suggested

---

[37] *Ibid.*, 70. "Staff" in this context means all employees.

by F. W. Taylor. In British army organization complete functionalization in Taylor's sense is not carried below the command of a Company (250 men). Below that level his description of the old form of industrial organization as "military" is partially applicable. Even at the next lower level, however, the Platoon (20–40 men), the Commander has a Platoon Sergeant, who acts in a staff capacity, relieving him of the detail of the interior economy of the platoon, and enabling him to concentrate on its leadership, training, and fighting efficiency — a greater degree of functionalization than is found in industrial enterprises not touched by Taylor's ideas. The comparative uniformity of the private soldier's duties and the moral necessity of associating him by every possible tie to the man who will actually lead him in battle, make functionalization at the lowest levels of command unnecessary and undesirable. Moreover in many matters he does receive the direct attention of functional specialists at his Company and Battalion headquarters. His Platoon Officer and Sergeant have a far more limited overall control than the old-fashioned foreman in industry.

There is, however, no reason why, under different conditions, functional control should not be carried right down to the individual if it is desirable to do so. Organization in the British Army could be so adapted merely by changing the duties of existing personnel. The Company Commander would become the "Shop Superintendent" and his Second-in-Command the "Assistant Shop Superintendent." The duties of the four Planning Room specialists might be allocated to the four Platoon Sergeants, and the four Platoon Officers become the foremen in the shop. They might have two groups of eight assistant functional foremen drawn from the Non-Commissioned Officers in charge of Sections.

But this arrangement would not offer any solution of the problem raised by functionalization carried to the higher levels of organization. Somewhere or other there must be co-ordinating points, especially when subordinate units are geographically separated. It is the extent of authority given to the manager at such points and its relation to functional authority which are in question.

As far as the "staff" itself is concerned, it is divided into branches which imply functionalization, at all events for the time being. While Staff Officers are not specialists, they carry out special duties. In the British Army there is first the broad division into the General Staff Branch and the three branches of the Administrative staff — dealing with:

Personnel (Adjutant-General's Branch).
Supplies, animals and certain classes of stores (Quartermaster-General's Branch) and with
Equipment, both maintenance and research (Branch of the Master General of the Ordnance)

respectively. These branches are again subdivided into sections. For example the General Staff Branch has sections for intelligence, operations, and training. This specialization within the staff is carried as far as possible, compatible with the staff's underlying function of co-ordination and the employment of the minimum number of persons necessary for the work.

In this way certain of the main aspects of administration are very highly functionalized in certain branches or sections. Investigation, which is most important in war in relation to enemy action (cf. the competitors' activities aspect of market research), is dealt with by the Intelligence. Forecasting is expressly the duty of the General Staff Branch. Organization on its formal side is a matter for the Adjutant General. Planning, in its broader aspects, is essentially a question for the Operations Section of the General Staff, though all branches and the specialized troops and services contribute their detailed aspects of a complete plan. Control on its systematic and formal side is largely confined to the Adjutant General's Branch. The accounts of war are balances in terms of men. Returns of strengths, casualties and prisoners are the basis of such accounting. But each section and branch assists in control, by statistics of the matters with which it is concerned and by constant personal visits to subordinate formations and units.

Command is the function of administration which it is most difficult for the chief to delegate. But the operative instruments of command are orders and instructions. All the formal work of preparing and issuing such orders and instructions is assumed by the staff, the work being usually functionalized into the two main groups of General Staff and Administration. Co-ordination, the fundamental reason for staff organization cannot in its nature be functionalized. It is provided for by the scalar structure of the staff itself, and in the British Army by a special arrangement under which the commander while

> "responsible for co-ordinating the work of his staff . . . may, on occasions, delegate it, with such reservations as he may think fit, to his senior general staff officer." [38]

Thus the duties of the staff are divided up and grouped by functions in a very large measure. In certain matters further functionalization is possible and probably desirable, e.g. in the control of clerical work. On the whole, however, Taylor's principle of one man, one function, is followed far more closely than in the majority of civil enterprises. His description of the older form of industrial organization as "military" does not correspond with the facts.

But it is the functionalization of levels of authority, the actual division of the work of administration, so that the chief is relieved of everything except its most personal aspects, the primary initiatives and the vital decisions on questions of major importance, which constitute the chief interest of the staff concept from this standpoint. Administration itself implies a number of functions, which can be specialized and delegated, provided the authority and responsibility vis-à-vis "line" superiors and subordinates, remain with the chief. A plan has many stages. So has its execution. The vital decision which sets the plan in motion may be brief in the time that it occupies and the form of its expression. But the detailed consequences are both exacting and intricate. Provided, however, that principal line subordinates understand that the vital decision is the chief's and that the detailed arrangements which follow are contributory to the plan, there is no reason why they should resist such arrangements when issued by their chief's "staff" even though those signing the actual documents are their inferiors in status.

---

[38] "Field Service Regulations," Vol. I.

20. PLANNING AND PERFORMANCE

Another of Taylor's main principles where the military parallel is of interest is the separation of Planning from Performance. Mooney and Reiley have observed that:

"Another common misconception concerning staff service must be disposed of, namely that it is in some way specially identified with the planning function. . . . If it were really the staff that plans and the line that executes, this would elevate the staff above the line in functional importance, a reversal of their true relationship. . . . On the Taylor system of functional foremanship, . . . every one of the planning bosses and likewise each performing boss has the authority of line decision with respect to his own functional job. It is ever thus in organization. The line plans, the line executes, the line does everything. In the line alone rests the authority to determine plans, the authority to execute such plans, and the responsibility for what is done." [39]

This comment appears to miss the essential point which is characteristic of "staff" functions in military life. It is true that authority rests in the line alone. It is true, as the authors point out, that

"thinking and doing are inseparable in every psychic movement and are therefore present in every activity."

But in a very real sense it is the "staff" that plans and the "line" that executes. Officers in command of line, specialist and service troops plan in respect of their own units and functions. As in the case of Taylor's foremen they have authority for line decisions with respect to their own functional jobs. The special characteristics of the "staff" officer's position is that his authority to plan with is that of his line superior, not his own, and he has no subordinates other than one or two junior "staff" officers and some clerks, to whom to communicate "line" decisions with respect to his own function.

A major aspect of the directive function of the chief is planning and the co-ordination of specialized plans. The great proportion of this work is delegated to the "staff." But the responsibility for execution remains with the chief and the chief's line subordinates. By very reason of his special position the "staff" officer, as an individual, is the purest example of the segregation of planning from execution which can be found. It is a purer example than Taylor's functional foremen, because they had authority for "line" decisions in respect of their own functions, as in the case of specialist troops and services.

The difficulties which have been encountered in practice may be traced to a single fact. Immediately the scalar claim is lengthened to five or six levels of authority it becomes impossible to preserve "line" responsibility and at the same time to co-ordinate effectively interrelated functional authorities whose "line" authority for their function runs through all these stages. "Staff" relationships are the solution of this problem, because they functionalize the planning aspect of command and thus present a clearer separation of planning and execution. A good staff somewhat resembles a Planning Room. With each advance in the technical aspect of war it resembles it more closely. A modern "creeping barrage" table with defined targets for

---

[39] *Op. cit.*, pp. 61 and 62.

every battery and every gun, "lifts" every half-minute, and so on is of the same order of detailed prearrangement as an instruction card. But it may be made out by a second-lieutenant assisting the "staff" at headquarters as orders to half-a-dozen Brigadier Generals.

Planning in this sense is necessarily anterior to execution in point of time. The "line" and specialists cannot act coherently without it. Since the "staff" "adheres" to the line, it "adheres" also to the authority of the line commander. In this sense "staff" functions precede the functions of officers of the "line" who are under the authority of the "line" superior. But this does not mean that "staff" are of greater importance than the "line." Their responsibility is greater, because it is more extensive. Marshal Foch said to students at the French Staff College before the war: "Remember, gentlemen, battles are never lost by the rank and file, always by generals." The staff, as part of a general, can help him to lose battles. But in war the only two functions of ultimate moment are the executive action of the soldier behind a gun or bayonet, and the leadership which puts him in the right place at the right time in the right heart. To link these two together, to maintain the one and to protect the other from all extraneous and secondary preoccupations, is the end of all intermediate functions whether of line, staff or service.

Other principles enunciated by F. W. Taylor also find expression in true "staff" organization. It is clear, for instance, from what has been said already that efficient "staff" work demands a comprehension and application of the "exception principle." It is the custom of the "staff" in the field to present to the commander daily statistics of strengths, casualties and other matters with explanations of all unusual figures.

Taylor insisted that

"one should be sure, beyond the smallest doubt that what is demanded of the men is entirely just and can certainly be accomplished." [40]

British army regulations read:

"The staff must be in a position to appreciate what is possible."[41]

Taylor stated that in his experience "almost all shops are under-officered." It is precisely the lack of officers specialized in "staff" functions which is creating current difficulties in co-ordination.

21. CONSEQUENCES OF LACK OF CO-ORDINATION

Two consequences of the lack of co-ordinating mechanisms in civil organization may be noted. First is the proliferation of Committees which is so characteristic of undertakings of all kinds. A Committee is a device for correlating different points of view. But it is an extremely expensive device. It is sometimes forgotten that the cost of any committee is the combined salaries of its members for the time spent at the committee or preparing for it. Possibly the popular saying that "the best kind of committee is a committee of one" is a subconscious recognition of the fact that many committees have only come into existence because an individual vested with the authority and possessing the capacity to do co-ordinating work has not been appointed.

---

[40] "Shop Management." [41] "Field Service Regulations," Vol. I.

In organizations there is a tendency to compensation, comparable to the tendency found in the human organism. Where essential mechanisms are not provided or decay, somehow and somewhere growth occurs to meet the functions of those mechanisms, often with great waste and at the risk of destroying the whole balance of the organism. As Mooney and Reiley have shown, committees may fulfil a genuine "staff" function. They may be designed to secure the "infiltration of a true service of knowledge . . . moving from the bottom upward." Too frequently they are based on "the need for organized procedure in the adjustment of differences," not only differences between the workers and the management, but between all kinds of "interests," specialized and otherwise. Their time-wasting capacities are notorious. In any event there is no reason why many of their functions should not be performed by individuals. An integrated system of shop stewards and a chief shop steward in contact with a Personnel Manager can provide such a service of information upwards in an industrial concern. The graduated "staff" positions in the Army are intended to do so as far as they extend, and do in fact do so.

More serious is the petrifaction of leadership which follows from an overload of administrative work. A British general has remarked that the huge armies of the great war "added vastly to administrative difficulties" and so "paralyzed generalship":

> "As the general became more and more bound to his office, and, consequently, divorced from his men, he relied for contact not upon the personal factor, but upon the mechanical telegraph and telephone . . . nothing was more dreadful to witness than a chain of men starting with a battalion commander and ending with an army commander sitting in telephone boxes, improvised or actual, talking, talking, talking, in place of leading, leading, leading."[42]

But this "disease of generalship," indicated by a soldier who understood "the immense value of a staff," if it is properly used, "if it is the general's servant, and not the general's gaoler," is endemic in civil life where there are no staffs at all. It is scarcely possible to meet a politician or a business man in a position of serious responsibility who is not overwhelmed with everyday work. He has no time to read, little time to meet those whom he administers. But the most constructive aspects of leadership are those which are exercised "face to face." The loss of the "personal touch" which is so often deplored is not due to the size or complexity of modern enterprises. It is due to the absence of "staff" organization. Administrators cannot see foremen and fields and factories for filing cabinets.

22. "Staff" Integrates "Line" and Function

If, as has been suggested, the confusion as to principles of organization in the world today is due to an attempt to compromise between the necessity for retaining "the scalar process" and the requirements of specialization emphasized by Taylor, it will follow that the "staff" conception, if it is a solution, must integrate these two essentials of organization. This is so. The "staff" concept in military practice as herein described, except in so far as it is not carried below the Company, accords very closely with Taylor's ideas. It is avowedly based on his well-known "exception principle." It secures that, in so far as is compatible with effective co-ordination,

---

[42] Major Gen. J. F. C. Fuller, "Generalship — Its Diseases and Their Cure."

one man is confined to one function: the "staff" itself, in the British Army, is specialized into four branches. It is a clear case of the separation of planning from performance. It accords with the irony which sometimes illumines human affairs that the difficulties of co-ordination caused in part by the genius of the man who wrote "throughout the whole field of management the military type of organization should be abandoned," may be solved by reference to the forms of organization which experience has forced upon the armies of the world.

23. Some Objections

In conclusion certain objections to the considerations which have been put forward may be considered. The prejudice against militarism which is so widespread among Anglo-Saxon peoples, will no doubt be encountered. It will be urged that the army is a "disciplined" force and that what is possible in the army is impossible or undesirable elsewhere. It should be considered whether in institutions where a high standard of discipline is not enforced the problem of co-ordination and the provision of mechanism to secure it, is likely to be less serious than in the case of armies.

The "practical" difficulties of applying technical principles in organization, even when their validity is admitted intellectually, are great. Personal factors obtrude. They cannot be ignored. But that they should always and on all occasions be given priority in consideration is fantastic. The idea that organizations should be built up round and adjusted to individual idiosyncrasies, rather than that individuals should be adapted to the requirements of sound principles of organization, is as foolish as attempting to design an engine to accord with the whimsies of one's maiden aunt rather than with the laws of mechanical science. Individuals are the raw material of organization. There is some freedom of choice, some elasticity for adjustment, in large enterprises a great deal. That an engineer in the wilderness should build a bridge of such materials as he can find is inevitable. That an engineer in a complex industrialized area should do the same is unthinkable. Even in the wilderness the trained engineer will build his bridge in accordance with principles. It will be a better bridge: there will be less strain and the materials will last longer.

Insistence on the personal standpoint in organization almost invariably implies an attempt to secure for some individual or for some group special privileges at the expense of their colleagues. It may be the chief who prefers to occupy his time with detail and his opportunities for straightening out personal situations with patronage. It may be subordinate officials who suspect that conservative insistence on the "status quo," and not their personal qualifications for positions of responsibility, is the best guarantee they have of whatever authority they at present enjoy. It may be elements in the rank and file who have developed "defence mechanisms" against some of the worst consequences of bad organization, and prefer to maintain their habits rather than to risk a change.

Whatever the motive underlying persistence in bad structure it is always more hurtful to the greatest number than good structure. It opens the way to every type of dishonesty and intrigue. Such things bring petty miseries every day and larger injustices very often. As Mooney and Reiley have observed:

"How often do we hear of business institutions that their organizations are all 'shot through' with politics. . . . Such conditions . . . are really due to inattention on the part of the management to the necessities of formal organization, and the application of its principles. . . . The . . . type of management, which regards the exact definition of every job and every function, in its relation to other jobs and functions, as of first importance, may sometimes appear excessively formalistic, but in its results it is justified by all business experience." [43]

More serious is the inertia of current practice. Men accept existing forms of organization at the point to which they have evolved as a matter of course. That they have been different in the past is ignored. The suggestion that enterprises for other purposes may have the same needs, be suffering from the same conditions, which have compelled that evolution, alone rouses resistance. The resistance is reinforced by what the French call "déformation professionelle," the tendency to look at all questions from a particular point of view, to assume that in respect of the individual's own profession what is must be best, which seems to result inevitably from the long and intensive practice of a particular calling. It is intellectually incapable of imagining alternative arrangements and insensitive to considerations other than those current in the given group. It is often associated with great disinterestedness and sense of public service.

24. The Evolution of Organization

From both these standpoints the evolution of the higher administration of the British Army is instructive. Today it is co-ordinated in a single department, the War Office. Everyone regards this piece of organization as a matter of course. Naturally an army must have one head, must be co-ordinated. In the year of Waterloo a British commander in the field had to deal with more than a dozen independent and separate ministers or departments in Whitehall on the affairs of his army. It required a hundred years of struggle, of incessant royal committees and commissions, of recurrent scandals due to maladministration, before the last vestige of conflicting authorities had disappeared and the constitutional and administrative position was finally consolidated. Certain significant stages in this evolution are illustrated in *Figure XII*.

At every stage the most eminent generals, the men who had suffered themselves under the worst effects of this regime in the field, fought reform — Wellington, Wolseley, perhaps the most extraordinary case of all, Airey who had been Quartermaster General in the Crimea and had seen the men perishing by hundreds for lack of the ordinary elements of workmanlike arrangements. In every case it was determined civilians, such as Esher, Cardwell and Haldane, who won the next step.

Today, the State is taking an increasing part in the administration of economic life. There are more than a dozen separate departments and offices in Whitehall each dealing with some particular aspect of the subject. The individual business man, the general in the field, has to co-ordinate their various services at the point of action somehow or other. Everyone regards it as perfectly natural. New semi-independent authorities are being created every year. Any suggestion of change of direction meets the insuperable objection "The Civil Service wouldn't like it."

---

[43] *Op. cit.*

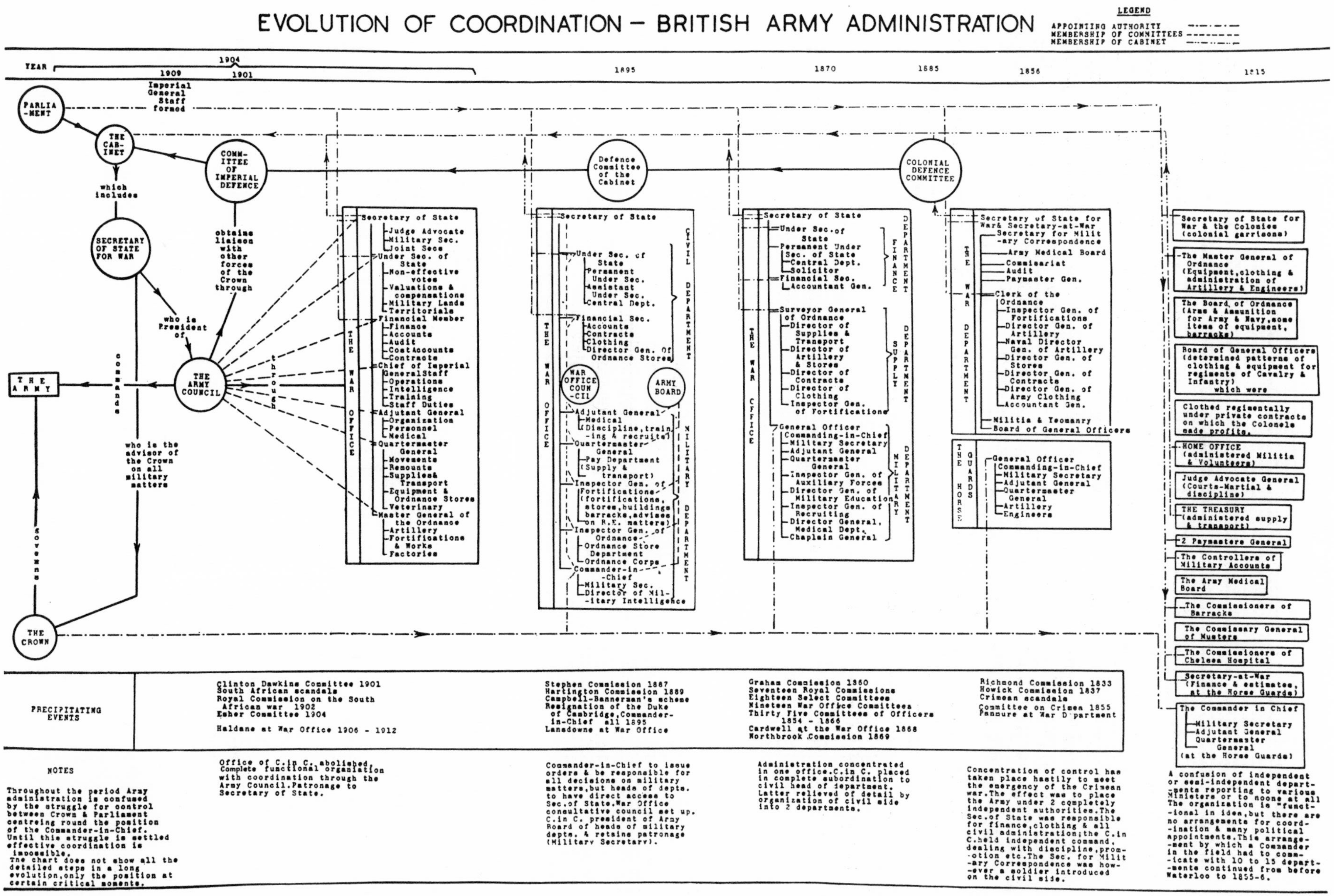

FIGURE XII. EVOLUTION OF CO-ORDINATION — BRITISH ARMY ADMINISTRATION

Herbert Spencer once wrote "socially as well as individually, organization is indispensable to growth; beyond a certain point there cannot be further growth without further organization." Rapid growth in scientific knowledge has placed an unprecedented strain on man's powers of organization. The effects of that strain are just becoming apparent. Knowledge of and interest in the technique of organization and in its basic principle of co-ordination, are as yet feeble. The common man fears the concentration of authority, lest he be unable to control it. The future of the Western nations hinges on their power to awaken that interest and to remove that fear. "Divide and rule" may be a sound motto for an agricultural despotism. For a machine-using democracy it is a passport to disaster.

> "But history records more frequent and more spectacular instances of the triumph of imbecile institutions over life and culture, than of peoples who have by the force of instinctive insight saved themselves alive out of a desperately precarious institutional situation, such, for instance, as now faces the peoples of Christendom." [44]

These words were written in 1914.

---

[44] Thorstein Veblen, "The Instinct of Workmanship," pp. 24 and 25.

III

THE PRINCIPLES OF ORGANIZATION

By

JAMES D. MOONEY

Vice President, General Motors Corporation

THE PRINCIPLES OF ORGANIZATION

The word *principle* signifies something fundamental. So also, in its human aspect, does the word *organization*. These two fundamentals, and how they relate, constitute the theme of this study.

Concerning the fundamentality of human *organization*, as such, a few words will suffice.

Most of us think of organizations as essentially something big; something that unites large numbers of people in some common purpose. Such combinations certainly do give high visibility to certain forms of human association, but the word organization itself means something far more basic.

The term organization, and the principles that govern it, are inherent in every form of concerted human effort, even where there are no more than two people involved. For example take two men who combine their efforts to lift and move a stone that is too heavy to be moved by one. In the fact of this combination of effort we have the reality of human organization for a given purpose. Likewise in the procedure necessary to this end we find the fundamental principles of organization. To begin with, the two lifters must lift in unison. Without this combination of effort the result would be futile. Here we have *co-ordination*, the first principle of organization. Likewise one of these two must give the signal "heave ho!" or its equivalent, to the other, thus illustrating the principle of *leadership* or command. Again the other may have a suggestion to make to the leader in the matter of procedure, which involves the vital *staff* principle of advice or counsel. And so on. Thus in every form of concerted effort principles of organization are as essential and inevitable as organization itself.

My own principal interest lies in the sphere of industrial organization, which of all major forms of human organization is, in its present magnitude, the most modern. For this the reason is evident. The vast present-day units of industrial organization are products mainly of one creating factor, namely the technology of mass production, and this technology, born of the industrial revolution, has been almost exclusively an evolution of the last century. In contrast other major forms of human organization — the state, the church, the army — are as old as human history itself. Yet if we examine the structure of these forms of organization we shall find that, however diverse their purposes, the underlying principles of organization are ever the same.

On the surface it might appear otherwise. For example we may think of *line* and *staff* as something peculiar to military organization — and so they are if we consider the origin of the terms only, and the particular functions to which they refer in military procedure. But if we take the broader view and consider *line* simply as the function of command, and *staff* as the service of information or counsel, we see at once that military organization can have no corner on these principles. The organizations of civil government have and of necessity must have the equivalent of these functions, so has church government, and so likewise has industrial organization.

The point here is that a principle, if it be truly such, must of necessity be universal in its own sphere, and so it is with the principles of organization. There is no principle in industrial organization as such that is not to be found in all of these other spheres, but it is erroneous to infer that industrial organizers have borrowed these principles of organization from these older forms. A principle, if it is truly such, is a universal, and a universal cannot be borrowed. It simply has a way of applying itself, and this is ever true, by whatever name we may be pleased to call it. If we can but recognize a principle when we see it, it is a simple matter to identify and co-ordinate what, for present purposes, I have called the principles of industrial organization.

Organization, as I have said, means concerted human effort, the kind of effort that is essential to the highest measure of success of any group undertaking. But what, in industrial organization, are the conditions necessary to the highest efficiency of such concerted effort? If we addressed this question to a score of representative industrial executives, we would of course get many valuable and inspirational answers. But I wonder how many of these answers would give the *structural* principles of organization the importance that I believe they deserve?

It may be asked why I emphasize the term "structural." The reason is that many people think of organization as in some way synonymous with administration or management. In every organization there is a collective job to be done, consisting always of the sum of many individual jobs, and the task of administration, operating through management, is the co-ordination of all the human effort necessary to this end. Such co-ordination, however, always presupposes the jobs to be co-ordinated. The job as such is therefore antecedent to the man on the job, and the sound co-ordination of these jobs, considered simply as jobs, must be the first and necessary condition in the effective co-ordination of the human factor.

The importance of the exact functional definition of each job as such, in its effect on the morale and general efficiency of an organization, may be shown by illustrations that are familiar in all business experience. How often do we hear it said of business institutions that their organizations are all "shot through" with politics. A superficial thinker might take this as a reflection on the personnel. If he should become acquainted with this personnel he might be surprised to find how good, potentially at least, it really is, comparing not unfavorably with the personnel of other institutions that function smoothly and harmoniously. Ten to one we must go to organization, rather than personnel, to find the real cause of the trouble.

Such conditions are really due to the inattention on the part of administration to the necessities of formal organization, and the application of its principles. When an employee is placed in a position, with duties ill defined in their relation to other duties, what happens? Naturally he attempts to make his own definition of these duties, and, where he can, to impose this view on those about him. In this process he encounters others in similar case, with friction and lack of co-ordinated effort as the inevitable consequences.

On the positive side orderly procedure gives way to the practice of "cutting cross lots"; on the negative side it results in the shirking of responsibilities, or, in popular phrase, "passing the buck." Such conditions become aggravated when management itself begins to take short cuts, without consideration of the longtime consequences. The two conditions usually go together, for the management that is inattentive to the definition of subordinate functions is almost sure to be just as disorderly in the exercise of its own. True co-ordination in the formal sense can only be effectuated through functional definition, and such co-ordination must begin at the top. Without it there will be friction, even at the top, and in these circumstances it is futile to look for co-ordinated harmony at any other point down the line. No one who has ever had personal knowledge of such conditions can question the importance of the exact functional definition of all jobs as such, in their relation to other jobs, in its effect on collective efficiency and collective morale.

The other type of management, which regards the exact definition of every job and every function, in its relation to other jobs and functions, as of first importance, may sometimes appear excessively formalistic, but in its results it is justified by all practical experience. It is in fact a necessary condition of true efficiency in all forms of collective and organized human effort.

It is such co-ordination that I have in mind when I speak of the structural principles of organization. A good job of organizing, in this sense, is a necessary condition of any efficient and successful management. I shall now endeavor to describe, as briefly as I can, those structural principles of organization, the application of which is necessary to this end.

Co-ordination, as we have noted, is the determining principle of organization, the form which contains all other principles, the beginning and the end of all organized effort. We must find the actual process, however, through which co-ordination becomes effective throughout an organization. Here I would distinguish between two forms of co-ordination, the *perpendicular* and the *horizontal*. I cannot conceive of a truly efficient organization of any kind that does not illustrate the operation of both of these principles.

The principle of perpendicular co-ordination is expressed in the single word *authority*. By authority I do not necessarily mean autocracy. In democratic forms of organization the supreme authority may be represented in the group as a whole, as it is under our government in the people of the United States. Nor is authority something that, under any system, can ever be segregated at the top. Responsibility without corresponding authority is inconceivable, and sound organization demands a clearly defined responsibility for every act, from the greatest to the smallest.

It follows, therefore, that authority must have a clearly defined process through which it projects itself throughout an entire organization, so that everyone in the institution participates in the exercise of this authority, according to the nature of his duties.

Here we come to what I conceive to be a vital distinction; that between authority as such, and the form of authority that projects itself through *leadership*. The difference may be seen in their relation to the organization itself. It takes supreme co-ordinating authority to create an organization; leadership, on the other hand, always presupposes the organization. I would define leadership as the form in organization through which authority enters into process; which means, of course, that there must be leadership as the necessary directive of the entire organized movement.

We know how leadership functions in the direction of this movement, and we are all familiar with the structural form through which it operates. We call it *delegation* of duties, but few realize how absolutely necessary to an orderly and efficient procedure is a sound application of this delegating principle.

Delegation is not a transfer of authority; it is a correlation of authority, and likewise of responsibility. The one to whom a task or a job is delegated becomes responsible for doing that job, but the superior who delegates this authority remains responsible for getting the job done. And this chain of correlated responsibility, which I call the scalar chain, extends from the top to the bottom of the entire organization, but always emanating from the top leadership, which is responsible for the whole.

Delegation, as a principle, is universal in organization, and no form of concerted human effort can be conceived without it. It begins where organization begins, in the simplest relations of superior and subordinate, and, no matter how vast the organization becomes, or how much the scalar chain may lengthen through sub-delegation, the principle of correlated responsibility remains ever the same.

But this process of delegation cannot and must not be conceived as an end in itself. It must have its own aim and end; in other words its own final purpose. This purpose is nothing less than the co-ordination of *functions*.

By functions I mean distinctions between *kinds of duties*. We know that authority is the determining principle of organization, but it is impossible to think of the variations of different jobs in terms of authority alone. Functionalism enters from the very first; from the first the central line of authority begins to throw off functions, and in the end it always breaks up into functional distinctions. Authority, represented in leadership, and operating through delegation of duties, has only one aim and purpose within the organization, namely the co-ordination of functions. And the efficiency of such co-ordination is the measure of the efficiency of the organization itself.

This is certainly true of the executive group. It is no less true of the organization as a whole, and equally true of every organization, whatever its purpose. We see this illustrated in a well organized factory, geared to mass production, with its countless individual jobs or functions, many of them seemingly small in themselves, but all of them fitting into the general scheme, and essential to the collective result. We see it again in another sphere in the perfect co-ordination of a symphony orchestra, where the co-operation of every individual musician is likewise essential to the collective harmony.

We must not think of functionalism, however, as something that always has primary reference to the function of the individual as such. *Departmental* functionalism, if I may call it by that name, is also a vital factor in nearly all forms of organization.

Take for example the military. The distinction between generals, colonels, majors, captains, etc., down to the high privates, is clearly scalar, and always defines itself as such. But just as clearly the distinction between the infantry and the artillery is functional, and the same applies to every other special function in military organization, including the auxiliary functions of supply and transport.

This same phenomenon of departmental functionalism appears in every sphere of industrial organization. It may be less evident in the sphere of production, where functionalism concerns itself mainly with individual duties. In the sphere of distribution, however, no matter what the nature of the product, there are four divisions of departmental functionalism that appear to be well nigh universal. These four are *finance*, *sales*, *supply*, and *service*.

If any of these four can be identified as the principal or determining function, it is obviously finance, and so it appears in most forms of distributive organization. The other three distributive functions appear in all kinds of relationships, according to the nature of the industry. In some industries supply and service are subordinated to selling in functional importance. In others this relation is reversed, and the two in combination appear as a far more important functional arm. The latter is generally true of all public utilities.

From the standpoint of organization, departmental functions of such importance require scalar organization from the top downward, such functions, at each stage of the scalar chain, adhering to the corresponding line authority. In this respect they clearly correspond to the line and staff functions in army organization, a subject on which I shall presently have more to say. The point I here wish to emphasize is that the organization of any function of such importance from the very top downward is an absolute essential to any truly efficient co-ordination of effort.

The necessity for such co-ordination, in order to attain a true efficiency of collective effort, is too obvious to require further illustration, but how to attain such efficiency carries us back to the process that assigns all functions. The scalar chain in organization, with its authority and delegation of duties, is the source of this co-ordination; it is here, in the way these principles are applied, that we may find the source either of a collective harmony or a functional discord.

So much for *perpendicular* co-ordination, operating through leadership and the delegation of authority, without which no organization can function. Another factor of equal importance is that of *indoctrination* in the common purpose, which is obviously essential to the true intelligence of concerted effort. Here enters the other great principle, that of *horizontal* co-ordination, which operates not through authority and the function of command but through the universal service of knowledge. This difference between the perpendicular and the horizontal forms of co-ordination brings us to the final distinction in functionalism, that between the *line* and the *staff*.

As students of organization we have become familiar with the military terms line and staff, and we have witnessed the extension of these terms to the sphere of industrial organization. But we are still prone to think of the line and staff distinction as in some way an evolution out of military forms.

My study of human organization refutes this notion. It is true that the terms line and staff are military in their origin, but that is all. The principles they describe are as old as human organization itself. In one form or another, and under various names, this distinction appears in other forms of organization — of church or secular government — from the beginnings of recorded history. In every form of organization we find the function of authority or command, and likewise the function of advice or counsel, the latter constituting a true service of knowledge. Thus the universality of this distinction, the true test of a principle, is clearly established. It is this same distinction that I have in mind when I contrast the principles of perpendicular and of horizontal co-ordination.

Authority, with its process of delegation, is of course essential in every organization, but experience proves that the service of knowledge is an equal necessity, and, furthermore, that such service is impossible through the contacts of command alone. Staff services, whether formally organized or not, are bound to grow up in every organization. Their formal organization, however, is demanded if we are to achieve the most efficient forms of concerted human effort.

Staff service, like line authority, begins at the top. In this phase it is informative and advisory to the top leadership. It has been defined as an extension of the personality of the executive — more ears, more eyes, and more hands to aid him in the formulation of his policies. These however are the informative and advisory phases of staff service. They become supervisory when all the formed policies of leadership are translated into execution. It is in the latter phase that we find how the service of knowledge is infused throughout an entire organization.

Here military organization furnishes an impressive example. We notice that military staff organization is scalar, like the line to which it adheres, following at each step in the scale the gradations of line authority. Even the smallest units of command have their own staff services. But more than this is needed if an entire organization is to be permeated with a true service of knowledge.

It is not the leader alone who has things to make known to his subordinates through the usual channels of staff service. These subordinates may likewise have something important to tell the leader; things that he should know in the exercise of his leadership. They may also have important things to tell each other, and this mutuality of things to be made known extends upwards, downwards, and sideways, from the very top to the bottom of the organized structure.

If we look about us in the sphere of industrial organization we may see examples of how such a service may be organized, prominent among them the interlocking committee systems. No intelligent movement toward a common objective is possible without such a service. If military organization, with its greater intensity of discipline, finds the service of knowledge so imperative, how much more evident the same need becomes in the case of every industrial objective. In all forms of organization, what I have called horizontal co-ordination is the principle that *indoctrinates* every member of the group in the common purpose, and thus insures the highest collective efficiency and intelligence in the pursuit of the objective.

In this outline of the structural principles of organization I have done no more than expose the scaffolding, the frame-work out of which it is made. In stressing the importance of this frame-work, I hope no one will think that I am overlooking the major importance of the human factor. Humanly speaking, the strength of any organization is simply the aggregate strength of the individuals who compose it. We cannot forget, however, that the strength of the individual, whatever that strength may be, can only attain the highest measure of effectiveness through soundly adjusted relationships, and it is here that we see the fundamental importance of these structural principles. If we truly co-ordinate the jobs as such, we shall find that the more efficient and harmonious co-ordination of the people on the jobs is immensely facilitated.

One question frequently asked is whether the development of personnel policies is properly a line or a staff function. The obvious answer is that it is both, for there can be no staff service in the segregated sense. Such service must always adhere to line responsibilities.

Nevertheless, in the development of personnel policies, the staff should be a potent factor. It is a point worth observing that in the general staff of our army the first division, or G-1, is the personnel division. This division, furthermore, has nothing to do with operations and training, which is the concern of a different section. It is concerned with personnel simply as individuals, and it advises concerning the movements of men in order that the right man shall always be found in the right job. Of course on the human side there is more to personnel policies than the mere fitting of the man to the job. Nevertheless this is always the prime essential — the one that must have first consideration in all personnel plans.

Finally, in all of this discussion concerning principles of organization, and how the application of these principles contributes to organized efficiency, we must keep ever in mind the fact that the prime importance of industrial organization, like every other form of human association, lies in its aim or object, and this leads us to the consideration of how the other great factors in human affairs, governmental and social, may affect its policies, aims, and even its destinies. Granted that efficiency is essential in everything that is worth the doing, we must not forget that efficiency is never an end in itself. It must always have an aim and purpose and it can only justify itself through the worthiness of this purpose. Worthiness in the industrial sphere can have reference to one thing only, namely the contribution of industry to the sum total of human welfare. On this basis only must industry and all its works finally be judged.

Even from the standpoint of efficiency in the pursuit of its objectives the record of industry during the last forty years leaves something to be desired. The growing efficiencies of industrial production during this period are familiar and we know what these efficiencies have accomplished in the lowering of production costs. What we also observe, however, during this same period, is that these producing efficiencies have not always had the effect they should have had in the reduction of price to the final consumer. And this fact brings us face to face with something that we all should know, namely that distribution, and the rising costs of distribution, and not production, constitute today the great unsolved industrial problem.

During this period the increasing efficiencies of production have created a dependence on ever larger and wider markets, and we have not developed the corresponding efficiencies in distribution that these conditions compel. The efficient production engineer has long been with us, but the distribution engineer is a more recent arrival, and in the proper relating of plants and products to markets he still has his own major problems to solve.

It is not such problems, however, but rather the moral problems growing out of the human relations in industrial organization that constitute our main concern at present.

Here we encounter the present-day problem of industry in its most vital aspect. Organizations, after all, are composed of people, and no organization can be any stronger than the people who compose it. To be exact on this point, the great internal problem of industry on the human side is and always has been the relation of the individual to the group, and the further fact that the reasonable continuity of this relation is one of the prime essentials of group loyalty. This brings us face to face with the problem of social security, now uppermost in the popular mind. Four and a half years ago, in June 1932 to be exact, in an address on "Current Problems of

Industrial Management," I made the prediction that if industry does not step up to this problem government will. We all know how that prediction has been fulfilled.

It is obvious that these later developments, which have made the government the sponsor for social security, do not help to improve the strength of industrial organization, for under present policies the security, if it indeed be such, appears to come from elsewhere. The fact remains, however, that industry, which always pays for everything, must finally pay the bills. What industry must continue to strive for are measures that will help to insure the continuity of the human relationship, without which no organization, however potent it may appear at any given time, can be assured of enduring strength. There is no escape from the fact that continuity of employment is the sole basis of enduring group loyalty, and this continuity, as all experience proves, is in turn dependent on reasonably stable industrial conditions. Nothing, as all experience likewise proves, can give absolute assurance of such conditions, but a much nearer approach is feasible through a scientific study of markets, and a sound relating of plants and products to markets, which should be the principal care of industrial engineering, now and hereafter.

In conclusion I would emphasize the fact that, despite these considerations, organization, and the sound application of its principles, must always remain a potent force in determining industrial destiny. Organization concerns procedure, and the attainment of any human group objective must ever depend, in great measure, on efficient forms of procedure. The lessons of history teach us that no efficiency of procedure will save from ultimate extinction those organizations that pursue a false objective; on the other hand, without such efficient procedure, all human group effort becomes relatively futile. It is in these facts, I believe, that we may see clearly the importance of these principles of organization, in their bearing on future industrial progress.

IV

THE ADMINISTRATIVE THEORY IN THE STATE

By

HENRI FAYOL

Translated from the French

by

SARAH GREER

Institute of Public Administration

ADDRESS BEFORE THE SECOND INTERNATIONAL CONGRESS OF ADMINISTRA-
TIVE SCIENCE AT BRUSSELS, SEPTEMBER 13, 1923

PUBLISHED BY KIND PERMISSION OF M. HENRI FAYOL, JUNIOR

IV

THE ADMINISTRATIVE THEORY IN THE STATE

In his address at the opening of the Congress of 1910 the President, M. Cooreman, gave the following definition of administration:

"By administration we mean three things connected but distinct: an ensemble of the executive power and the exercise of this power; the body of functionaries and employees; and the administrative personnel.

"The executive power as we understand it here, has for its object the maintenance of order, public security, the guarantee of a just and free use of common property, the management of the public wealth, the execution of the laws and the preparation and putting into effect of measures of general interest."

According to this definition the science of administration would include only knowledge relative to the services, agencies, the personnel and the operation of public administration. In fact the Congress of 1910 had in view only the administration of public affairs.

The meaning that I have given to the word *administration* and which has been generally adopted, broadens considerably the field of administrative science. It embraces not only the public service but enterprises of every size and description, of every form and every purpose. All undertakings require planning, organization, command, co-ordination and control, and in order to function properly, all must observe the same general principles. We are no longer confronted with several administrative sciences but with one alone, which can be applied equally well to public and to private affairs and whose principal elements are today summarized in what we term the *Administrative Theory*.

This seems to be also the opinion of those who planned this conference, for in their invitation we find the following:

"The importance of administration has grown steadily since the first Congress of Administrative Science held in Brussels in 1910. In consequence we have felt strongly the need of good administrative methods, and men such as Fayol, Solvay and Taylor have in recent years worked out certain formulas (or a synthesis of principles) which should in their opinion govern an administration.

"Belgium has made many successful experiments in this vast field. The Ministry of National Defense has just been reorganized according to the principles of Fayol. Some important steps in this direction have also been taken by the Ministry of Agriculture."

Following the example of Belgium, France has recently been inspired to reorganize the Department of Posts, Telegraphs and Telephones according to the Administrative Theory. In an act presented to the Parliament in July, 1922, the Government said as follows:

"Already many government activities in foreign countries have put into operation the administrative methods that we wish to introduce into the administration of the Postal Department. In Belgium the Minister of National Defense has published a brochure which contains an outline of the ideas of M. Fayol which have been successfully put into operation in his department.

"France must not be the last country to apply modern methods to public administration."

We must not be deluded, however, by these official statements for in reality, the essential principles of the Administrative Theory do not seem to have been applied in their entirety. Even the organization and operation of industrial undertakings seldom conform to them, while governments are only waking up to the theory of administration and so far have limited themselves to certain questions of detail, without attacking the real problem.

The essential principle of the Administrative Theory is the great importance of management and this importance increases with the size of the undertaking. No enterprise can be successful without good management and every enterprise which is poorly managed is doomed to failure. This principle is as true for the State as for private industry. In my opinion, if the operation of the public service causes so much vexation it is because it is not well managed. The manner in which the subordinates do their work has incontestably a great effect upon the ultimate result, but the operation of the management has a much greater effect. The Congress of 1910 was concerned only with the work of the subordinate governmental employees, ignoring the machinery which is of first importance in the operation of any business. It is of this machinery that I am going to speak today.

I will first take up, from the point of view of the Administrative Theory, what should be the rôle, the means of operation and the structure of the high command in the public service, then I will glance at the manner in which these problems are understood and solved. I shall take up here only the question of agencies and shall not touch upon personnel. I assume that all the members of the Congress are familiar with the Administrative Theory. A résumé of it will be found at the end of the printed report of my address.[1]

Rôle, Means of Operation and Structure of the High Command in the Public Service

The structure of the high command in the public service has the same general aspect in all modern states; under different names we find almost everywhere a Prime Minister, ministers and directors.

The Prime Minister has authority over the entire governmental enterprise. It is his duty to conduct the enterprise towards its objective by endeavoring to make the best possible use of the resources at his disposal. He is the head of the ministers and must see that all essential functions are carried on. Each minister is in charge of a group of activities and is the head of the directors of his group. Each director is in charge of a certain activity and is the head of all the employees in his activity.

According to the worth of the men who occupy these three grades of responsibility and according to the means of operation at their disposal, this general plan of the high command in public administration has results ranging from the best to the worst.

Rôle

Let us see what is the principal rôle of the high command in the public service. In a great enterprise like the state, this rôle is essentially administrative; it consists

---

[1] This résumé is not given here, since an outline of Fayol's theory is to be found in L. Urwick's: "The Function of Administration with Special Reference to the Work of Henri Fayol," Paper V, pp. 115–130.

in preparing the operations of the various governmental services, in seeing that they are carried out and in watching the results. To prepare the operations is to *plan* and *organize;* to see that they are carried out is to *command* and *co-ordinate;* to watch the results is to *control*.

The preparation of the operations is the result of a twofold effort of planning and organization. To plan is to deduce the probabilities or possibilities of the future from a definite and complete knowledge of the past. To organize is to define and set up the general structure of the enterprise with reference to its objective, its means of operation and its future course as determined by planning; it is to conceive and create the structures of all the services that compose it, with reference to the particular task of each. It is to give form to the whole and to every detail its place; it is to make the frame and to fill it with its destined contents. It is to ensure an exact division of administrative work by endowing the enterprise with only those activities considered essential and with careful determination of the sphere of each of them. Thus in organization, the theoretical concepts of planning are translated into facts.

Execution is the result of command and of co-ordination. To command is to set going the services defined by planning and established by organization.

An order when given, sets into motion simultaneously in all the grades concerned, authority and responsibility, initiative and discipline.

But command would be powerless to ensure the complete execution of the will of the chief, if it were not supplemented by co-ordination. To co-ordinate is to bring harmony and equilibrium into the whole. It is to give to things and to actions their proper proportion. It is to adapt the means to the end and to unify disconnected efforts and make them homogeneous. It means establishing a close liaison among services specialized as to their operations, but having the same general objective.

Control is the examination of results. To control is to make sure that all operations at all times are carried out in accordance with the plan adopted — with the orders given and with the principles laid down. Control compares, discusses and criticizes; it tends to stimulate planning, to simplify and strengthen organization, to increase the efficiency of command and to facilitate co-ordination.

Such is the administrative rôle that our theory assigns to the high command in the public service, a rôle in which the Prime Minister, the ministers and the directors have each a part corresponding to their functions.

This rôle is much the most important one for each of these three upper grades, but it is not their only one. Besides his administrative rôle, the director of a public service must see to the carrying on of all important functions in accordance with the orders he receives from the minister. He must naturally follow closely the professional operations characteristic of his service (financial, military, judicial or industrial), and this requires of him an outstanding technical ability in his field.

The minister receives his directions from the Prime Minister, interprets them and transmits them to his immediate subordinates. He controls the actions of these subordinates and represents his Ministry before Parliament.

The Prime Minister, placed at the summit of the administrative hierarchy through the confidence of the Chief of State and of Parliament, has charge of the interests of the country as a whole. He selects the ministers and submits their names to the Chief of State and to Parliament for approval; and on important questions gives them their directions or indicates the course to be followed. He plans, organizes, commands, co-ordinates and controls the public service as a whole. Grave questions of general interest constantly demand his attention and take a great deal of his time and he must also maintain relations with foreign powers. All of this imposes upon him an enormous responsibility which is often beyond the strength of a man most capable physically and mentally.

Such is the rôle of the chiefs at the three upper levels of public service.

Means of Operation

What are the means of operation at their disposal? Let us suppose that the personnel of each activity at every rank of the hierarchy are efficient and equal to their tasks. Let us also suppose that Directors, Ministers and the Prime Minister are equal to their calling. Will this suffice to ensure the efficient operation of the Government? Without hesitation I say No.

Staff

Whatever their ability and their capacity for work, the heads of great enterprises cannot fulfil alone all their obligations of correspondence, of interviews, of conferences and of countless other duties; they must ensure command and control, superintend reports preparatory to decisions, have plans of operations drawn up; encourage and effect improvements. Thus they are forced to have recourse to a group of men who have the strength, competence and time which the Head may lack. This group of men constitutes the Staff of the Management. It is a help, or reinforcement, a sort of extension of the manager's personality, to assist him in carrying out his duties. The Staff appears as a separate body only in large undertakings and its importance increases with the importance of the undertaking. The staff of a Prime Minister, of each Ministry and of each Direction includes: a secretariat, consultants and accountants. The Prime Minister has also a Council for Improvements or Reforms.

Administrative Tools [3]

Administrative tools are essential to the management of any great public business. They are a vast documentation which includes the present, the past and the future, to which the élite of the personnel contribute and which, together with its other sources of information, enables the management to make under the best possible conditions, decisions whose consequences and repercussions can be foreseen.

It is the practical means by which planning, organization, command, co-ordination and control are carried out. It is obvious that in order to manage an undertaking the manager must have a thorough understanding of it. He must be conversant with all that concerns its objectives, its needs, its resources (raw materials, plant machinery, capital, staff, surroundings, etc.), but the acquisition of this knowledge requires a great deal of time and effort, and if studies have not already been made and clear and complete reports prepared, the manager in office may lack the information that he requires and a new manager remain for a long time ignorant of the most essential information about the business.

---

[3] Outillage administratif.

I am going to describe briefly the administrative tools that I used during fifty years in a great mining and metallurgical undertaking. Naturally the different parts of the machinery were adapted to the nature and importance of each of the units which formed the concern, but the general outline of the documentation was always the same, and it can be used in every kind of undertaking. It is as follows:

1. General Survey. — A general survey (of the present situation as well as of the past and the probable future of the business); this survey is made for each unit and also for the business as a whole. The review of the *past history* of the concern is made in order to recall the reasons which determined the founding of the business, the changes it has undergone, and the results obtained. The study of the *present situation* relates to the actual condition of all the parts and of the whole of the resources and needs of the undertaking envisaged from every point of view. The *probable future* is that which is foreseen in taking into account the past, the present and any economic, political and social changes that may take place.

In order that this survey may be made efficiently, it is necessary to have an experienced head, expert in the management of men, capable of getting a loyal and active co-operation from his subordinates and taking a large part of the responsibility that the survey implies. From this study should emerge the general scheme and the directives which serve as a basis for the *Plan of Operations*.

2. Plan of Operations. — The plan of operations is the union or synthesis of various plans: annual, long term, short term, and special. It is a sort of picture of the future where approaching events are set forth clearly and remote events appear vaguely in proportion to their distance. It is the progress of the undertaking foreseen and prepared for a certain length of time. The need of a plan of operations is recognized by all, but the practice is not yet general. Many private undertakings leave much to be desired in this respect; while in government, planning is still the exception and not the rule, because the preparation of a plan requires a great effort on the part of the higher personnel and also a competent and stable head, aided by a good staff.

3. Reports or Proceedings. — The report on operations carried out is the complement of the plan of operations.

Reports of subordinates to their superiors are established for each rank of the hierarchy; they are daily, weekly, monthly or annual, and are a powerful method of control. The use of the plan of operations and the detailed report by each grade of the service permit us to realize two highly important administrative objectives, which are the sense of responsibility among employees and confidence among the administrative authorities.

4. Minutes of Conferences between Heads of Departments. — There is a weekly conference of heads of offices, bureaus and departments with the manager. Each office head gives an account of the work of his department, its accomplishments and the difficulties encountered. After the discussion the manager makes his decisions. Everyone leaves the conference knowing what he has to do and knowing also that he must give an account of it. In one hour the manager has reviewed the principal happenings of the past week and the plans for the following week, and this is a powerful method of co-ordination and control for him.

The minutes of this conference, where all the activities of the business are unfolded and explained by the leading participants are of the greatest importance to the general management. No report or any amount of correspondence could give him such a perspective of the personnel.

5. Organization Chart. — Organization charts, with branches like genealogical tables, permit us to seize at a glance, better than we could with a long description, the organization as a whole; the various activities and their boundaries; the ranks of the hierarchy; the position occupied by each employee, the superior to whom hê reports and the subordinates under his control. The organization chart draws the attention to overlappings and encroachments, to dualities of command and to offices without incumbents. It is a kind of model which shows the imperfections of the staff as a whole and which can be used each time the whole or any part of the organism is reorganized or modified. Accompanied by a clear definition of the functions of each, it defines their responsibilities and permits us to decide quickly what employee we should apply to, in order to deal with a certain matter.

These administrative tools are indispensable in the management of large enterprises. They permit the carrying out under good conditions, of planning, organization, command, co-ordination and control, or in short, efficient administration, which without them would not be possible.

I should like to call attention to two very important administrative results which we can accomplish by their use and whose general absence in government is one of the chief reasons for the inefficient operation of the public service: the sense of responsibility among employees and confidence among administrative authorities.

Responsibility

A plan of operations for an·activity, drawn up by the head of the activity, places an obligation upon him, whatever his rank in the hierarchy. Most of the heads of activities take part in drawing up the plan of operations. The weekly, monthly or annual report, by contrasting plan and accomplishment, shows to what extent these obligations have been fulfilled, and from this springs the sense of responsibility. Without a plan there is no obligation, and without a report there is no comparison of accomplishment with plan, and thus no responsibility in either case. The absence of plans and reports creates a general irresponsibility among employees of the State.

Confidence Among Administrative Authorities

In a corporation, confidence among the directors results from the fact that the plans of the chairman are known and approved by the board of directors who are constantly kept in touch with activities and results, while in the state a minister takes charge of a department about which he knows little and which he administers without a serious or definite plan. Both the Parliament and the employees are ignorant of his intentions, and uneasiness and distrust prevail. But let us suppose a plan of operations drawn up by the employees, agreed upon by the minister and submitted by him, first to the Cabinet and then to Parliament. There is thus a unity of opinion. The Parliament knows what the minister intends to do; regular reports show that the plan is being faithfully carried out and confidence takes the place of the distrust which now prevails among government officials.

The co-operation that is established among employees in all ranks of the hierarchy by the preparation of reports, is another advantage of administrative tools. This constitutes a real participation in administration by minor employees and is perhaps the best participation that could be devised.

Administrative tools have many other virtues. They imply that no one will embark upon any course of action without having foreseen the consequences. This means putting planning into operation, and thus an imperfect machine will not be destroyed without a better one to replace it. One would not turn over a government undertaking to private enterprise, or the reverse, without being quite sure that the change would be beneficial to the Nation. By putting these administrative tools into operation in the state we might bring about a considerable modification in the orientation of public opinion.

STRUCTURE AND ORGANIZATION

Given the rôle and means of operation of the high command in the public service, what should be its structure and organization? We will assume that Directors, Ministers and Prime Ministers are amply endowed with physical, intellectual and moral qualities, as well as with general culture, and will leave these aside to confine ourselves to questions of competence and of organization.

Director

The Director of a governmental activity must have the following qualities and competence, necessary to the head of any great private enterprise: administrative ability; professional competence appertaining to the enterprise; general notions on all essential functions, and stability. If he can keep his post for ten years he is considered stable, if he cannot stay in one place longer than a year or two he is unstable. He should be supplied with a good staff and good administrative tools.

The Minister

The Minister must be a good administrator, able to plan, to organize, to command, to co-ordinate and to control. He should have a wide general knowledge of the affairs for which he is responsible, but he is not required to have a special competence in the various professions characteristic of his department, this being the function of the Directors. The importance of stability has not yet been realized by parliamentary governments and this is not one of the requirements for a minister. He must, however, have platform eloquence, for he plays his principal rôle in Parliament. There he is the representative of the activities under his administration and must ask for necessary funds for them and defend his requests against attacks. He is called a good minister if he wins the approbation of the deputies and senators, but more than parliamentary eloquence is needed to direct a ministry. It is conceivable that a good lawyer might become a brilliant minister in a few weeks, but his talent as an orator would not make him a good administrator. Finally the minister should be provided with a good staff and good administrative tools. His staff should include accountants independent of those under the directors.

Prime Minister

The Prime Minister should above all things be a good administrator. He cannot be expected to have a profound personal knowledge of all the problems incident to the functioning of the government enterprise, but usually he has had long political experience and with the assistance of a good staff and good administrative tools he can make decisions with a thorough knowledge of the case. His staff should include a secretariat, special consultants, accountants and a Council for Improvements and Reforms. The Prime Minister must possess parliamentary eloquence to a high degree.

The Actual State of Affairs

The above would be the recommended organization of the high command in the public service according to the Administrative Theory. It would be interesting to see to what extent this idea is grasped and carried out in the various constitutional States, but today I must confine myself to a rapid glance at the situation in France, feeling convinced that I could apply most of my observations and conclusions to the other countries.

Prime Minister

In France, for several decades the Prime Minister has been surrounded by from twelve to fifteen ministers and several under-secretaries of state. Besides general administrative supervision over the government as a whole, the Prime Minister is in charge of one of the government departments and usually one of the most important. As Prime Minister he has neither a secretariat, nor accountants, nor special consultants, nor a Council for Improvements and Reforms. He has besides, no administrative tools. He would not even have an office or attendants but for the government department of which he is in charge.

Aside from his personal worth which is usually high, the Prime Minister has at his disposal none of the various means of operation recognized as indispensable if he is to fill properly his office as Head of the Government. He has too many ministers to direct, and it is absolutely impossible for him to administer the Public Service as a whole efficiently and at the same time to be head of a department. There we have an extraordinary and incredible fault in organization. Whatever the circumstances that brought about this state of affairs there is no reason to maintain it in the face of the enormous harm that it causes the Nation. The remedy lies in the suppression of portfolios, in the reduction of the number of ministers, in the setting up of a staff, and in administrative tools.

Minister

In order to ensure the successful operation of his department the Minister should be a good administrator with a certain competence in the affairs of which he has charge.

He should receive orders from only one chief and have but a small number of subordinates directly under him. But in actual fact the Minister is seldom a good administrator who has learned to plan, to organize, to command, to co-ordinate and to control, and he has rarely had any training for his position. He is responsible for the activities of his department to the Prime Minister and to Parliament, but he renders no report to either. If there is any happening out of the ordinary, of such a nature as to arouse Parliament or upset the Cabinet, the Minister discloses it and the President intervenes.

The Minister usually lacks the administrative ability, professional competence and time which are necessary to the head of a great enterprise.

On taking office he finds himself immediately confronted with a great number of problems, of which he has no knowledge but which urgently demand attention. He has no documentation to enlighten him, he seldom has a staff of special consultants and he is unable to consult the head of the Government, who is too busy to follow the details of current affairs. To add to this he usually finds that he must deal directly with some twenty subordinates. Swamped, submerged and unable to make decisions from first hand knowledge, the Minister generally abandons the attempt to exercise any executive authority and it is difficult to tell what to dread most, his active intervention or his inaction. Current operations are ensured somehow by directors acting independently of each other, like the ministers, without co-ordination. It is a system of water-tight compartments.

Thus it is not a matter for surprise if certain activities which are partly under two departments wait long months for decisions which should be made in a week, and if those which are under two ministries wait indefinitely. It is also not surprising that ministers who might seriously influence the interests of the state, find themselves powerless to carry out the least reform. The remedy lies in a better recruitment of government personnel and in introducing the use of good administrative tools. The Cabinets also would probably last longer under a better functioning of government, and their present harmful instability be lessened.

Directors

The Head of a government activity as in the case of the Manager of a big private undertaking, should have the following qualities: administrative ability, professional competence and stability. This combination of qualities is sometimes met, but it may also happen to be completely lacking.

On November 4, 1920, I delivered to M. Louis Deschamps, Under-Secretary of State, a report which he had asked me to make on the organization and operation of the Department of Posts, Telegraphs and Telephones of which he was Director General. The report began thus: "During the past year I have been studying the government undertaking of P.T.T., and I have noted many faults of administration of which the following are the most outstanding:

1. An unstable and incompetent chief at the head of the undertaking;
2. No long term plan;
3. No budget;
4. Abusive and excessive interference from members of Parliament;
5. No incitement to enthusiasm and no reward for services rendered;
6. Absence of responsibility."

Chance had brought me into contact with one of the great enterprises where the usual faults of public administration were most pronounced and I set myself to prove that most of these faults are the result of bad management. To remedy these defects the Government, citing the Administrative Theory, has recently proposed to set up a committee of consultants without changing in any way the method of recruiting the directorate. Now let us see, according to my survey of 1920 how this recruitment is made: "A ministerial crisis arises. The composition of the new ministry appears in the Officiel of January 16. The Under-Secretary of State, Monsieur A., lawyer and deputy, holding the office of Director General of the P.T.T. is replaced by the Under-Secretary of State, Monsieur B., lawyer and deputy. January 17, Monsieur B. comes to the office and meets Monsieur A. These gentlemen talk together for a few minutes, then Monsieur A. takes his leave, having already emptied the drawers of his desk. There has been no presentation of the heads of departmental activities to the new chief and no plan of operations is given to him for his guidance.

"Thus takes place a handing over of office in one of the most important administrations of the Government. The chief who is leaving took office twelve or fifteen months earlier without knowing anything of the great undertaking he was called upon to direct, and the new chief is in the same position and will probably leave after the same interval." A head thus recruited has neither stability nor competence and it is highly probable that he is not gifted with administrative ability, nor does he have a good staff nor good administrative tools. The Administrative Theory condemns the illusion that under these conditions, the administration of the P.T.T. could be improved by the addition of a committee of consultants. The appointment of such a committee is generally an admission of helplessness on the part of the Administration and a way of lulling the vigilance of those interested. Even if all the subordinate personnel were very efficient the undertaking would not function well with a mediocre head. It is like an individual all of whose limbs are sound, but who has a diseased brain. We must realize that while all possible reforms may be carried out under a good management, no serious reforms can be carried out under a poor management. The Administration of the P.T.T. evidently does not understand the Administrative Theory.

This is not the case in another great French Administration — the Army. Planning and organization are constant preoccupations with our great military chiefs; authority, discipline, unity of management, unity of command, and subordination of individual interests to the common good are constantly kept in mind. The National Military School has received the Administrative Theory with favor because it recognizes in it a synthesis of the ideas that it advocates. But these ideas have not yet reached the ministries, and so the abuse of written communications continues to prevail, and a Minister has twenty assistants where the Administrative Theory says that a manager at the head of a big undertaking should not have more than five or six.

The persistence of faults of organization in the directorate of the P.T.T., taken as an example, gives an idea of the difficulty presented by the reform of the public service, and this difficulty has recently given rise in several countries to special organisms called Reform Commissions, or Economy Commissions.

Councils for Improvements

The Administrative Theory supposes that in every great enterprise there is a permanent council for improvements whose function it is to make researches on all possible improvements in the enterprise and to carry them out under the auspices and authority of the director.

An organism of this kind seems to me indispensable in order to study and carry out reforms in the Enterprise of Government, which perhaps, more than any other, is in constant need of them.

A firm determination and continued action are needed to overcome the resistance that ignorance, routine and individual interests oppose to reforms. Temporary manifestations in which the higher authorities take little part can have no important results. Continued action requires a special permanent organism.

The firm determination of a Head, such as the Prime Minister, must be based upon a profound conviction of the need for reform and on an accord with the President and with Parliament. This accord in turn must have the support of favorable public opinion.

M. François Marsal, Minister of Finance, appointed in 1920 a High Commission of Inquiry to look into the question of possible retrenchments in the budget. M. Maurice Bloch, Procureur Général of the Cour des Comptes was chairman of this commission, which was succeeded in August, 1922, by the Economy Commission (Commission Supérieure des Économies) under the chairmanship of M. Louis Marin. The Commission has found many defects of organization and function in most of the government services, but when its work is finished in a few months and its findings and recommendations are embodied in a report, what will be the fate of the latter? We have seen that the Prime Minister is much too busy to study a voluminous and complicated document requiring a great deal of special knowledge, and we also know that he has no group of men around him whose duty it is to perform this task for him. The Ministers are too absorbed by their routine duties and too uncertain of their tenure to devote themselves to difficult studies which take time and whose recommendations they cannot put into effect, and which can only create embarrassment for them. As for the Directors, whose tranquillity has been disturbed by the Commission and who have sometimes been severely taken to task by it, they usually have no sympathy for the reforms it proposes.

Under these conditions it is highly probable, not to say certain, that this attempt at reform will be futile like most of those which have preceded it.

It would be otherwise if there were a permanent Council for Improvements or Reforms associated with the Prime Minister. This council would have for its mission to guide and direct studies on reforms in the various departments and offices and to see that they are carried out. The creation of such a body should be carefully studied by competent authorities and the following set-up is suggested only as a tentative plan:

The Council for Improvements should be composed of five members:

The first would have charge of planning, organization, command, co-ordination and control, or in other words, of administration;

The second of financial problems;

The third of the organization of accounting and statistics;

The fourth of legal matters;

The fifth should be a business man.

The Council for Improvements should be represented in each government department by a liaison officer subordinate to the Minister, and particularly charged with the duty of keeping him in touch with the studies being made in his department.

The Council itself should be in charge of the improvements to be made in the machinery of the superior services of the state.

In the work of governmental reform the directing powers of the state need to be helped, sustained and encouraged by public opinion. Public opinion, however, is not prepared for this: unenlightened upon the projects for reform and ignorant of the benefits to be derived from them, it remains indifferent and sceptical. I believe it could be aroused by imbuing it with the idea that there are important reforms both necessary and possible, and that among their results might be a considerable reduction in taxes and a very appreciable decrease in the cost of living.

Public opinion may be guided in the direction of reform by a knowledge of the principles and rules of the Administrative Theory and we can help to spread this by teaching it in the institutions of higher learning. But the effect will be slow and we can hasten it by immediately putting into use administrative tools (*outillage administratif*) in all the public services.

At the same time we can endeavor to arouse public opinion by showing the economic advantages which should result from the projected reforms. It is for this reason that I present to the Congress the following estimates which do not pretend to be rigorously exact, and which for me are only a means of interesting public opinion.

I have endeavored to put into figures the pecuniary interest which the Management of Government has for us. This interest is composed of two elements, one of which is easily determined — it is the cost of government as represented by its annual budget plus its extraordinary requirements (immovable assets, supplies, etc.). If the administration is efficient, these expenditures, however high, are justified — the country has its money's worth. If on the contrary the administration is bad, the expenditures constitute a total loss. But we rarely find that either term can be applied sweepingly, for we seldom find an administration completely good or completely bad. The truth is that good and bad are mixed in varying proportions. Is it rash to assert that under the best administrations there is room for reforms that would lower the cost of government without curtailing its services? What then shall we say of the other administrations? Taking the public services as they are, the good with the bad, in order to form an idea, can we not estimate at 10 per cent of the ordinary and extraordinary budget, that part of the expenses of administration that should interest public opinion, in the sense that the country will spend it or not according to whether the business of government has been efficiently managed or otherwise?

But this is only one element of the situation. The second is the repercussion, good or bad, that the operation of the government necessarily has upon the general economic life of the Nation. We cannot possibly estimate this in figures, but every one knows that it represents a huge sum. Taking, for example, the French government service of the P.T.T., where the capital actually invested is estimated at one billion francs, the coefficient of 10 per cent would show an economy of 100 million francs as the advantage of a good management over a bad one; and when the proposed future capitalization of two billion francs has been effected, there would be an economy of 300 millions, without counting the much more important advantages that would accrue to the country as the result of a better administration of the service. If this calculation were extended to all the activities of the state, the result would be a great many billions, and billions of economies means reduction of taxes, more abundant production and decreased cost of living.

The High Commission of Inquiry (Comité Supérieur d'Enquête) under M. Maurice Bloch, estimated at about two billions the amount of savings that could be realized without any important administrative reorgnization, by simply cutting down appropriations and demanding more efficiency from the various government services. The High Commission for Economy (Commission Supérieure des Économies) under M. Louis Marin estimated that a complete reorganization of the Government under a new plan would result in an economy of four or five billion a year. Such, according to this estimate, is the cost to France of a bad management of public affairs. This is not in contradiction with the estimate of the Commission of Enquiry nor with that I have made above for the P.T.T. If we add to this the inconveniences of every kind that are the result of an inefficient government and the money the inhabitants failed to earn for the same reason, we are led to double the above sum and we find ourselves confronted with the formidable figure of eight or ten billions.

In a country of less than forty million inhabitants, this sum represents a loss of more than 200 francs to each person — 100 francs lost and 100 francs not earned. To the average family consisting of parents and two children, an inefficient government costs more than 800 francs a year: the half of this sum that corresponds to the actual loss, should be deducted from the family income, for it goes to the state for taxes. The other half affects the very basis of the family fortune, for it applies to wealth in process of formation, whose development is paralyzed for individuals, without any immediate or remote profit to the state. It is true that this estimate cannot pretend to be really or even approximately exact, for the income and wealth of the inhabitants are not uniformly affected by inefficient government, but if the mean indicated is necessarily not exact, the calculation that leads to it is based none the less on the uncontrovertible principle that all French citizens bear a part of the expense of government and have an interest in the good management of public affairs.

Whatever their economic status all French citizens bear a part of the expense of government. Even though taxes on wealth and income reach only a fraction of the taxpayers, taxes on commodities strike all without distinction. All of these taxes could be reduced if the needs of the state were less, and especially if there were effected that indispensable condition to any important economy, the reorganization of the High Command of the Public Service. We are therefore forced to maintain that the mass of citizens, and not only the most fortunate, bear under the guise of a reduction of income the disastrous effects of our inefficient administration.

The taxpayers of all countries have an interest in the good management of public affairs, and hence in administrative reform. The abusive levies effected by the state directly or indirectly on the revenues of capital and labor form an obstacle to thrift, hamper the formation of new wealth and in consequence rob production of its means of development. Industry, agriculture and commerce are not alone to suffer from this state of affairs: the consumer bears also the unpleasant consequences, since every restriction of economic activity is manifested by diminished comforts and a rise of prices.

These considerations seem to me of a nature to interest the public in administrative reforms and to encourage the Managers of the State to study them and put them into effect. I am anxious to have the Congress share this opinion.

What is my conclusion? It is that the essential condition for a successful operation of the Public Service is a good High Command, and a good High Command entails a good staff and good Administrative Tools.

V

THE FUNCTION OF ADMINISTRATION

With Special Reference to the Work of Henri Fayol

By

L. URWICK, O.B.E., M.C., M.A.

Chairman, Urwick, Orr and Partners, Ltd.
Consulting Industrial Engineers
formerly
Director of the International Management Institute
Geneva

A lecture delivered before the Institute of Industrial Administration, 13th November, 1934

V

THE FUNCTION OF ADMINISTRATION

WITH SPECIAL REFERENCE TO THE WORK OF HENRI FAYOL

This paper has a threefold purpose:

I. It calls attention to the work of a famous French industrialist which is perhaps too little known in this country. More than any other European who has lived in this century, Henri Fayol is responsible for directing minds to the need for studying administration scientifically. He has laid down broad lines which no subsequent student should neglect.

II. But his logical analysis of the operations involved in business and particularly of the function of Administration stops quite suddenly when he begins to talk of principles: he becomes empirical in his presentation and attitude. This sudden check in his thought will be shown to be due to the "practical man fallacy," inevitable in the light of his background and experience. It is an intensely interesting example of the limitations imposed on scientific study by immediate administrative responsibility.

III. Despite his own practical attitude and refusal to consider a logical arrangement of the principles, it will be found, on closer examination, that his general treatment of administration can be presented as a complete, logical scheme. Within that scheme are two subsidiary systems. The one deals with the structural and the other with the human aspects of administration. The former has been arranged to correspond with the scheme of the principles of organization developed by Mr. Mooney, President of the General Motors Export Company. The latter has resulted from arranging the balance of Fayol's principles and administrative duties on the same general lines.

Three points of interest arise from this study:

(A) Despite the fact that Fayol's work was, apparently, not known to Mooney, a statement of principle corresponding to each head of Mooney's analysis is discovered in Fayol's empirical lists. These principles deal with structure.

(B) The remaining principles do exactly correspond to a second scheme dealing exclusively with the operating or personal aspects of administration. That constitutes fairly effective proof that Fayol's refusal to consider structure and operation separately was, in fact, the cause of his failure to push his very logical handling of the function of administration to its conclusion.

(C) Despite this avowed refusal to continue along logical lines, the general arrangement presented does, in fact, use up the whole of his principles and administrative duties exactly. One, "impose penalties for mistakes and blunders," is used in two places. Otherwise there is neither repetition nor omission. The successful, practical organizer was being far more logical than he himself realized or was prepared to admit.

These considerations, if accepted, appear to the author to strengthen greatly the general contention that a scientific analysis of the arts of administration and organization can be developed. It is hardly necessary to emphasize the importance of this conclusion, if it is valid, not only for business administration, but for political science. Many exact scientists have emphasized in recent years the lack of balance between our knowledge of research devoted to the material aspects of nature and our knowledge of social organization. The possibility of a science of management, or, as Fayol would say, of government, is the only concrete hope before humanity of an ordered and satisfactory solution of the economic and social problems which that lack of balance has created.

Henri Fayol was born in 1841 and died in 1925. He qualified in 1860 as a mining engineer and entered the great coal and metallurgical concern of Commentry-Fourchambault. In 1866 he was appointed Manager of the Commentry collieries, to which were added in 1872 the collieries of Montircq. In 1888 he was appointed General Manager of the Company Commentry Fourchambault & Decazeville, which at the time was in a most critical condition. He was brilliantly successful. When in 1918, after thirty years of practical command, he handed over to his successor, the concern was on a firm basis of prosperity, endowed with remarkable financial stability and assets of unusual value.

His career, thus passed entirely with one organization, is typically European. It is in marked contrast in this respect to F. W. Taylor's varied experience. But in the scientific enthusiasm with which they approached practical problems, both men were remarkably alike. Taylor experimented with high speed steel and the technique of cutting metals: Fayol with shafting, timbering, subsidence, and a geological survey of the coal resources of the Commentry field. M. C. E. Guillaume won the Nobel prize in 1921 for researches undertaken at the Imphy factory with Fayol's assistance and encouragement. Both men were scientists before they were managers. Both men gave the devotion of their later lives to putting science into management. Taylor worked from the individual worker at his bench upwards. Fayol worked from the Managing Director downwards. Their contributions are essentially complementary.

Fayol always insisted that his success was due, not to any personal qualities, but to the methods he employed. His later years were dominated by the desire to prove that, with scientific forecasting and proper methods of management, satisfactory results are inevitable. Shortly before his retirement he expounded his theory of administration in two lectures before the Society for the Encouragement of National Industry. These lectures formed the foundation of his famous book, "Industrial and General Administration."[1] He applied his ideas to public administration in a report on the French postal and telegraph services, published under the title "The State Cannot Administer."[2] They were further crystallized by the foundation of an organization in Paris for their development and teaching — The Centre of Administrative Studies.

Fayol's thesis, which is illustrated graphically in Table I, starts with the proposition that all the operations which occur in business undertakings can be divided into six groups:

---

[1] Except where otherwise stated, all references are to *Administration Industrielle et Générale* by Henri Fayol, Dunod, Paris, 1925. English and German translations were published by the International Management Institute, Geneva, in 1925. The English translation by J. A. Couborough is entitled *Industrial and General Administration*. References show the page in the French and English editions preceded by a capital F and E in each case.

[2] L'Incapacité industrielle de l'Etat: les P.T.T. — Dunod, Paris, 1921.

1. Technical Operations (production, manufacture, etc.).
2. Commercial Operations (purchases, sales and exchanges).
3. Financial Operations (finding and controlling capital).
4. Security Operations (protection of goods and persons).
5. Accounting Operations (stocktaking, balance-sheet, costing, statistics, etc.).
6. Administrative Operations (planning, organization, command, co-ordination, control).

He defines administration as "to plan, organize, command, co-ordinate and control." In explanation of these terms he writes:

"*To plan* means to study the future and arrange the plan of operations.

"*To organize* means to build up the material and human organization of the business, organizing both men and materials.

"*To command* means to make the staff do their work.

"*To co-ordinate* means to unite and correlate all activities.

"*To control* means to see that everything is done in accordance with the rules which have been laid down and the instructions which have been given."

TABLE I
HENRI FAYOL'S ANALYSIS OF THE OPERATIONS WHICH OCCUR IN BUSINESS
GOVERNMENT

("To govern an undertaking is to conduct it towards its objective by trying to make the best possible use of the resources at its disposal; it is, in fact to ensure the smooth working of the six essential functions")

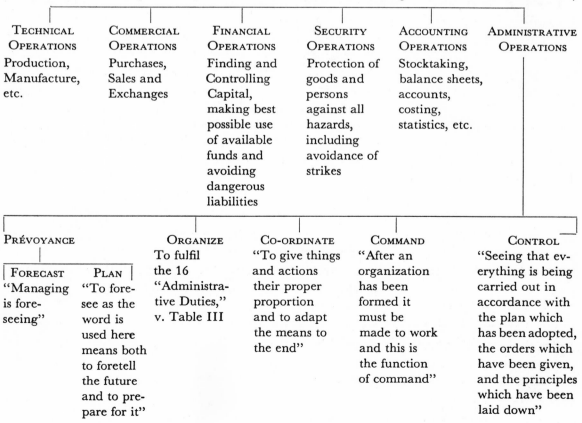

TECHNICAL OPERATIONS	COMMERCIAL OPERATIONS	FINANCIAL OPERATIONS	SECURITY OPERATIONS	ACCOUNTING OPERATIONS	ADMINISTRATIVE OPERATIONS
Production, Manufacture, etc.	Purchases, Sales and Exchanges	Finding and Controlling Capital, making best possible use of available funds and avoiding dangerous liabilities	Protection of goods and persons against all hazards, including avoidance of strikes	Stocktaking, balance sheets, accounts, costing, statistics, etc.	

PRÉVOYANCE		ORGANIZE	CO-ORDINATE	COMMAND	CONTROL
FORECAST "Managing is fore-seeing"	PLAN "To fore-see as the word is used here means both to foretell the future and to pre-pare for it"	To fulfil the 16 "Administra-tive Duties," v. Table III	"To give things and actions their proper proportion and to adapt the means to the end"	"After an organization has been formed it must be made to work and this is the function of command"	"Seeing that everything is being carried out in accordance with the plan which has been adopted, the orders which have been given, and the principles which have been laid down"

(From "Industrial and General Administration," English edition.)

He adds: "Administration regarded in this way must not be confused with government. To govern is to conduct an undertaking towards its objective by seeking to make the best possible use of all the resources at its disposal; it is, in fact, to ensure the smooth working of the six essential functions. Administration is only one of these functions, but the managers of big concerns spend so much of their time on it, that their jobs seem to consist solely of administration."[3]

Thus Fayol begins his theory with a classification along functional lines of the main groups of activities to be found in business. He then deals with Administration, breaking it down into five main aspects. It may be noted, however, that his term *prévoyance*, which has been translated by "planning" in the English edition, really covers two or more separate and distinct processes. He says *prévoir* (literally "to foresee") as used here means both to foretell the future and to prepare for it; it includes the idea of action. *La prévoyance* is found in innumerable forms and at many different points; it becomes most concrete and obvious in the plan of operations (*programme d'action*) which is at the same time its most effective instrument. In illustrating his idea he describes the method of drawing up the plan of operations in a big mining and metallurgical firm. The details which he gives of these forecasts, particularly on the financial side, are in effect a complete summary of the principles which have subsequently attained so much prominence in business practice under the title of Budgetary Control.

His general introduction to the study of administration concludes with what, in the author's view, is one of the most important features of his invaluable contribution: "Whatever the function being considered, the chief characteristic of the lower employees is the special ability appertaining to the function (technical, commercial, financial, etc.) and the chief characteristic of the higher employees is administrative ability. Technical ability is the most important quality at the bottom of the industrial ladder and administrative ability at the top." As Fayol observes, "the technical function has long been given the degree of importance which is its due, and of which we must not deprive it, but the technical function by itself cannot ensure the successful running of a business; it needs the help of other essential functions and particularly of that of administration."

Many of the failures to conduct large combinations of firms successfully may be traced to lack of administrative knowledge in men who have been highly successful in charge of smaller concerns, that is in positions demanding a relatively larger proportion of technical capacity. A man with high administrative qualifications who has never been inside a steel or biscuit works *may succeed*. A man with all the knowledge of steel or biscuit making in the world, but who lacks the requisite level of administrative knowledge and capacity *will certainly fail*.

Unless and until Fayol's thesis on this point wins universal acceptance, avoidable losses will occur. They will be due in large measure to failure to recognize the appropriate balance of qualities in those selected to fill the higher executive positions in business. At the same time the arts of administration and management will receive less study than they deserve or than is necessary for the training of future generations.

---

[3] F. p. 59; E. p. 35.

So long as technical capacity and experience are treated as superior qualifications for higher posts, it is inevitable that administrative ability should be regarded as an empirical and secondary consideration, something the technical man "picks up" in the course of his career.[4]

At this point, however, Fayol abandons any further attempt to analyze administration logically. Of the principles of administration he writes: "There is no limit to the number of principles of administration. Every administrative rule or device, which strengthens the human part of an organization or facilitates its working, takes its place among the principles, for so long as experience proves it to be worthy of this important position." He then lists fourteen of such principles, summarized in the second column of Table IV, and adds: "I shall leave the review of principles at this point, not because the list is exhausted — it has no precise limit — but because it seems to me particularly useful at the moment to endow the theory of administration with about a dozen well-established principles, on which public discussion can conveniently be focussed." The reason he gives for abandoning a logical arrangement is a sound one. He wishes to insist on elasticity in the application of administrative principles: "The same principle is hardly ever applied twice in exactly the same way." This is a fundamental concept in administration. His discussion of the principles is extremely suggestive and illuminating. But, it is open to question whether the reason which he gives, sound though it is, was his real reason for leaving his logical analysis aside.

When he comes to deal with organization as an aspect of administration, he does not distinguish clearly between designing the structure of an enterprise and providing the personnel to carry out the various groups of activities thus demarcated. The phrases which he uses, *organisme social* and *corps social*, are virtually untranslatable in English. They have been rendered by "social organism" and "the staff as a body." The term organism is, however, always used of a living entity. And it is clear that he regards organization wholly from this standpoint.

He says, for instance, that the staff of an enterprise as a body is frequently compared to a machine, a plant or an animal. He objects to the first comparison on the ground that it might leave the impression that "like the parts of a machine, the mechanism of administration cannot transmit power without some loss. This is not correct; the mechanism of administration, that is, every intermediate link in the chain, can and must be a source of energy and ideas; there is in each of these links, or men, a power of initiative which, if properly used, can considerably extend a manager's range of activity."[6] On the other hand, he is in considerable sympathy with the two organic comparisons and particularly the second — "the part played by man in an organization is analogous to that of the cell in the animal."

Indeed he writes somewhat slightingly of any attempt to isolate the structural factor: "If we could eliminate the human factor, it would be easy enough to build up

---

[4] Fayol's insistence on the importance of administration should not be taken to imply any justification for the creation in any enterprise of a special administrative group or class. A situation such as that revealed by the Bridgman Report on Post Office Organization in Great Britain ([5]) where the chiefs of the technical functions occupied a secondary position, and were separated from the chiefs of the operating divisions and from the administrative chiefs by a special Secretariat or Headquarters, inevitably leads to conservatism and lack of enterprise. Decisions tend to become merely administrative. Responsible executives are insulated from the discipline and stimulation of direct contact with technical development. Cross-functionalization breaks down.

[5] C.M.D. No. 4149. Committee of Enquiry on the Post Office, 1932 Report.   [6] F. p. 83; E. p. 46.

an organization; anyone could do it if they had some idea of current practice and had the necessary capital. But we cannot build up an effective organization simply by dividing men into groups and giving them functions; we must know how to adapt the organization to the requirements of the case, and how to find the necessary men and put each one in the place where he can be of most service; we need, in fact, many substantial qualities." [7]

Just because Fayol was a practical man of long experience, this attitude was probably inevitable. The responsible administrator cannot divorce himself from the human factor. Enterprises are built up of living persons engaged in a joint undertaking and thus partake of the character of living organisms. To regard them as purely mechanistic is to open the door to every kind of error. But in so far as it is claimed that Fayol's work establishes a theory of administration — a claim which has certainly been preferred by his disciples — his concept of organization sets limits to his thought.

It is impossible for humanity to advance its knowledge of organization, unless the factor of structure is isolated from other considerations, however artificial such an isolation may appear. Existing confusion in the world's affairs makes such an advance in knowledge essential if social order is to be preserved. It is just because responsible administrators of all kinds, who inevitably carry the greatest weight with public opinion in such matters, *cannot, owing to the nature of their task, achieve such an intellectual detachment*, that our progress in the sociological sciences lags behind our growing command of physical resources.

The statesman cannot consider what is the most effective form of organization as a technical question, without at the same time taking into account the traditions of local patriotism, the activities of the press, the current emotional tendencies of the population, all the thousand and one contemporary influences which may constrict what is desirable to what is possible. The captain of industry administering a vast enterprise should never lose sight of the quality and personal idiosyncrasies of the managers at his disposal, of the temper of his workers, of the drift of public demand for his own and allied products. Because they are "practical men," because it is their duty to make the best they can of a complex human situation, they would be doing less than their duty if such considerations did not form a constant background to their thought.

Yet, it is only by achieving the isolation of one or more factors in a problem that science advances its frontiers. Medicine is concerned with the preservation of life. But it gains knowledge from anatomy. The art of administration demands knowledge of the human factor. But that does not mean that it is impossible to study the structure of enterprises anatomically, to isolate organization and treat it as a technical problem.

Fayol's analysis of organization starts with a list of the administrative duties which every organization shall be designed to accomplish. This list is shown in the first column of Table IV. It does not correspond exactly with his list of principles. But the major discrepancies, where there is no principle corresponding to an administrative duty, are covered by the fact that there is one of his aspects of administration corresponding to each such administrative duty.

---

[7] F. p. 83; E. p. 46.

Having noted these characteristics of Fayol's exposition, let us turn for a moment to two authors, who have made an attempt to analyze organization considered as structure. In 1931, Messrs. J. C. Mooney and A. P. Reiley published, under the somewhat misleading title "Onward Industry," an analysis and historical comparison of the principles of organization as manifested in governmental, religious, military and industrial institutions. Their general scheme of principles is outlined in Table II. The logical standard which they set themselves was a high one. It was founded on Louis F. Anderson's *Das Logische, seine Gesetze und Kategorien.* Felix Meiner, Leipzig, 1929. Broadly speaking, it postulates that every principle has its process and effect. But, if the principle, process and effect have been correctly identified, the process and effect

TABLE II
MOONEY AND REILEY'S ANALYSIS OF THE PRINCIPLES OF ORGANIZATION

	1. PRINCIPLE	2. PROCESS	3. EFFECT
1. The Co-ordinative Principle	Authority; or Co-ordination *per se*	Processive Co-ordination	Effective Co-ordination
2. The Scalar Process	Leadership	Delegation	Functional Definition
3. The Functional Effect	Determinative Functionalism (Legislative)	Applicative Functionalism (Executive)	Interpretative Functionalism (Judicial)

(From "Onward Industry")

will each be found to have their own principle, process and effect. Thus the whole statement correlates into a complete square of nine items.

Without going into detail, their table may be expanded as follows. The purpose of all organization is to unify effort, that is co-ordination. Co-ordination finds its principle in authority. Authority enters into process with the scalar chain, that is the hierarchy or "line," as it is sometimes called. Its effect is the assignment and integration of functions. The scalar process has its own principle in leadership. But leadership can only enter into process with delegation and its final effect is always the definition of function. Somewhere at the end of all delegation, what is delegated is responsibility for the performance of a particular task. In all forms of organization, three main functions can always be distinguished — the determinative or legislative, the applicative or executive and the interpretative or judicial. These are related as principle, process and effect.

In comparing Fayol's work with the theory of Mooney and Reiley, it occurred to the author that if the apparent empiricism in Fayol's presentation is, in fact, due to the "practical man" fallacy, to a refusal to distinguish between structure and operation, then the introduction of this distinction as a basis of classification might reveal a much greater degree of logical coherence in his principles and administrative duties and a much closer correspondence with the more formal scheme of Mooney and Reiley than appear on the surface. In short, the claim that he has laid down the outline of a theory of administration would be largely substantiated. The author believes this to be the case. Fayol's immense practical experience, while it tempted him to ignore the importance of logical analysis, secured him against dealing with inessentials. And as a consequence of the unity of principle which is fundamental in all effective administration, his statement of essentials, while unco-ordinated in form, does in fact lend itself to a completely correlated arrangement.

In the first place, his general analysis of the function of administration divides it into the five elements of *prévoyance*, organization, co-ordination, command and control. But, as has been pointed out, the term *prévoyance* really covers two separate conceptions, to foretell the future (forecasting) and to make a plan to meet it (planning). It will be noted that these six aspects of administration readily fall into three groups of two, related to each other as process and effect. Thus the process of forecasting results in a plan: organization has for its purpose and effect co-ordination: command issues in control. At this stage of his argument Fayol was not concerned with underlying principles — only with the processes of administration. If, however, it is possible to discover the underlying principles in other parts of his work, it is legitimate to apply them to complete the scheme.

The underlying principle of any form of administration which aims at scientific precision and integrity must be investigation or research yielding information. Administration must proceed on a basis of facts. While Fayol nowhere states this categorically, it is implicit in his discussion of planning. He defines the characteristics of a good plan of operations as unity, continuity, flexibility, and *precision*. Of this last quality he writes: "A plan must be as precise as is possible in view of the unknown forces which influence the results of an undertaking. As a rule, it is possible to trace the line of action for the near future with quite a considerable degree of accuracy, while just a general guide is enough for operations which are some distance ahead; before the time comes when they will have to be carried out, *more information will be available*, which will allow the line of action to be more accurately determined."

The process of forecasting is reflected in process by the establishment of an organization. And Fayol clearly indicates the principle which should underlie organization in his second administrative duty: "See that the human and material organization are suitable for the objects, resources and needs of the undertaking." This principle may be termed appropriateness. It is a fundamental consideration which must qualify the purely intellectual process of forecasting before it takes shape in human and material arrangements for action.

Similarly, a plan, however prudent, accurate and farsighted, remains a plan, a project, until staff are set to work to carry it out. That is to say, it enters into process with command. But it is possible to conceive a plan without action, just as it is possible to conceive of a great quantity of commanding without a plan. The reason for a plan, the conception which links it with command has also been stated by Fayol in his tenth Principle and fourteenth Administrative Duty — "ensure material and human order."

But if these three principles — investigation, appropriateness and order — are added to the six elements of administration, there is immediately the outline of a logical scheme for the function of administration as a whole, similar to that developed by Mooney and Reiley in relation to the principles of organization only. Thus the fundamental principle of administration, which is investigation, enters into process with forecasting which takes effect in a plan. Forecasting has its own principle,

TABLE III
HENRI FAYOL'S ELEMENTS OF THE FUNCTION OF ADMINISTRATION CORRELATED INTO A COMPLETE LOGICAL SCHEME

FORECASTING, PLANNING are the two parts of Fayol's PRÉVOYANCE.
ORGANIZATION, CO-ORDINATION, COMMAND, CONTROL, are the other four original elements.
(INVESTIGATION), (APPROPRIATENESS), (ORDER), are principles found or implicit in other parts of Fayol's exposition.

	1. PRINCIPLE	2. PROCESS	3. EFFECT
The function of 1. ADMINISTRATION must depend on the basic principle of Investigation	(INVESTIGATION) which is implicit in Fayol's discussion of Planning, and enters into process with Forecasting	FORECASTING which is part of Fayol's "Prévoyance," and results in Planning	PLANNING which is the other part of Fayol's "Prévoyance"
2. FORECASTING has its own principle in Fayol's 2nd Administrative Duty (Appropriateness)	(APPROPRIATENESS) "See that the human and material organization are suitable." It enters into process with Organization	ORGANIZATION which has the effect of securing Co-ordination	CO-ORDINATION Cf. "The internal objectives of Organization are co-ordinative always" (Mooney and Reiley)
3. PLANNING finds its principle in Fayol's 10th Principle and 14th Administrative Duty, viz.: (Order)	(ORDER) "Ensure material and human order." It enters into process with Command	COMMAND and its effect is Control	CONTROL

process and effect in appropriateness, organization and co-ordination. Planning finds its principle in order, enters into process with command and results in control. This scheme is shown in diagram in Table II.

If, however, Table III is examined closely, it will be noted that read horizontally its second and third columns correspond closely with the distinction which has been drawn between the structural and operating aspects of administration. Forecasting, organization and co-ordination are abstract processes. They consist in determining what is wanted to achieve the objective of the enterprise in the given circumstances, what groups of activities are required to provide what is wanted, and how those groups should be related. They ignore the human factor. Planning, com-

TABLE IV
FAYOL'S ADMINISTRATIVE DUTIES AND PRINCIPLES COMPARED

ADMINISTRATIVE DUTIES (F. p. 78; E. p. 42)[x]	PRINCIPLES (F. p. 28; E. p. 19)[x]
1. See that the plan of operations is carefully prepared and strictly carried out	Nil. (Fayol's "Prévoyance")
2. See that the human and material organization are suitable for the objects, resources and needs of the undertaking	Nil. (Fayol's "to organize")
3. Establish a management which is competent and has singleness of purpose	Nil. (Fayol's "to command")
4. Co-ordinate operations and efforts	5. Unity of management (Fayol's "to co-ordinate")
5. Make decisions which are clear, distinct and precise	Nil.
6. Make careful selection of staff — each department has a competent and energetic head: each employee where he can be of most service	Nil.
7. Define duties clearly	Nil.
8. Encourage the desire for initiative and responsibility	13. Initiative
9. Reward men fairly and judiciously for their services	7. Remuneration
10. Impose penalties for mistakes and blunders	2. Authority
11. See that discipline is maintained	3. Discipline
12. See that individual interests do not interfere with the general interest	6. Subordination of individual interests to the common good
13. Pay special attention to unity of command	4. Unity of command
14. Ensure material and human order	10. Order
15. Subject everything to control	8. Centralization
	9. The hierarchy (Fayol's "to control")
16. Avoid red tape	14. Esprit de Corps
[x]References to Fayol's "Administration Industrielle et Générale": French edition shown' 'F"; English edition shown "E"	Principles listed by Fayol for which he does not show equivalent administrative duties: 1. Division of labor 11. Equity 12. Stability of staff

mand and control, on the other hand, are concrete. They are processes of realization or operation. They are intimately concerned with obtaining the best results from the human factor.

If this point is conceded, three consequences follow:

(A) A complete statement of the principles of administration calls for the addition to the table of two subsidiary logical schemes, the one giving the principles of organization and co-ordination and concerned with structure, and the other the principles of command and control and concerned with the human factor.

(B) If Fayol's empirical lists of principles and administrative duties are really logical and complete, it will be found that one of his statements corresponds to each principle, process and effect in these subsidiary schemes and no more. There will be no principles or administrative duties superfluous and every aspect of both schemes will be provided for.

(C) If Fayol's thought is consistent with the principles of Mooney and Reiley it will be sufficient to adopt their scheme to cover the structural aspect of administration and to show where Fayol has corresponding principles or administrative duties.

This correlation has been attempted in Table VI which is an expansion of Table III to include the two subsidiary systems of principles. I may mention that there is no Table V.

Following Mooney and Reiley, organization and co-ordination are treated as the processive and effective aspects of the same structural activity. Command and control are similarly treated as the processive and effective aspects of the same operating activity. In the first case Mooney and Reiley's scheme of principles has merely been inserted, and the appropriate statement from Fayol's lists placed under each heading. In the second case a fresh scheme of principles based on those of Fayol's principles or administrative duties which bear upon the human factor has been constructed. In addition, where any of Fayol's principles or administrative duties were merely restatements of his original six elements they have been put in the appropriate place in the main scheme.

The principles of command and control are those which bear upon the human factor. The underlying purpose of command and control is to secure that all activities subserve the common interest. The principle expressing this purpose is centralization. It enters into process with appropriate staffing and its effect is *esprit de corps*. Appropriate staffing depends on the principle of selection and placement. It enters into process with the stimulation of the individuals selected by rewards and sanctions. Its effect is to release each individual's initiative in the interests of the undertaking. *Esprit de corps* depends primarily on equity. It enters into process with the enforcement of discipline. Its effect is stability of staff.

On the whole the table substantiates the view of Fayol's Principles and Administrative Duties suggested above. The scheme as a whole is logical and self-consistent. *All* Fayol's statements are included. There are no gaps and only one Administrative Duty (No. 10) is used twice. Administrative Duties 1 and 8 are each divided into their structural and operating aspects. There are no superfluous statements. The subsidiary schemes correlate with the general scheme, and, with one exception, with each other.

The exception is interpretative functionalism. The fact that it is omitted, that Fayol has no operative principle or administrative duty corresponding to the judicial function in government, strengthens the argument as to the "practical man" fallacy. It is exactly the discrepancy one would expect. As Mooney and Reiley have pointed out, there is a general failure to identify and isolate the judicial or interpretative function in business organization. Even today the business executive, like the primi-

TABLE VI

RECONCILIATION OF FAYOL'S ANALYSIS OF THE FUNCTION OF ADMINISTRATION AND HIS PRINCIPLES AND ADMINISTRATIVE DUTIES WITH THE LOGICAL ARRANGEMENT OF THE PRINCIPLES OF ORGANIZATION SUGGESTED BY MOONEY & REILEY

BLOCK CAPITALS - Fayol's Analysis of Administration   (BLOCK CAPITALS) in brackets - Headings implicit in or introduced to complete Fayol's Analysis

Cursive Type(Underlined)- Mooney & Reiley's Principles—*Cursive Type* - Titles of Principles of Operation introduced by the Author

Small Type within inverted commas - Actual quotation of Fayol's Principles & Administrative Duties,the actual number quoted shown in brackets preceded by P or AD

	1. PRINCIPLE	2. PROCESS	3. EFFECT
THE ADMINISTRATIVE FUNCTION — Administration is not government.To govern is to coord-inate the six essential functions of which Administrat-ion is one.To govern an undertaking is to conduct it towards its objective & the outline of its objective and policy are therefore "given" before Administration starts	(INVESTIGATION) The basis of any scient-ific Procedure must be facts.Investigation is therefore the first prin-ciple of Administration	FORECASTING(PRÉVOYANCE) Investigation enters into process with a forecast of the future	PLANNING(PRÉVOYANCE) And takes effect in a plan of action
2.FORECASTING must be in terms of the objective and policy of the undertaking "See that the plan of operations is carefully prepared"(AD1)	(APPROPRIATENESS) "See that the human & mat-erial organization are suitable for the objects, resources & needs of the undertaking"(AD2)	ORGANIZATION It enters into process by the Provision of a suitable Organization	COORDINATION and achieves its effect in Coordination
It therefore finds its underlying principle in appropriateness			
THE PRINCIPLES OF ORGANIZATION & COORDINATION - THE STRUCTURAL ASPECTS OF ADMINISTRATION			
As shown by Mooney Reiley Organization & Coordination have their own system of principles	*The Coordinative Principle* "Coordinate operations & efforts"(AD4)	*Authority or Coordination per se* "Unity of Command" (AD15:P4)	*Processive Coordination*
			Effective Coordination
	The Scalar Process "The Hierarchy"(P9)	*Leadership* "Unity of Management"(P5)	*Delegation* "Encourage the desire for responsibility"(AD8)
			Functional Definition "Define duties clearly" (AD7)
	The Functional Effect "Division of Labour"(P1)	*Determinative Functionalism* "Make decisions which are clear,distinct & precise"(AD5)	*Applicative Functionalism* "See that the plan of operations is strictly carried out"(AD1)
			Interpretative Functionalism "Impose penalties for mis-takes & blunders"(AD10:P2)
It therefore finds its underlying principle in order	ORDER "Ensure material,and human order"(AD14:P10)		
3.PLANNING The purpose of Planning is to secure systematic action "See that the plan of operations is strictly carried out"(AD1)		COMMAND operates through command "Establish a management which is competent and has unity of purpose"(AD3)	CONTROL & results in control "Subject everything to control"(AD15)
THE PRINCIPLES OF COMMAND & CONTROL - THE HUMAN ASPECTS OF ADMINISTRATION			
Command & Control have also their own system of principles	*The General Interest* "See that individual int-erests do not interfere with the general interest"(AD12:P6)	*Centralization* Command is Protection of the general interest.Its main principle is there-fore Centralization "Centralization"(P8)	*Processive Centralization* Centralization operates through appropriate staffing
			Effective Centralization And results in Esprit de Corps
	Appropriate Staffing "Each department has a competent & energetic head"(AD6) depends on selection & placement	*Selection & Placement* "Make careful selection of staff - each employee where he can be of most service"(AD6) & enters into process through	*Rewards & Sanctions* "Reward men fairly & jud-iciously for their serv-ices"(AD9:P7)"Impose pen-alties for mistakes"(AD10)
			Initiative resulting in initiative - "Encourage the desire for initiative"(AD8:P13)
	Esprit de Corps "Esprit de Corps"(P14) depends primarily on	*Equity* "Equity"(P11)	*Discipline* operates through"Discip-line"(AD11:P3)&"avoid-ance of red tape"(AD16)
			Stability and results in "stability of staff"(P12)

tive king, is law-maker, administrator, police, judge and jury all rolled into one. The extended use of industrial courts is a sign of reaction against this position. It is also interesting to note that in one factory where a joint appeal committee was established to deal with disciplinary cases, the members chose as their neutral chairman, the company solicitor. A number of dismissals were quashed by the committee on the ground that the evidence that the defendant had in fact committed the misdemeanor alleged by his manager was insufficient to satisfy a court of law.

Because Fayol was relying on his "practical experience" as an industrialist, it did not occur to him to question this absence of any separate judicial function. It was universal in industrial practice and only becomes anomalous and manifest when industrial organization is compared with military or governmental examples. In this connection, however, it may also be noted that equity is given as the basic principle of *esprit de corps*. In so far as the workers feel that this identity of executive and judicial functions in one person is inequitable, to that extent will business administration fail to achieve complete *esprit de corps* because in this respect it will appear tyrannical.

With this exception, the degree of correspondence is remarkable. Despite his own admission of empiricism in stating his principles, Fayol's thought is susceptible to schematic presentation. All the aspects of his theory of administration can be shown to correlate with each other, and to have their exact counterparts in Mooney and Reiley's scheme of the principles of organization. These facts are a testimony to the great weight of Fayol's authority in this field and further evidence of the essential unity and logic which underlie successful organization in practice. They constitute the strongest possible argument for intensifying the attempt to build up a recognized technique of organization and to secure that all who are likely to be responsible for administration are trained systematically in this technique.

Indeed the unique character of Fayol's work cannot be overemphasized. For the first time a successful business leader of long experience submitted, not the work of others, but his own duties and responsibilities to close scientific analysis. He viewed what he had to do as an administrator with a detachment as rare as it is valuable. In the first quarter century of the scientific study of business management, his is the only European figure worthy a place beside that of F. W. Taylor. To Taylor belongs the glory of the pioneer. He it was who initiated the idea that management and administration might be studied scientifically. But Fayol showed beyond question, what Taylor himself appreciated, but what many of his imitators have failed to emphasize, that better management is not merely a question of improving the output of labor and the planning of subordinate units of organization, it is above all a matter of closer study and more administrative training for the men at the top. Seldom in history can two men working in an identical field have differed so sharply in methods and in the details of their careers and yet have produced work which was so essentially complementary.

As was suggested in opening the lecture, the evolution of a science of administration has a wider significance than the facilitation of business operations. It must have its repercussions in politics, in government, in every aspect of social life. It will change many things. But it is the author's conviction that only by developing such a science can we hope to arrive at any solution of the problems presented to us by the immensely rapid advance in and application of the sciences bearing on material things which have occurred during the last century. We must know more of social organization or a mechanized economy will run amuck with civilization. That is his excuse, if excuse is needed, for troubling you with a somewhat complicated piece of analysis.

VI

THE NEED FOR THE DEVELOPMENT OF POLITICAL SCIENCE ENGINEERING

By

HENRY S. DENNISON

Dennison Manufacturing Company, Framingham, Mass.

REPRINTED FROM THE AMERICAN POLITICAL SCIENCE REVIEW,
VOL. 26, APRIL, 1932

THE NEED FOR THE DEVELOPMENT OF POLITICAL SCIENCE ENGINEERING

In the early days of factory management, when the problems and conditions were relatively simple, it fell to the lot of all sorts of human folk to manage the various jobs involved. Each used his own peculiar method and, naturally enough, it came into general belief that ability in management was an instinctive knack, that managers were born, not made, that few if any rules could be laid down, and that little could be learned by one from another. Even in the earliest days, a small handful of men called attention to the fact that management measures and forms of organization could be better or worse adapted to their uses; but for generations the suggestion passed unheeded.

As the problems and conditions of factory management grew more complex and exacting, more men came to believe that the art of management was something more than an intuitive and highly personal knack. Before the Great War, a fair nucleus was beginning to study the art from the point of view of the forces involved, and with an eye to causes and effects. And the war experience of manufacturing strange materials, shifting conditions upside down, built up this nucleus into a very fair working minority.

The first studies of management were largely descriptive. Forms of organization and management methods were described in detail, often with the result that those who read would try to take over the plans and the forms and the measures just as they were and apply them to their own tasks. This was the hey-day of the organization chart, when the anatomical structure of the organization for factory government was worshipped almost as if it were an end in itself. The troubles that arose when one tried to take over bodily the structure of one corporation or its card systems into a different problem at first set back the whole movement, and then forced studies which were more than merely descriptive. At the present time, we are beginning to accumulate fundamental material to form the basis of an art of management, which will be the application of the pertinent social and psychological sciences.

I

Now a factory or business organization is, after all, one sort of social group — a group of human beings, each with his individual nature, attempting to work together for some more or less definite end. A nation or a state is another sort of social group, living together and in no remote sense working together for common ends, whose management is the art we call governing. For the study of this art of governing I am proposing a shift of emphasis comparable to that which has taken place in studying the art of factory management, that is, a shift from the descriptive to the analytical; and from the analytical immediately to the engineering point of view, which focuses upon the natural material and psychological forces found in a given social group and the measures and structures of organization which can be applied to them in order to work toward its fundamental purposes. It is the approach, not of the historian or of the moralist, but of the student of applied science, the engineer.

It will be granted at once that the problem is immensely more difficult than the problems which the nascent art of industrial management has to face; that in fact it is probably the most difficult of all human problems. It will be granted, also, that the sciences which this art of governing must learn to apply are themselves in a germinal, or at best embryonic, state. But two practical considerations outweigh any objections that can be raised.

In the first place, few of the physical sciences advanced much beyond their embryonic stages until applications began to be attempted. Engineers fooled with the laws of physics and chemistry, and tried to make them work somehow, long before those laws were in any solid sense established; and these very attempts to make them work keyed up and directed the pure scientist in his further researches, so that he could elaborate or strengthen or amend these very laws. There is much in the history of the physical sciences to warrant the belief that they never could have grown to their present state unless the engineer had made successful and unsuccessful attempts at application, and had brought back the results of these attempts into the laboratory with a demand for further research. It can, therefore, be properly inferred that progress in the social sciences will likewise depend upon earnest, even if sometimes unsuccessful, attempts at the application of what is so far known.

Secondly, there stands the pressing need for progress in the art of governing, and especially in the art of self-governing. No human need today is greater. The very progress itself of the physical sciences and their application has plunged us into a world in which, if we cannot manage ourselves, we may flounder to our destruction. A benevolent and far-seeing czar of all the world might in fact wisely command progress in the physical sciences and their application to stand still until progress in the social sciences and their application should catch up. There being no such czar, progress in physical engineering will continue and so make necessary a still more rapid progress in social engineering.

Four factors have in these modern days combined to bring this need for the study of government from an engineering point of view to the place which justifies the use of the word "overwhelming." First, the development of industrial and commercial processes, intensive and extensive, and the new complications and interrelations of all social and individual life which this development has brought about. Second, the steady reduction, since the great ages of discovery, in the proportion of new lands practicable for settlement — a reduction to a point today at which it is no longer a considerable factor in economic and social life. Third, the growth, intensive and extensive, of the deeply grounded social idea that the final purpose of all government must somehow include the satisfactions of all the people rather than the satisfactions of a god, a dynasty, or a small ruling group. And, fourth (and likely enough derived from the other three), the growth of an underlying demand for more general security, even at the cost of some reduction in the rate of progress in material well-being.

These four factors are enough to warrant the belief that the greatest need of today, and of the next fifty years, is progress in the art of government. The present slogans of the business world which protest against any participation of government in economic affairs have many followers; but it is distinctly possible that the complexities and the pervasiveness of economics will force every sovereign government into economic participation, economic influence, even sometimes into economic control. As a matter of fact, ever since the high tide of geographic pioneering, which turned somewhat before the end of the last century, the governments of the world have exerted more and more influence upon economic life; and this largely at the natural demand of first one and then another group of business men themselves. Taking into account this clear trend of the past, and the lessons, both positive and negative, of the great Russian and Italian experiments in the future, it is on the whole a safer guess that we will see from year to year more government in business, rather than less.

But if a governing machine, built to fit the needs of a relatively simple agricultural and trading community, is loaded with the task of participation in an infinitely complex industrial structure, it is as certain that there will be a serious breakdown as that two and two make four. If the structure of the governing organization is to be regarded as sacrosanct and cannot be altered to meet the rapidly changing needs of the modern community, it is true enough that we ought to have less government in business rather than more. But if the trends of the past are any guides to the future, we then find ourselves lost in a dilemma: Government both must and must not increase its participation in the economic life of this nation.

The business answer to this dilemma has in recent years been that business must govern itself; that is to say, when put frankly, that the business world itself must build up a governing structure — a government. But when such propositions are examined in detail in any realistic fashion, problems of enforcement and of relative sovereignty arise which are insoluble. The political community and the economic community interweave and overlap to such an extent that they are indistinguishable. The government of one is in fact the government of the other, and any attempt to bring down to cases a discussion of business self-government forces into clear view the fundamentally anomalous situation in which we find ourselves today.

For it can be said in a very valid sense that the whole of society in the civilized world lives today as one society under two social systems — the economic system and the political system — between which there is practically no effective correlation; two systems which many times become mutually incompatible. If, therefore, it should turn out that the business world can build for itself a government, it will be a wholly justifiable prediction that this business government will be more powerful than, and finally rise over, the political government; in which case we shall finally have a government which not only participates in, but which is, the government of the business and economic world.

But if the probability of this participation of political government in the economic world is discounted to the minimum, there still remains the job of the political world itself to cope with the complexities of modern society. In any case, the crucial need is for a study of the *art* of government, which regards the word "art" as a careful application of scientific knowledge and principles to the realistically analyzed forces of a given social situation.

II

If political science is to furnish the basis for this engineering approach to the problems of government, it must view any community it is studying as a field of forces — psychological, biological, and physical. In view of what it can discover about these forces, it must determine the measures and structure of government which can be expected to use these forces and to relate them so as to bring about development in the direction of the fundamental purpose adopted by and appropriate to a particular social group.

At the very beginning, this fundamental purpose will need clarification, for the purposes of government have been in the past and are today various; and they are not, and have not very often been, clearly known or stated. There have been communities whose deepest purpose was the service of a god or gods, and others whose purpose was the satisfaction, wealth, power, or glory of a monarch. Some have aimed chiefly at the preservation of the status quo; others at defense against aggressive neighbors; some at the preservation or advance in wealth of an hereditary aristocracy or of the owners of property; and others, again, rather vaguely at the spiritual, mental, or material progress of the largest number of its people. Whatever the purpose may be, it is important to realize that its nature is from the point of view of an engineer one of the primary determinants of the measures of governing and of the forms of organization which are to be adopted.

Of most concern in the modern world is the vague and ill-defined purpose included in what is often called the democratic ideal. When it is worked out in any definite way, it seems to be a reaching for progress toward the fullest use and growth of each man's powers in the service of his fellows, and the enjoyment of such pleasures as contribute to the refreshment or enhancement of such powers. But it is still so vague as to serve much more often as camouflage for the narrow aims of a small group than as a determinant of government policies.

It is with the true democratic ideal before him that a student of political science writes:

> "It seems to me decidedly true that the time has come for a study of government from the following three angles: (1) government as the resultant of certain forces in the community, which forces dictate (a) the direction and objectives of the activity of government, (b) the nature of its structure and its organization; (2) government as an organization for the attainment of certain objectives which are in part devised by government itself and are in part dictated to it from the outside; and (3) government as an agency having power to influence very strongly, and in some instances actually to create, the forces which in turn (a) influence the structure of government, (b) influence the objectives of government, (c) facilitate or impede the ability of government to attain its objectives." [1]

This way of specifying the needed study brings out at once the peculiar difficulties of the task due to the continuous interaction which takes place among the factors involved — the fact that causes do not stay causes, but are themselves altered and affected by their own effects — the principle which in the biological and social sciences has been called the principle of "circular response." These difficulties must be faced from the beginning, and will discourage all but the strong heart. They mean, certainly, that while specialization in so complex a subject is essential, yet integration of the specialized studies must take place, as it were, simultaneously. The engineer in political science will find, as physicians have found, that the specialist is essential to progress but cannot be left to run the show alone.

---

[1] A letter from Professor John Dickinson.

III

With some reasonably adequate idea of general objectives, the political science engineer must make progress in his understanding of the forces which must be dealt with; and here, particularly, is a realistic study necessary, for in the first place it is the forces in a given community, not abstract mankind-at-large forces, which are to be known. The stage of education and of culture, the peculiar conditions inculcated by "social inheritance," the special habits of mind and of vocation, make literally all the difference in the world. There are, of course, no two communities, no two nations, and no two states, principalities, or cities within any nation, in which the complex of forces is the same in their aggregate composition — just as there are no two business concerns in which the composition of forces is exactly the same, nor in any single community will they stay always the same, but will change with time and under the influence of such governing measures as are applied to them. The problem is in dynamics, not statics.

The engineer will realize that the powers upon which the government of any community can draw are just those forces which actually exist among its membership. While these original forces may be enhanced, weakened, or redirected as time goes on, none can be counted upon at any given moment which is not then to be found there.

A government must, therefore, find active among its members sufficient energy arising from biological, or from economic, political, or other social pressures, to serve its main purpose. This necessary energy may be very little, as in an isolated tribe located in a rich country, or very much, as in a nation with an itch for conquest; it may be sufficiently aroused by the pressures of physiological nature or of social tradition, with little interference of a political sort, or it may demand incessant and varied political activity. Whether simple or immeasurably difficult, the problem lies on the front doorstep of any government that, by whatever pressures may yield the most satisfactory net results, the energies sufficient to its main purpose be aroused among its members.

But whether physiological, social, or political, these pressures are upon human beings, and upon just those human beings of whom the community is made up; and hence must be so adapted to the natures of just these men and women that there is a net yield of the required results. The practical problem of a government is to know as much as it can about the nature of its peoples and the influences actually at work among them, to judge when, where, how, and how much to interfere with the influences of physiological nature or social custom then acting upon its members, and to decide to what extent to alter, lessen, or add to the pressures it is already exerting.

The principal channels through which a government can bring its measures to bear upon a man are his desires to preserve his life, to avoid pain and discomfort, to mate, to preserve his family, to increase their standard of living, to enjoy companionship and social approval, to satisfy his curiosity and his moral or aesthetic demands. These desires and others which move men will practically never be free to find their satisfactions as they wish. They will be limited by each other, by physical nature, by the struggles of other men to fulfill their own desires, by traditions or unwritten laws, and by government. Just how much or how little any given government should spur, limit, or steer any of these desires is a practical question to be settled with reference to the government's accomplishment of its fundamental purpose. In one case, this purpose may best be accomplished by leaving the control of men's activities to tradition or to their mutual interferences, with little affirmative governmental action; in another case, a different purpose — or even a similar purpose but in a different environment — may be served best by very broad and active government controls. No general principle can be laid down that for all governments and all peoples, under all circumstances, government control is *per se* good, bad, or indifferent.

The measures which a government may use to spur, direct, or limit the attempts of its members to satisfy their desires will include propaganda or propagandist education, tariffs, subsidies, taxes and tax exemptions; it may make regulations as to mating and family life, working conditions, and the rights and duties pertaining to property.

Many of the measures of a government must, of necessity, be negations and prohibitions. Naturally, where large numbers of corporations, institutions, or individuals are to be dealt with, the chief means of guidance must be negative, since it is more often possible to define the line of undesirable behavior than to select from among a large and rapidly developing variety of possible desirable behaviors the ones best for any individual case. In simple communities, it might be possible to prescribe a goodly bit of a man's life; in complex societies, it is more likely that the definitely undesirable areas will be proscribed, leaving open to individual choice a wide range of neutral or desirable action.

But no regulation expressed in language can be clear in its application to all cases, even in a relatively simple and stable society; a series of interpretations of its application to a variety of cases may after a time give it practical clarification unless changes in conditions take place. In a changing community, judicial interpretations may be almost continuously necessary, leading, perhaps, to periodic alterations in the regulatory measures, each of which in its turn will need its own series of interpretations.

The limits of its appropriate activities are determined by the circumstances in which a government finds itself, and by its purposes. They may extend to the most intimate actions and thoughts of its members in a theocracy whose purpose is the service of a god or gods through obedience to a minute code; they may go almost as far under such a dictatorship as in Russia or Italy today; and so in close gradations the limits may narrow down nearly to zero, as in a moving frontier belt where each man's will and his power to exert it as against any other are the only limitations upon his acts. A people who have come by their early training to desire above all things peace and quiet and security will accept, and in fact demand, a close direction and regulation which would bring a restless folk to revolution.

A government may be doing its best to ensure stability or to cultivate material progress; in most modern communities, it will be doing something toward both of these ends. As a result, unless there is a strong central planning and balancing power, a government will find some of its departments in fundamental conflict, as where the agricultural department urges restriction in planting while another department opens up new lands for cultivation. In this case, as in hundreds of others, some central clearing house with a persistent view to the fundamental purpose must have the facilities for balancing and integrating any differing or conflicting measures. In the simpler static communities, such integration is easy and rarely needed, but as communities grow in complexity, and especially where some sort of progress is part of their purpose, the need grows rapidly.

For protection and stability, a government uses its police and courts, fire departments, insurance, charities, an army of defense, and the like. For material progress, it may build roads, cultivate health, encourage invention, the expansion of business and industry, practical education and research. For spiritual progress, it may encourage schools, the church, and the protection of what it considers moral, and help in the discouragement of what it considers non-moral attitudes and acts. In modern communities, non-governmental agencies and associations will be doing much of this work — for good or ill; any government must take such organizations or efforts into account and decide to encourage, suppress, or let them run; it has responsibility commensurate with its actual power, whether it acts or fails to act.

The total of education — by homes, schools, churches, papers and periodicals, unions, clubs, lecture halls, and political meetings — through personal contacts, radio, and movies, results in what is called a public opinion, which may be vague or concrete, mixed or simple, fixed or changeable, as the circumstances determine. As one of the forces to be taken into account by government, public opinion may be almost negligible, as in an illiterate and phlegmatic society governed by a powerful autocrat, or virtually self-determining, as among a group of energetic pioneer settlers. In either case, it can best be studied as a resultant of the influences which created it rather than as a thing in itself.

The very foundation upon which public opinion at any moment builds itself is the body of beliefs, theories, prejudices, or superstitions with which a people have become indoctrinated early in life, and which have, therefore, gained the strength of habit. Those which result primarily in mental or emotional attitudes we may call its traditions; and those which are reinforced by physical activity, its customs. They are not unalterable any more than are other kinds of habits, but they can be changed only when conditions or influences conforming to the laws of habit-change are brought about or bring themselves about.

The abstract validity of theories of government or of human rights — whether they be called moral, legal, or natural — is from a strictly engineering point of view wholly impossible to determine. For the government engineer, the only question of fact is what appeal the various theories make in any given social group — what force they exert or may exert, and, hence, what reactions follow them or may be expected to result from them. For him, the classic question of the violability of contract by a sovereign is the question of the results to be expected in the group in question, if this or that sort of contract is violated. For him, the problems of the rights to liberty, property, or happiness, or the demands of loyal service, are to be subjected to a realistic analysis into the strength of their roots and the probable influence they will exert toward or away from the fundamental purposes of the government. If he is also a student of ethics, he will analyze them with the technique of ethics as well; but as government engineer he must focus upon them as sources of influence among the whole field of forces he has to survey. He will recognize that going theories, like the men who hold them, are the joint product of heredity and environment; immediate changes, therefore, are to be expected only through changes of circumstance or educational influence. And customs, because in them mental habit is reinforced by physiological habit, he will recognize as even more powerful and difficult to change.

V

It is with a view to the attainment of its fundamental purpose, and with an understanding of the physical and psychological forces which it can call forth from the people, that the problems of governmental structures are to be approached. It is as true in government engineering as in any other branch of organization engineering that structure is most wisely to be considered as a means, not an end. But since its structure affects both the members of an organization and the effectiveness of its operating measures, it must, therefore, be determined and judged by its effectiveness, through its influences upon men and measures, in accomplishing the purposes the community holds.

Not infrequently, an intense enthusiasm for a given structural form will fuse or confuse it with purpose; it is vital to government engineering that the two, if actually different, should be kept clearly separate, or if one and the same, should be so understood. For it is as easy for men whose real purpose may be the goal of the utilitarians, and who have seen a democratic form work their way in one case, to make democratic forms their goal in all cases, as it is for aristocrats whose real purpose is to preserve aristocracy as a form to convince themselves that they are doing it for the "greatest good of the greatest number." Democracy, if thought of as a form of governmental structure, must submit to a practical inquiry as to whether it is the form for any given group through which the accomplishment of its purpose may be made most likely or least difficult. Democracy, however, is sometimes implicitly regarded, not so much as a form, but rather as the determination, for better or for worse as may happen, by the whole of a group of people of their own behavior. When this idea is made explicit and there is actually no other fundamental purpose but self-determination intended, then structure and purpose are more nearly one, and the main problems are as to what details of structure help most in the determination by a people of their own course of life.

In any government there will be a number of different activities through which the main purpose is to be striven for; in a complex society, these will be many and varied. In any group, therefore, larger than a patriarchal household, more than one man will be needed, and work and responsibilities must be apportioned — the structure of government must be departmentalized. To decide how this can best be done involves a listing of the tasks and analysis of the physical means and the human abilities demanded by each of them. But only in the simplest and most stable societies can these separate tasks, once provided for, be left without constant re-direction and coordination with each other. This demands their grouping into sub-sub-departments, and these into sub-departments and again into departments, which themselves must be related together in some one or another effective way. Moreover, as structure increases in complexity there is need of many cross relationships among many of its primary and secondary groupings which fall under different departments.

Departmentalizing is so fundamentally necessary as to be practically universal in any governing task which is beyond the powers of one man. The main principles which direct its best use have, therefore, been worked out through wide experience; although in changing communities, with their changing and enlarging tasks and the growing differences in their inter-relationships, the reorganizations needed to make application of these principles take place very slowly. Much less thoroughly worked out are the methods and principles by which co-ordination among departments and sub-departments can be attained. This becomes especially necessary and especially difficult as a society comes to rely less and less upon physical compulsion and threats of compulsion, and as its governmental undertakings become more varied. In modern communities where economic projects, and where the facilities of communication, cross and recross those state lines and national lines which set bounds to the limits of government authorities, the needs for co-ordination have far outrun the development of its technique.

Since any government structure is made up of men, men must somehow be selected for its tasks. The selection may be by birth — an eldest son, a youngest son, or a daughter — by tests of strength, of fighting power, by appointment, by examination casual or elaborate, by lot, or by joint action of some designated people, that is, by election. The choice of method is a practical problem involving consideration of the nature of the place to be filled, the nature of the folk in the community, the existing government structure and the purpose it serves.

But, to be adequate, any method of selection must include a sufficient knowledge of the qualities and abilities the task calls for and the individual characteristics of the men from among whom selection is to be made. Some tasks, especially in modern communities, will need for their fulfillment a considerable degree of public support, and will require of the men who undertake them qualities which can call forth public acceptance; these will, therefore, be filled often by some more or less general election. The principles of government organization will demand, however, that such places be not complicated by adding to them tasks for which special technical abilities are needed. The guiding principles, indeed, of all departmentalizing, or specific task-setting, require that each job be determined upon, so far as is possible, in such a way that it will be reasonably likely that men able to do it can be drawn from the available material. For most of the separate tasks necessary to be performed in the management of a modern state, this is not difficult; the main trouble has been how to define the requirements of the job and analyze the characteristics of the possible candidates so that an adequate selection machinery might be set up.

For the efficient performance of a task, as well as for the proper selection of its performer, a clear definition of it is essential; and not merely of the task conceived of separately, but of its relationships to other tasks as well. It is often easy to forget that an essential part of each separate task is to maintain all proper co-ordinate relations with other tasks. Any type of analysis or cutting up into parts seems to exert a fascination which specializes and particularizes the mind, and so delays and interferes with the companion process of synthesis.

Finally, if the structure of a government is to be fitted to its people and its purpose, it must take into account the probabilities of changes that may occur. In settled and relatively isolated societies, change may be very slow. But in newer communities and those where considerable changes in educational technique, in population, in economic environment, or inter-community relationship, take place, provision for appropriate steps in structural reorganization are essential. It is very rare that a governmental structure suited to one set of circumstances is well suited to any other. As early as 1901, Lord Bryce said: "Nobody now discusses the old problem of the Best Form of Government, because everybody now admits that the chief merit of any form is to be found in its suitability to the conditions and ideas of those among whom it prevails." [2] The penalty of undue stability must, therefore, be confusion, revolution, rebellion, or conquest.

It is perfectly obvious that much fuller stores of knowledge than we now hold must be at our command before any application of political science fit to be called engineering can be made. Yet all the applied sciences have grown from inadequate beginnings by instant progressive attempts to make useful application of whatever is known. It is these attempts and their inadequacies and partial failures which have given impulse and direction to the search for the needed facts and to the experiments in method. It seems impossible to develop an engineering art otherwise. It is none too early, then, for the beginnings to be made in the application of scientific knowledge and method to the art of governing — in the development of an objective and realistic Political Science Engineering.

---

[2] "Studies in History and Jurisprudence," Oxford Press, 1901.

VII

THE EFFECTS OF SOCIAL ENVIRONMENT

By

L. J. HENDERSON, T. N. WHITEHEAD AND ELTON MAYO

From the Graduate School of Business Administration, Harvard University, Boston, Mass.

THIS STUDY IS TAKEN FROM A PAPER READ BY T. N. WHITEHEAD BEFORE THE BRITISH ASSOCIATION FOR THE ADVANCEMENT OF SCIENCE AND PUBLISHED IN "THE HUMAN FACTOR" (LONDON) 9, 381, 1935, UNDER THE TITLE OF "SOCIAL RELATIONSHIPS IN THE FACTORY"; IT IS REPRINTED BY KIND PERMISSION OF THE EDITOR, DR. C. S. MYERS. IT IS ALSO A PAPER READ BY DR. L. J. HENDERSON BEFORE THE HARVARD UNIVERSITY TER-CENTENARY CELEBRATION, HARVARD SCHOOL OF PUBLIC HEALTH, BOSTON, AUGUST 24, 1936, AND PUBLISHED IN THE JOURNAL OF INDUSTRIAL HYGIENE & TOXICOLOGY, VOL. XVIII, NO. 7, SEPTEMBER, 1936.

THE EFFECTS OF SOCIAL ENVIRONMENT

The human aspect of modern industrial organization attracted no great attention from industrialists until the advent of the European War of 1914; after the outbreak of hostilities the need to accelerate and to maintain production of various necessities quickly provoked a formulation of the problem. Apparently no one had ever sufficiently considered the enormous demand upon industry that would be made by a war-machine organized upon so heroic a scale, for armies counted in millions were a gigantic innovation. Nor had anyone considered the effect of the strenuous and sustained exertion imposed upon those who worked to provide supplies. The authorities in England speedily became aware of a "national lack of knowledge of the primary laws governing human efficiency." In particular, there was "need for scientific study of the hours of work and other conditions of labor likely to produce the maximum output at which the effort of the whole people was aimed." The actual conditions of work set in the munition factories were, in the early days of the struggle, admitted to be progressively detrimental to the worker and consequently unfavorable to that maintenance of output for long periods upon which success in large part depended. Inquiries undertaken by Dr. H. M. Vernon and others appointed by the *British Health of Munition Workers Committee* were effective; the introduction of shorter hours of work, of rest pauses and of other humane innovations resulted in the restoration of morale and the maintenance of production.

The stimulus to inquiry provided by this situation has continued to operate in the years that have elapsed since 1918, and much has been learned of the human factors that are involved in industrial organization for work. Another paper given at this symposium, by Dr. D. B. Dill, will present some of the most recent and interesting findings by physiology in the problem of fatigue. In addition to physiology, psychology has been summoned by industry to aid its determination of appropriate working conditions for the human being in action. In many of these inquiries, and rightly, the worker is considered and studied as an individual. Up to the present there have been few attempts to study the social conditions of work — that is to say, the effect upon morale and production of the situation created by the interrelation of several human beings in an industrial department. This paper is designed to give a brief account of two experiments at the Hawthorne Plant of the Western Electric Company which in a sense stumbled upon this problem as an exceedingly important aspect of industrial administration.

Officers of the Western Electric Company were probably moved to begin the researches of 1927 at Hawthorne by two chief influences. The one may be described as a general interest in the problems of the incidence of "fatigue" and "monotony" in factory work. This took its rise, remotely, in the publication by the English Industrial Health Board of its studies of the conditions of work in munitions factories and other industrial plants during and after the War. The other influence may be attributed to the fact that, as good engineers, these same officers were aware that Company policies with respect to human beings were not so securely based as policies with respect to materials and machines. Mechanical processes, the type and quality of materials used, were based upon carefully contrived experiment and knowledge; the human policies of the Company, upon executive conceptions and traditional practices. In determining the human policies, the Company had no satisfactory criterion of the actual value of its methods of dealing with people. A mechanical process as studied in a modern factory will in some way reveal an inefficiency; a traditional method of handling human situations will rarely reveal that it is rooted in mere use and custom rather than knowledge. The hope that an experimental method of assessing the human effect of different working conditions might be discovered must be regarded as counting for something in the development of the experiment. The object was not to increase production but to discover facts. Where production could be accurately observed, records were kept; but this was arranged merely as an essential part of the experimental procedure.

The original "test room" was installed in April, 1927, and continued to operate until 1932, when, for reasons not connected with the experiment, it was abandoned. The principal results here presented have been described by T. N. Whitehead. The operation selected for study was that of the assembly of telephone relays. Five girl workers were transferred from their usual work surroundings into an experimental room, within which their work was supervised by specially appointed observers. Arrangements were made for the continuous and accurate record of individual output and for other observations that were considered appropriate. It will suffice for our present purpose if we say that the output of the test room workers continued to rise slowly for a period of years. In its upward passage this major gain ignored almost completely experimental changes arbitrarily introduced from time to time by the officers in charge of the experiment, including modification of the hours of work, the introduction of rest periods, etc., except those that modified the social organization of the group.

Thus it became evident that the group was performing two distinguishable, but mutually dependent, functions. On the one hand, the group was performing its technological, or economic, function; on the other hand, the activities of the group were being so modified and controlled as to heighten the social solidarity of the group within itself, and also to stabilize its relations with other groups.

As time went on, the interplay between the economic and the social functions of industrial groups became the central subject of the Western Electric researches. Although the girls' work itself was not altered, the general conditions in the test room differed in a number of respects from those to which the girls had previously been accustomed. They were informed as to the nature of the experiment, and their cooperation was invited. The girls were paid, as before, on the same system of group piece work; but their previous group had contained over a hundred individuals, while in the test room the group, for purposes of payment, consisted of only five members. They were told to work at a comfortable pace, and no emphasis was laid on achieving any given level of output; in fact, they were warned against "racing" or forced output in any form. Conversation was permitted; on occasion it was general, while at other times it was confined to pairs of neighbors. In addition to these innovations, certain other experimental changes were introduced from time to time. The length of the working day was varied, as were also the number of working days in the week, rest pauses were introduced, and so forth.

Figure 1 is a photograph of the girls at work. They are sitting in a row along their work bench, and opposite them are trays containing the necessary parts for assembly. Immediately in front of each girl is a small jig to assist her in building the relays.

Numerous records were kept by the supervisor in charge. Since an automatic instrument recorded, to a fraction of a second, the instant at which each girl completed every assembled relay, we have the minute-to-minute output of each individual over a period of five years. Other records relate to quality of output; reasons for temporary stops; the length of time spent in bed every night; periodical medical reports, and so on. Room temperatures and relative humidities were taken hourly and the Chicago Weather Bureau has supplied similar records for outside conditions. In addition to these, a number of other records were kept.

The supervisor and his assistants made extensive daily notes of conversation, and of the relations developing between the workers. The workers were also separately interviewed by an experienced person on a number of occasions in another room. In all, we have volumes of contemporary observations bearing on the characters and

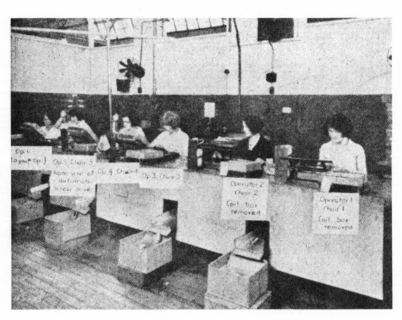

FIG. 1.—Girls at bench assembling relays. (Thanks for reproducing these illustrations is due the editors of *Human Factor*.)

dispositions of these girls, their mutual relations, their conversations and attitudes, their home situations, and their leisure hour acquaintances and activities. All this information was collected with the knowledge and consent of the girls themselves; and, as evidence that this consent was real, we may add that two suggested records were vetoed by the girls and so were never kept.

Figure 2 shows the weekly output rates for each of the girls in the test room. Each point, or short horizontal bar, indicates the average number of relays assembled per hour by the worker for the given week.

It will be noticed that girls Nos. 1 and 2 did not enter the test room until the beginning of 1928, when they replaced the original girls 1A and 2A. Similarly, No. 5 left the Company in the middle of 1929, and returned about 10 months later. During this interval her place was taken by No. 5A. In this short account no further mention will be made of Nos. 1A and 2A, but No. 5A entered into the life of the group too vitally to be ignored, and she will be referred to in due course.

All these girls were experts at relay assembly, having already had several years' experience, but it is noticeable from the figure that in every case their output rate increased substantially, the average increase being somewhere in the neighborhood of 30 per cent.

Of great interest are the wave-like irregularities exhibited by each graph. Some of these "waves" last for months, and others only for a week or two. Moreover, the

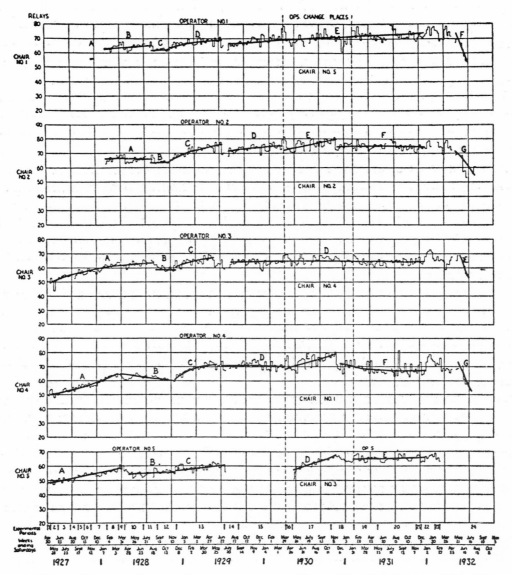

Fig. 2.—Weekly output rates for girls in test room. Each point or short horizontal bar indicates the average number of relays assembled per hour by the worker for the given week.

available output figures show that similar irregularities occurred with durations of as little as a minute or two upwards. At first it was supposed that these variations in working speed might be related to the experimental changes deliberately introduced, or possibly to other changes in physical circumstance, such, for instance, as temperature, or the worker's own physical state. But a careful analysis of the data forced us to the surprising conclusion that irregularity in speed of work substantially failed to correlate with any changes of physical circumstance. This applied equally whether experimental changes, irregular changes of natural circumstances, or those cyclical changes involved in the passage of time were considered.

Since working speed was in fact very variable, and yet so insensitive to changes in physical circumstance, changes in the girls' social relations were next examined as being possibly connected with variations in working speed. And this time positive results were obtained. Speed of work varied markedly with changes in the sentiments entertained by the workers towards each other, towards their supervisors, and towards the group as such. To give a social history of the test room from 1927 to 1932 would be to give an explanation of the major trends shown in these graphs.

We have already remarked that these graphs show an average increase of speed of about 30 per cent. In any ordinary sense they are not learning curves, for the workers all had several years' experience in this particular work, and they had reached a more or less steady state as regards speed and skill.

Nevertheless, the plateaux and spurts are decidedly suggestive. It was the organization of human relations, rather than the organization of technics, which accompanied spurts in these cases. This illustrates the futility of attending exclusively to the economic motivation of workers, or to their physical conditions of work. These things are of high importance; but no group of workers can be expected to remain satisfied, or to co-operate effectively unless their social organization and sentiments are also protected.

In looking at Figure 2 once more, each graph can be imagined as the resultant of a number of wave-like disturbances of differing wave-lengths each superimposed upon the other. An ocean, such as the North Atlantic, only too frequently provides us with an analogy. So often it is simultaneously disturbed from shore to shore by ripples, waves, oceanic rollers, and by tides — four different types of wave-like disturbances, differently produced, and each with its characteristic range of wave-lengths. In similar fashion a work speed graph can be thought of as simultaneously disturbed by superimposed fluctuations of very different wave-lengths, or better, *time-spans*, for in this case the length of the wave is measured in units of time.

By means of a statistical device it is not difficult to break down a work speed graph into a family of curves, each curve containing only those fluctuations lying between certain limits of wave-length, or time-span, and such that, if the ordinates of all these curves be added together, the original graph results. This has nothing to do with harmonic analysis; it is just a device for examining all disturbances of approximately similar time-spans in isolation from the others.

This analysis has been performed by Whitehead for each of the work speed graphs in Figure 2. For instance, among others, one curve has been prepared for each girl, showing all those fluctuations of speed whose time-spans lie between 1 and 4 weeks — all other fluctuations have been eliminated from these particular curves. And these 1–4 week time-span curves have been compared with one another to see in what degree the speed fluctuations of one girl correspond with those of another.

The accompanying figures give this information for typical dates throughout the experiment. Figure 3 refers to April, 1928. The five circles represent the five relay assemblers in the order in which they sat, the distinguishing number of each girl being placed within her circle. When the speed fluctuations of two girls show a significant correspondence in the 1–4 weeks time-span, then the pair in question are joined by a line; for example, the pairs 1–2 and 3–4. The figures against the lines indicate the strength of the correspondence stated in percentages, and when this correspondence amounts to 50 per cent or more this is indicated by a thick line. These figures do not refer to correlations (r), but to the squares of correlations (r^2), and are called "determinations."

Determinations have certain theoretical and practical advantages as compared with correlations; but the point to remember is that a determination is always numerically smaller than its corresponding correlation. Thus a correlation of 0.8, or 80 per cent, corresponds to a determination of 0.8^2, or 64 per cent. All the determinations shown in the following figures are positive unless otherwise indicated.

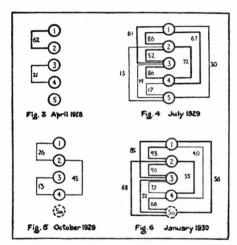

FIGS. 3–6.—Correspondence in output fluctuations.

With this preliminary explanation let us examine Figure 3. The relay test room had been running for about a year, but Nos. 1 and 2 had been members of the group only for the last 3 months of that time. As the figure shows, these two girls "determinated" quite strongly. No. 2, of Italian origin, was undoubtedly the leading member of the group. She was the fastest worker, showed the highest score in an intelligence test, and possessed the most forceful character in the room. This girl was ambitious and at times hoped to obtain a secretarial post, but circumstances had prevented this. At the date in question, April, 1928, her mother and sister had recently died, and No. 2 ran her father's house, looked after her younger brothers, and was the principal wage-earner of the family. In the main shop, No. 2 had found little scope for satisfaction, but the test room seemed to offer a greater outlet for her ambitions and energies, and she threw herself into the new situation with vigor. Her friend, No. 1, of Polish origin, possessed a more placid disposition and contentedly followed her strong-minded neighbor. This friendship lasted throughout the five years of the experiment.

Workers 3 and 4, both of Polish origin, had been friendly since the beginning of the experiment, although they had little in common except their chance propinquity. Neither possessed conspicuous qualities of leadership, though it appears that, in the absence of No. 2, No. 4 might possibly have assumed a dominant position in the group.

Characteristically, No. 5 shows no correspondence in her speed fluctuations with any of the others. A Norwegian by birth, she had lived in the States only a few years and spoke English with difficulty; and this, combined with the fact that she was married, older than the others, and of a phlegmatic disposition, prevented her from ever entering fully into the life of the group.

So Figure 3 shows determinations between two pairs of friends, but nothing that could be described as a general state of mutual influence as between the five girls.

Figure 4 illustrates the state of affairs fifteen months later, in July, 1929. Here every girl "determinates" significantly with every other girl, and in many cases the degree of determination is decidedly great. It will be noticed that every determination exceeds 50 per cent, except those involving No. 5 which never exceed 30 per cent.

During the fifteen months separating Figures 3 and 4, the group had been acquiring common activities, interests and loyalties. To a large extent the group had taken their discipline out of the hands of the supervisor and were performing this function for themselves. To give only one instance: when a girl wished for a half day's leave of absence she had to obtain permission from the supervisor. But a custom had become established by which no girl could ask for such permission unless the group sanctioned it. This leave was seriously debated by the group and not always granted, and we do not think the supervisor ever reversed the decision of the group in this matter. Group solidarity had developed with No. 2 as the unofficial but acknowledged leader; and Figure 4 shows the extent to which the girls were influencing each other in respect to speed fluctuations in a particular time-span.

Figure 5 shows an almost complete collapse of group solidarity only three months later, in October, 1929. In the interval between Figures 4 and 5, No. 5 had left the Company's employment of her own free will, and had been replaced by another relay assembler, No. 5A. This last girl was selected at the request of No. 2, the two having been close friends for some years.

No. 5A was in all respects more congenial to the group than her predecessor; she was of the same age as the others, unmarried, good-tempered and co-operative. Nevertheless, No. 5A was unaccustomed to working with her new associates and quite unused to the type of integrated group activity of which she had no previous experience. The result was that, in the 1–4 weeks time-span, she "determinated" with no one. But, even more significant, other pairs not involving No. 5A also failed to show much mutual influence. Solidarity had fallen all round in consequence of an unassimilated social element, and this in spite of the fact that No. 5A was more popular than her predecessor.

However, this state of affairs did not last long, and three months later (Figure 6) we find the highest state of integration ever observed in the group in this particular respect. No. 5A had established herself as a participating member of the group and being better adjusted in her surroundings than No. 5, determinations are higher. Every individual determinates with every other; the mean value of all the determinations is 64; and the least is 37, corresponding to a correlation coefficient of 0.6.

Taking Figures 4 and 6, the only cases here presented of complete determinations, the mean values of the determinations for neighbors are 66; for two individuals separated by one other, 57; for those separated by two others, 47; for those separated by three others, 43.

Figure 7 shows another change by June, 1930, five months later. Two events occurred to account for this. In the first place the girls had changed seats, as can be seen from the figure.

This rearrangement was introduced for experimental reasons in April of 1930, and was maintained for ten months. A change in seating may not seem important to those whose occupation permits them some liberty of bodily action during working hours, but it made a great difference to the relay group. Their work necessitated some degree of visual attention, as well as continuous finger and arm action; it thus determined the position of the body with respect to the work-bench. So, of necessity, intimate conversation could only be carried on between neighbors, although general conversation in a raised tone of voice was not uncommon. Thus a change of seating order involved new associates, an entirely different perspective of the whole group and consequently the need for a new orientation.

Shortly after this change No. 5 requested the Company to take her back and to place her again in the test room. The circumstances surrounding this request were pathetic and the request was granted. But the responsible official had not realized the extent to which this action would be resented by the remainder of the group. The fact was that No. 5A was decidedly popular and was supporting an invalid father.

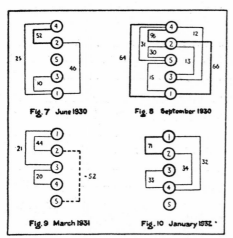

FIGS. 7–10.—Correspondence in output fluctuations.

Her removal from the test room resulted in a small drop in her wages (she was given a somewhat different occupation), and it was supposed to increase her chance of being laid off as a result of the industrial depression, which was then in its early stages. For both these reasons the reinstatement of No. 5 was disliked by the group, and this dislike was transferred to No. 5 herself. In Figure 7 No. 5 has no relations with anyone, and other determinations are few and relatively weak. However, by September of 1930, three months later, the group began to show signs of reintegration (Figure 8). How far this might have gone it is impossible to say, for shortly afterwards the girls were put back into their original order of seating. The result is shown in Figure 9. Not only has integration in this respect collapsed, but Nos. 2 and 5 show a marked negative determination (the corresponding correlation equals 0.72). It will be remembered that No. 5A was a close friend of No. 2, and at this time the latter rarely spoke to No. 5 except to snub her. The result is seen in the variations of their working speeds; when one worked faster the other worked slower. Their speeds varied in anti-phase. This is the only instance of a negative correlation in the 1–4 weeks' time-span, though more frequent instances are found in some of the other spans.

The occurrence of this one negative determination involving No. 2 should perhaps be considered in connection with the fact that the total of her determinations contributed about 40 per cent more than their proportional share to the total of all the determinations of Figures 3–10. In other words, determinations in which No. 2 is involved are approximately twice as great as those in which she is not involved. This presumably is the mark of her leadership, and it is possible that the one negative determination may be partly due to the same influence.

Finally, Figure 10 shows the situation about ten months later, in January, 1932. By this time the depression was at its height, many employees had been laid off and quite evidently the process was bound to continue. For this reason, as well as others, the tone of the relay group had been gradually changing from optimism to resignation. The future was a matter for dread rather than hope, and No. 2 in particular was again restless in the feeling that her ambitions were not being realized. The self-discipline of the group showed signs of deteriorating, and the ten months separating Figures 9 and 10 resulted in little growth of solidarity. The group had lost its spring. No. 5 was no longer the object of active resentment, but she was effectively outside the common life and practically never spoke to any of the other girls.

We have briefly compared synchronization of fluctuations, in the 1–4 weeks time-span, with the social sentiments of the workers, themselves; and it appears that these two factors tend to vary in close accord with one another. This accord was considerably more detailed than has been explained. Moreover, the story is much the same whatever time-span be considered. For fluctuations have been examined with individual endurances of a minute or two, at one end of the scale, up to those having endurances of nearly three months at the other extreme.

In every case, the degree in which the speed fluctuations of two workers correspond relates itself in some fashion to their mutual sentiments; though the type of social sentiment involved does depend somewhat on the length of the time-span chosen.

The second experiment we report has been fully described in a monograph entitled "Management and the Worker," by F. J. Roethlisberger and W. J. Dickson. A study of a bank-wiring room, it constituted the final experimental phase at the end of five years' inquiry at the Hawthorne plant. "The method of study was novel in that it utilized two types of investigation simultaneously. One type consisted of an indirect conversational interview, the other of direct observation. The interviewer remained as much as possible an outsider to the group, and the interviews were held by appointment in a private office. The observer was stationed with the group in the rôle of a disinterested spectator. His function was to keep records of performance, and of events and conversations which he considered significant. . . . The attention of both investigators was fixed upon the same group, and the one simply attempted to get information which the other could not get as well, or could not get at all." [1]

The situation that was revealed in this method of study was very different from that which obtained in the relay assembly test room. Whereas in the test room the collaboration of workers with management was at a high level and the aims of the two groups apparently in perfect accord, the situation in the bank-wiring observation room was quite otherwise. The spontaneous social organization of the latter group seemed to order itself about a certain sentiment of fear or doubt with respect to managerial intention. The group had arrived at a conception of a day's work which was less than the "bogey" set for the department. This decision was not the result of careful consideration or logical process; it had "just happened." And the output records showed a "straight-line" production which was closely in accord with the group conception of a day's work. There were a variety of methods by which group discipline was enforced; no individual escaped the group decree. As a result of these practices, the departmental efficiency records did not reflect the actual situation. The official incentive plan was not functioning as it was intended. The group had so organized

---

[1] W. J. Dickson, "Actual Behavior in a Shop." Paper read to Personnel Research Foundation, January 25, 1935.

itself — in a purely spontaneous fashion — that the intentions of the engineer organizers were defeated.

To show how completely the informal organization of the group had defeated the official plan, we quote certain findings made by W. J. Dickson, the officer in charge of the investigation. In the original test room experiment, study of the performances of the girl workers after a period of years showed that the comparative achievements of the individuals in respect of output gave a ranking order that coincided very closely with the order assigned by intelligence and vocational tests. Quite a contrary situation revealed itself in the bank-wiring room. The relative rank in output of the various workers was compared with their relative rank in capacity as measured by tests of intelligence and dexterity. "This comparison showed that there was no relation between their ability as measured by these tests and their actual performance. The lowest producer ranked first in intelligence and third in the dexterity tests. The man who scored highest in the dexterity test ranked seventh in intelligence and seventh in output. The man who scored lowest in the dexterity test shared first place in intelligence and ranked fifth in output. This then was a situation in which the native capacities of the men were not finding expression in their work. In order to see whether differences in earnings accounted for difference in output, these two factors were then compared. Here again no relation was found. The man who ranked first in earnings ranked fourth in output, and the man who ranked lowest in earnings ranked fifth in output. Two of the men received the same wages, yet one produced an average of 16 per cent more work." [2] Dickson goes on to point out that careful analysis of all the available data showed that these differences in output related themselves approximately "to the individual's position in the group." That is to say, differences in output related themselves to the social controls established by the informal grouping and not to individual capacity or to economic or logical considerations. Dickson's conclusions, briefly summarized, follow. He expresses a caution that these conclusions apply specifically to the group under observation and are not to be interpreted as generalizations.

1. Output for these operators was a form of social behavior. Their own peculiar concept of or feeling about a day's work was the idea about which the informal grouping was organized. Individual differences of performance were related rather to the individual's position in the group than to his actual capacity.

2. In this situation the supervisory controls established by management had failed. The whole logic of the technical organization was implicated in this failure.

3. The problems encountered were not due to a logical insufficiency in the wage plan. Such plans assume that a worker is primarily moved by economic interest and that he will act logically. The study shows that social considerations outweigh the economic and logical; the workers' actions were based upon non-logic and sentiment — in other words, upon social routine procedures.

4. The study has some interest for vocational work in selection. In the conditions described, scientific selection and placement do not ensure a corresponding efficiency.

5. The conflict of loyalties involved in the dissonance between the official and the actual organization leads to worry and strain, not only for the supervisor but also

---

[2] W. J. Dickson, *op. cit.*

for the workers. There is reason to believe that the girl workers in the test room, whose work closely reflected their capacities, experienced a feeling of release from this type of strain.

Roethlisberger and Dickson have elsewhere pointed out [3] that situations such as that described are commonly misinterpreted. It is supposed, for example, that there is a necessary hostility somewhere implicit in the relations between management and the worker, and that restriction of output is consciously contrived. But this type of explanation misses "the essentially non-logical character" of the situation. It is only those who assume that economic interests dominate the individual and that clear logical thinking serves these interests who can argue thus. And it is the assumption, and not the fact, that drives them in this direction. "Logically it could be argued, for example, that it was to the economic interest of each worker to produce as much as he could and to see that every member of his group did the same. But, in actuality, the the workers saw to it that no one's output ever exceeded a certain limit. Had they been asked why they limited their output in this way, they would probably have expressed fears of a possible 'rate reduction.' *Yet none of the men in the bank-wiring observation room had ever experienced a reduction of rates. But they acted as though they had.* This behavior was not directly in line with their economic interests, nor was it based on the facts of their own experience with the company."

There are other observations which make the hypothesis of a necessary hostility between management and workers untenable. The Western Electric Company has a long and consistent record of fair dealing with its employees. Both overtly in a very low labor turnover and verbally in the interviewing program, employees have shown a manifest appreciation of the company's attitude. "In the interviews of 1929, when over 40,000 complaints were voiced, there was not a single unfavorable comment expressed about the company in general." It seems to be clear that the hostility hypothesis is an inference from the insufficient assumption of economic interest and logical thinking as fundamentals of human association; it is not an inference from the facts.

"Upon examining more closely the behavior of employees," it became evident that "many of their actions were of the nature of mechanisms to resist too rapid changes in their environment." The opposition to change was not only reflected in all their tactics to keep output constant, but was also implied in all the reasons they gave in justification of their actions. Roethlisberger and Dickson, therefore, conclude that the chief function of the informal groupings which organize themselves on the working line is "resistance to change or any threat of change in their established routines of work or of personal interrelation." This is a very ancient and well-known character of human association.

Scientific management has preferred to work with explanations or hypotheses that are simple and logical. This would be admirable, if one were not guilty of what A. N. Whitehead terms "the fallacy of misplaced concreteness." [4] But no study of human situations which fails to take account of the non-logical social routines can hope for practical success. Roethlisberger and Dickson give two reasons for the failure

---

[3] "Management and the Worker, Technical vs. Social Organization in an Industrial Plant." Harvard Business School, Bureau of Business Research, Boston, 1934.

[4] A. N. Whitehead, "Science and the Modern World," The Macmillan Company, New York, 1926.

of the technical plan in the bank-wiring department. They begin by distinguishing between the technical organization and the informal social organization of the employees. The technical organization is chiefly remarkable "for its logically contrived character" which makes for rapid change. And, just as capacity for change characterizes the technical organization, so resistance to change characterizes the informal employee groups. As a result the employee groups feel that they are constantly under fire — in the sense that it is as if the technical experts were constantly battering to pieces any routines of collaboration that the workers develop. This rouses resistance, first, because "the worker is at the bottom level of a highly stratified hierarchy. *He is always in the position of having to accommodate himself to changes which he does not initiate.*" Second, "many of the changes to which he is asked to adjust rob him of the very things that give meaning and significance to his work. His established routines of work, his personal relations with fellow-workers, even the remnants of a cultural tradition of craftsmanship — all these are at the mercy of the technical specialist. He is not allowed either to retain his former traditions and routines or to evolve new ones of any probable duration. Now, the social codes which define a worker's relation to his work and to his fellows are not capable of rapid change. They are developed slowly and over long periods of time. They are not the product of logic, but of actual human association; they are based on deep-rooted human sentiments. Constant interference with such codes is bound to lead to feelings of frustration, to irrational exasperation with technical change in any form." Ultimately, therefore, the disrupted codes revenge themselves by giving rise to informal employee organizations which are opposed to the technical authority.

Scientific management has developed a logical flexibility which in itself is admirable. As applied to industrial organization, however, this flexibility perhaps creates more problems than it solves; it is at least true that social sentiments and routines of association find difficulty in adjusting themselves to the rapid "shift." But scientific management has never studied the facts of human social organization; it has accepted the nineteenth-century economic dictum that economic interest and logical capacity are the basis of the social order. It would seem possible, therefore, that scientific management has itself done much to provoke that hostility between management and workers which now so inconveniently hampers every development towards "rationalization."

There remains comfort, however, to be drawn from the series of experiments at Hawthorne. These experiments:

1. Have called attention to an important group of facts — the facts of spontaneous social organization at the working bench. These facts are of such a nature that they escape the notice of physiological and psychological inquiry.

2. The experiments strongly suggest that the excellent results obtained in the original test room were largely due to the achievement of a comfortable equilibrium between the technical organization, or plant authority, and the spontaneous social organization of the workers themselves. This equilibrium is not generally found in working departments or in other factories.

The facts that we have been considering have revealed and have led us to describe certain characteristics of two social systems, one experimentally (though accidentally) produced, the other a spontaneous formation whose existence had been ignored. Now there can be little doubt that any group of people who work together sooner or later take on some of the characteristics of such a system, and thereafter so act that their behavior can only be conceived as the resultant of social forces as well as of economic forces and of those psychological forces that are private to the individuals. Social organization is, in fact, a human need; it is, in some measure, necessary and inevitable. Its mere existence disciplines the members and gives rise to sentiments, often very strong sentiments, of loyalty, of personal and group integrity, and not infrequently of pride. No. 2 of the test room, commenting after the event on the decline of output toward the end of the long experiment, at a time when the effects of the depression were at their worst, remarked, "We lost our pride."

Not infrequently the proprieties of the spontaneous social system call for more consideration than the strictly economic interests of the group or the psychological properties of the individual members of the system. This is because the social forces are nearly always strong, and sometimes dominant. Like that of the family, the social organization of any group is *felt* as a real thing, indeed as something far more real than the technical organization of a factory; and spontaneously formed human relations are felt to have a meaning and a value that are lacking in purely hierarchical relations or in those relations that are involved in merely working together in time and place, according to an arbitrarily determined plan.

These statements, assuredly, are platitudes; but they are platitudes that are nearly always forgotten by most men of action in action. Yet, it is urgently necessary that they should be always remembered, — remembered and acted upon. Whenever men work together search should be made to discover and to characterize the social systems that have spontaneously arisen, for these are the worlds in which the individual members feel themselves to be living, just as a mother feels herself to be living not so much in a particular house, in a particular street, in a particular town, as in her family.

If you are talking with, giving orders to, planning for, making use of a man who is living in a world — or *feels* that he is living in a world — of which you are ignorant, whose existence you do not suspect, is it possible that what you say to him, what you command him to do, what you plan for him, what you use him for, will have for him the same meaning that it has for you? Is it not more probable that what seems to you good for him will to him sometimes seem bad, both for himself and for his fragile and insecure social system, which he values and which gives meaning and color to his life? And is there any ground for thinking that what is logical and reasonable to you will be so to him? If you do not know his axioms, it is probable that your axioms will not be his, and, besides, he cannot, in general, be persuaded by reason but only by an appeal to his sentiments. How shall you appeal to sentiments that you do not know?

The stability of the world in which he feels — however non-logically, however irrationally — that he is living — however vague, however unanalyzed his feeling — is of first importance to every man. That world is largely made up of his human social relations and of the sentiments that habitually arise in the course of his habitual performance of the routines and rituals of daily life. Change too rapidly imposed from without, for him is evil, because his social system cannot change very rapidly without breaking; it is bound together by sentiments, which change slowly and resist change, because rapid change is destructive of routines and rituals, of habits and of conditioned behavior. Such change is painful even to a dog.

The social environment is what sentiments, routines and rituals make it. From the most perfect family in the world take away the sentiments, the routines and the rituals, and the residue will be unrelated individuals. No doubt the social environment (the various social systems) of a factory is in many ways less important and far less perfect than the social system of a good family. But in several respects it is the same kind of thing and, as experiment shows, it is in several respects so important that it cannot be neglected by anyone who wishes to plan wisely, or even merely to know what he is doing.

The environment is at once physical, chemical, biological, psychological, economic and sociological. As a rule, we all have the strongest feelings about its sociological properties and the least intellectual awareness of them. Often these are the most important properties of the environment. Let us study, weigh, modify and use them.

VIII

THE PROCESS OF CONTROL

By

MARY PARKER FOLLETT

THE FINAL LECTURE IN A SERIES DELIVERED AT THE LONDON SCHOOL
OF ECONOMICS IN 1932

PUBLISHED BY KIND PERMISSION OF MISS ELIZABETH BALCH AND DAME
KATHERINE FURSE, G.B.E.

VIII

THE PROCESS OF CONTROL

Our subject tonight is Control. Of course that is what we have been talking about all along — when we were considering orders or authority or leadership or co-ordination. This final talk therefore may be considered partly as a summary of the other four.

In our best managed industries, we notice two points about control: (1) control is coming more and more to mean fact-control rather than man-control; (2) central control is coming more and more to mean the correlation of many controls rather than a superimposed control.

In regard to the first point, notice how often the word control is used in the sense of fact-control. We hear, for instance, of Inventory Control. We used to think the Inventory helped us in *our* control, we did not talk of it as if it were in itself a control. We hear, again, of Budgetary Control. This means that where you have cost-accounting and unit-budgeting, the general manager and the head of a department are both subject to an impersonal control. The head of a department does not receive an arbitrary order from the general manager, but both study the analyses and interpretations which cost-accounting and unit-budgeting have made possible.

Control is becoming less personal in the old-fashioned sense; control and fact-control are becoming synonymous.

My second point was the correlation of controls. The ramifications of modern industry are too wide-spread, its organization too complex, its problems too intricate for it to be possible for industry to be managed by commands from the top alone. This being so, we find that when central control is spoken of, that does not mean a point of radiation, but the gathering of many controls existing throughout the enterprise.

Genuine control then, that is, fact-control and correlated control, is within the situation.

With this in mind as our guiding thought, namely, that each situation should generate its own control, and in the light of our previous talks, what can we say are the principles of control? This is the same as asking what are the principles of organization. For the object of organization is control, or we might say that organization *is* control.

Four fundamental principles of organization are:

1. Co-ordination as the reciprocal relating of all the factors in a situation.
2. Co-ordination by direct contact of the responsible people concerned.
3. Co-ordination in the early stages.
4. Co-ordination as a continuing process.

My first principle, co-ordination as the reciprocal relating of all the factors in a situation, shows us just what this process of co-ordination actually is, shows us the nature of unity. We considered unity last week, but I want tonight to penetrate further into its meaning. We saw last week the process by which any two people may combine their different kinds of knowledge and experience. I compared it to a game of tennis. Let us now take more than two. There usually are more than two concerned in any decision. Take four heads of departments. You cannot envisage accurately what happens between them by thinking of A as adjusting himself to B and to C and to D. A adjusts himself to B and *also* to a B influenced by C and to a B influenced by D and to a B influenced by A himself. Again he adjusts himself to C and *also* to a C influenced by B and to a C influenced by D and to a C influenced by A himself — and so on. One could work it out mathematically. This sort of reciprocal relating, this interpenetration of every fact by every other fact, and again by every other fact as it has been permeated by all, should be the goal of all attempts at co-ordination, a goal, of course, never wholly reached.

You will understand that I am simplifying when I speak of A, B, C and D adjusting themselves to one another. They are of course at the same time adjusting themselves to every other factor in the situation. Or it would be more accurate to say that all the factors in the situation are going through this process of reciprocal relating.

If anyone finds this principle difficult to accept, I would suggest that it is a principle which he has already accepted in regard to facts. Any fact gains its significance through its relation to all the other facts pertaining to the situation. For instance, if you have increased sales, you are not too pleased until you find out whether there has been an increased sales cost. If there has been, or one out of proportion to sales, your satisfaction disappears. Merchandizing shows you this principle at work. For merchandizing is not merely a bringing together of designing, engineering, manufacturing and sales departments, it is these in their total relativity.

This may seem a rather clumsy phrase, total relativity, but I am trying to express a total which shall include all the factors in a situation not as an additional total but as a relational total — a total where each part has been permeated by every other part.

The possible examples from business management of the working of this fundamental principle are innumerable. Take a situation made by credit conditions, customers' demand, output facilities and workers' attitude. They all together constitute a certain situation, but they constitute that situation through their relation to one another. They don't form a total situation merely by existing side by side.

It is necessary to emphasize this because while it is customary nowadays to speak of "the total situation" — you find that phrase often in articles on business management — that phrase, total situation, means to many people merely that we must be sure to get *all* the factors into our problem. But that is by no means enough for us to do, we have to see these factors each one affecting every one of the others.

Many examples of this come to mind at once. Take an instance of a social worker. She is dealing with a girl of a difficult temperament, who has a nagging stepmother, is working at a job for which she is not fitted, and has evening recreations of not the most wholesome character. It is obvious that here you have a situation, a whole, made up not of its parts but of the interacting of the parts. Perhaps it is because the girl is working at something she is not interested in that makes her seek over-excitement in the evening. And so on. The most successful social worker is not the one who deals with these separately, but who sees them in relation to one another.

This is the first requirement of statesmanship. We shall get no control over economic conditions until we have statesmen who can meet this requirement. We shall get no grip on our economic affairs until we acquire a greater capacity than we seem to have at present for understanding how economic factors interpenetrate at every point.

I am talking in all this of the nature of a unity. This, which is a matter of everyday experience to business men in their problems of co-ordinating, happens to be considered by some scientists the most important thing in present scientific thinking. The most interesting thing in the world to me is the correspondence between progressive business thinking and certain recent developments in the thinking of scientists and philosophers. Such biologists as G. S. Haldane, such philosophers as Whitehead, such physiologists as Sherrington, are telling us that the essential nature of a unity is discovered not alone by a study of its separate elements, but also by observing how these elements interact.

I could give you many examples from the sciences. I am going to take a moment to give you one, although it may seem far from my subject, simply to bring home to you this remarkable correspondence in thinking in such entirely different fields. I found this in an article in a Journal of Zoology — a very different subject from business management! The article was on the local distribution of wild mice, and the whole point of the article was that this distribution, while controlled by food and water supply, by nesting material, by climatic conditions and by antagonism between species, while controlled by these, was controlled by them only as they were related to one another, that the behavior of the wild mice was governed by an environmental complex, that it was not influenced by these various factors one by one.

I thought this expression, "environmental complex," strikingly like what I have been trying to say to you in describing the nature of unities, very much like what I called a relational total as distinct from an additional total. And business men, as I have said, see this every day. The ablest business man, or social worker, or statesman, the ablest worker in any field, looks at an "environmental complex," sees the solution of his problem depending on the interacting of the elements of that complex.

This seems to me a principle of the utmost importance for industry or for any joint endeavor. This seems to me as important a principle for the social sciences as Einstein's theory of relativity has been for the natural sciences. They are both, it may be noticed in passing, concerned with relativity. I believe that the principle of relativity in the realm of social theory will displace as many of our old ideas in the social sciences as Einstein's has in the natural sciences. And I think it greatly to the honor of progressive business thinking that it is taking a lead here — a lead which I am sure must be followed eventually by statesmen, national and international.

Before I leave this point, let me call particularly to your attention that this reciprocal relating, co-ordinating, unifying, is a process which does not require sacrifice on the part of the individual. The fallacy that the individual must give up his individuality for the sake of the whole is one of the most pervasive, the most insidious, fallacies I know. It crops up again and again in one place after another. In some of the businesses I have studied, I have been told that the head of a department should subordinate the good of his department to the good of the whole undertaking. But of course he should do no such thing. His departmental point of view is needed in the whole. It must indeed be reconciled with all the other points of view in the business, but it must not be abandoned. Just as we have been told by an eminent authority in international matters that men should not denationalize themselves but internationalize themselves, so I should say to the heads of departments that they should not de-departmentalize themselves but inter-departmentalize themselves. In other words, departmental policy should be an integral part of what is known as "general policy." General policy is not an imaginary "whole," an airplant, it is the interweaving of many policies. Whether we are talking of the individual man, or individual department, the word should never be sacrifice, it should always be contribution. We want every possible contribution to the whole.

My second principle was co-ordination by direct control of the responsible people concerned. We saw last week that in some industrial plants, control is exercised through cross relations between heads of departments instead of up and down the line through the chief executive. This seems sensible, as these are the people closest to the matter in hand. Moreover, if my first principle was right, if the process of co-ordination is one of interpenetration, it is obvious that it cannot be imposed by an outside body. It is essentially, basically, by its very nature, a process of auto-controlled activity. It is the same as with the individual. We know that every individual has many warring tendencies inside himself. We know that the effectiveness of an individual, his success in life, depend largely on these various tendencies, impulses, desires, being adjusted to one another, being made into one harmonious whole. Yet no one can issue a fiat by which I am adjusted, I can only be helped to adjust myself. It is the same with a group, with a group of executives, for instance. Here, too, the process is one of self-adjustment. This being so, it is essential that they should have the opportunity for direct contact.

My third principle was co-ordination in the early stages. This means that the direct contact must begin in the earliest stages of the process. We see how this works in the correlation of policies in a business. If the heads of departments confront each other with finished policies, agreement will be found difficult. Of course they then begin to play politics, or that is often the tendency. But if these heads meet *while* they are forming their policies, meet and discuss the questions involved, a successful correlation is far more likely to be reached. Their thinking has not become crystallized. They can still modify one another. Their ideas can interweave. I should say that one of the fundamental ideas for business management is that the making of decisions and the correlation of decisions should be one process. You cannot, with the greatest degree of success for your undertaking, make policy forming and policy adjusting two separate processes. Policy adjusting cannot begin after the separate policies have been completed.

I speak of the correlation of departmental policies, yet the principle of early stages should, I believe, begin to be operative far earlier than with the heads of departments — with heads of sub-divisions, with foremen, and, where you have union-management, co-operation with the workers themselves. In the union-management plan of the Baltimore & Ohio Railroad, the adjustment of trade unions and management begins down in the lowest shop committees. We see this also in the Canadian railways. The same principle should guide us where we have shop stewards or employee representatives on committees. That is, we shouldn't put to these representatives of the workers finished plans in order merely to get their consent. We should bring them into the game while the plan is still in a formative stage. If we don't, one of two things is likely to happen, both bad: either we shall get a rubber-stamped consent and thus lose what they might contribute to the problem in question, or else we shall find ourselves with a fight on our hands — an open fight or discontent seething underneath.

These two principles — direct control and early stages — which I have seen in operation in some of our industries, governed some of the Allied co-operation during the War, and are vigorously advocated by Sir Arthur Salter in his "Allied Shipping Control." He thinks that adjustments between nations should be made not through their Foreign Offices, but between those who exercise responsible authority in the matters concerned, that is, between departmental ministers. This corresponds, you see, to what I have said of the cross-relations between departments in a business. And in regard to the principle of early stages, Sir Arthur shows us most convincingly that a genuine international policy cannot be evolved by first formulating your national policy and then presenting it as a finished product to confront the policies of other nations. For the only process, he tells us, by which completed policies can be adjusted is that of bargaining and compromise; if you want integration, he says, the process of the interpenetration of policies must begin before they are completed, while they are still in the formative stage.

It seems to me extraordinarily significant that we should find these principles recognized in such different fields as those of business management and international relations. It means that our ablest thinkers, men who are at the same time thinkers and doers, have found a way of making collective control collective *self*-control — that is a phrase used by Sir Arthur and I think it a remarkably good one — collective *self*-control.

My fourth principle was co-ordination as a continuous process. Just as I think that co-ordination cannot be enforced on us, but must be done by ourselves, just as I think it must begin in the earliest stages, so I think it must go on all the time. I do not think that the various people concerned should meet to try to unite only when difficulties arise. I think that continuous machinery for this purpose should be provided.

One reason for this is that there is then a greater incentive to discover the principles which can serve as guides for future similar cases. If an industrial plant has continuous machinery for co-ordination, and if it makes some classification of problems, then when a fresh problem arises it will be able to see the points in which that resembles a certain class of problems and it can ask, "Have we evolved any principles for dealing with problems of that kind?" One of the interesting things about the League of Nations as one watches its work at Geneva is that many in the Secretariat are trying deliberately to discover the principles underlying the decisions made in order that they may be taken as precedents in similar cases arising later. A member of the political section of the Secretariat said to me: "Our treatment of every question is two-fold: (1) an attempt to solve the immediate problem; (2) the attempt to discover root causes to help our work in the future."

Another advantage of continuous machinery for co-ordination is that then the line is not broken from planning to activity *and from activity to further planning*. A mistake we often tend to make is that the world stands still while we are going through the process of a given adjustment. And it doesn't. Facts change, we must keep up with the facts; keeping up with the facts changes the facts. In other words, the process of adjustment changes the things to be adjusted. If you want an illustration of this, consider the financial and economic adjustments between nations. When one financial adjustment is made, that means only that we have a fresh financial problem on our hands, the adjustment has made a new situation which means a new problem. We pass from problem to problem. It is a fallacy to think that we can solve problems — in any final sense. The belief that we can is a drag upon our thinking. What we need is some process for *meeting* problems. When we think we have *solved* a problem, well, by the very process of solving, new elements or forces come into the situation and you have a new problem on your hands to be solved. When this happens men are often discouraged. I wonder why; it is our strength and our hope. We don't want any system that holds us enmeshed within itself.

In order, however, to get the fullest benefit of continuous machinery for co-ordinating, in order to utilize our experience, get the advantage of precedents, be able to formulate principles, we must learn how to classify our experience. I do not think any satisfactory method for that has yet been worked out. I was present once at a meeting of heads of departments in a large shop, and heard one of these heads say in regard to a case they were discussing, "We had a problem like this two or three years ago. Does anyone remember how we treated that?" No one did! We talk much about learning from experience, but we cannot do that unless we (1) observe our experience, (2) keep records of our experience, and (3) organize our experience, that is, relate one bit to another. Unrelated experience is of little use to us; we can never make wise decisions from isolated bits, only as we see the parts in relation to one another.

I have given four principles of organization. These principles show the basis of control, show the process of control, show that control is a process. They show us control as self-generated through a process of the interweaving of the parts. The degree of correlation is the measure of control: the more complete the reciprocal adjusting, the more complete the control.

We find this principle also in the sciences. I said a few moments ago that scientists are finding that the nature of the unities they deal with is governed by a certain principle and that that is the same principle which we find in the co-ordinations that appear in the running of a business. I want now to go further and say that both scientists and business men find that this principle of unity is the principle of control, that is, that organization is control.

Biologists tell us that the organizing activity of the organism is the directing activity, that the organism gets its power of self-direction through being an organism, that is, through the functional relating of its parts.

On the physiological level, control means co-ordination. I can't get up in the morning, I can't walk downstairs without that co-ordination of muscles which is control. The athlete has more of that co-ordination than I have and therefore has more control than I have.

On the personal level I gain more and more control over myself as I co-ordinate my various tendencies.

This is just what we have found in business. Let me remind you how often we have noticed this even in the few illustrations I have had time to give you in these talks. We saw last week that if the price of a certain article has to be lowered, the situation will not be controlled by the production manager's solution of the problem, nor by the sales manager's. The situation will be controlled when these two men and the others concerned unite their different points of view. We saw that if the personnel manager tries to force his opinion of a worker on the foreman, or the foreman tries to force his point of view on the personnel manager, the situation will not be controlled.

The question of the debt to America will find no satisfactory solution if either America tries to force her will on England or England tries to force her will on America. We shall have control of the situation only if England and America are able to unite their different points of view, only if we can find what I have called in these talks an integration. A writer in the *Observer* last Sunday spoke of the divergence between English and American opinion on the debt question, but added that there were indications that we might yet be able to get the hyphen back into Anglo-American opinion. That expresses wittily and concisely what I have taken two hours to say to you. His hyphen is a symbol of my integration. If instead of an English opinion and an American opinion, we can get an Anglo-American opinion, that unity will mean control of the situation.

But this is in the nature of an aside. What I was doing was looking back over our four talks to see what indications we had that this conception of unity and control as synonymous is gaining ground today in the running of business or of any enterprise. One very clear indication, I think, is the fact that in seeking for leaders we are not thinking first of the ability to dominate people. The head of one of the women's organizations in the War told me that on one occasion when a woman offered herself for work, she was asked by the board which received applications what she considered her qualifications for an officer's position. She replied, "Because I have had so much to do with blacks." The board were amused; they had in their minds quite other qualifications for officers' positions than that of being a disciplinarian.

The leader has not only to deal with people but with situations. I think I may say now what I could not say so definitely in my talk on leadership because we had not then considered this subject of correlation, that an understanding of the process of correlation is one of the chief requirements of leadership. We all see this every day. If my maids don't get on well together, it isn't enough for me to command them to do so, and it certainly isn't enough for me to preach brotherly love. I must find out just what adjustments to each other they find difficult to make and show them how to correlate those particular differences. I think this matter of brotherly love has been terribly exaggerated, as between people or between nations. There is no use in preaching that to us unless we are told *how* to live in brotherly love. I know plenty of people who want to, who simply don't know how to. It is of course a good thing for men and women of different nations to feel kindly toward one another, but it won't meet emergencies unless we know how to integrate our differences, or, to use the language of the *Observer* correspondent, unless we know how to put the hyphen in.

I had two chief points to make about control. One, which I have been considering, that it comes from unity, organization, integration. The second is that control is a process. We have had indications of that, too, throughout these talks. Let me mention one. In my first talk I spoke to you of obedience. It was difficult for me to say all that I wished to about that until we had got to this place in our thinking. I think we should consider obedience as one moment in a continuous process. If I obey and do my work in the best way possible, obey intelligently, that obedience may get incorporated in the next order. With this conception you don't see order and obedience as two entirely different things. You see them as part of a whole. You see a process; one moment in that process we may call an order, another moment we may call obedience. Life is continuous and it is for us to see the connection between one moment and another. Life is whole and it is for us to see it whole. To realize that our aim is control, and to recognize that obedience contributes to that control as well as the order, is I think to get the whole fun out of working together, whether we are the ones who obey or the ones who order.

If you look at business not theoretically, but as it is, you don't find the board of directors controlling the general manager and the general manager the sales manager and the sales manager the salesman. You see that all the time many are sharing in the control, that they are taking part in a process.

I must take the precaution here to repeat to you what I have said before, that as I am talking largely of tendencies in these talks, I can say few things that are a hundred per cent true. We know that a board of directors may have a certain policy, as, for instance, in regard to labor, and that policy must be accepted throughout the plant. But in the daily routine of buying and manufacturing, advertising and selling, what I have said is true.

And if control is the process of the inter-functioning of the parts, if the most perfect control is where we have the inter-functioning of all the parts, then I think the workers should have a share, not from any vague idea of democracy, not because of their "rights," but simply because if you leave out one element in a situation you will have just that much less control. It has been found that piece-rates cannot be wholly decided by an expert, the question of fatigue cannot be wholly decided by psychologists, the cost of living cannot be wholly decided by statisticians. And so on.

And it is because of this conception of control which I have been giving you that I cannot believe in "workers' control" as advocated by some in the Labor Party. I think managers and workers should share in a joint control. This to my mind is so important that I am sorry it could not have a larger place in these talks.

We aim then at co-ordination in business because we know that through unity an enterprise generates its own driving force. And this self-generated control does not coerce. But I do not think that this kind of control is sufficiently understood. Everyone knows that our period of laissez-faire is over, but socialists wish to give us in its place state control, and they mean by that state coercion — we find again and again in their pamphlets the words force, coerce. Those using these words are making the fatal mistake, I believe, of thinking that the opposite of laissez-faire is coercion. And it is not. The opposite of laissez-faire is co-ordination.

Others who do not believe in state control are urging National Planning Boards of experts to co-ordinate industry. If these boards were to be composed of the heads of industry or their representatives we might hope to have the kind of self-adjusting, of self-correlating which I have been describing to you, but I have not seen any plan which allows for this process. Therefore I do not believe that as at present conceived they will bring us any appreciable degree of co-ordination. The policies of our different industrial and economic organizations will have to be adjusted to one another by changes not imposed by an outside authority, but voluntarily undertaken, no, not exactly undertaken, but spontaneously brought about by the process of interpenetration. In order for this to be done, the planning boards will have to be composed of the heads of the industries themselves, of course with expert economists on the board as well. I think the consideration of planning boards a splendid step in the right direction. I am only hoping that before we establish such boards we shall see that both their composition and their functions are in line with the more progressive thinking on organization.

The period of laissez-faire is indeed over, but I do not think we want to put in its place a forcibly controlled society whether it is controlled by the State or the socialists or the experts of a planning board. The aim and the process of the organization of government, of industry, of international relations, should be, I think, a control not imposed from without the regular functioning of society, but one which is a co-ordinating of all those functions, that is, a collective *self*-control.

If then you accept my definition of control as a self-generating process, as the interweaving experience of all those who are performing a functional part of the activity under consideration, does not that constitute an imperative? Are we not every one of us bound to take some part consciously in this process? Today we are slaves to the chaos in which we are living. To get our affairs in hand, to feel a grip on them, to become free, we must learn, and practice, I am sure, the methods of collective control. To this task we can all devote ourselves. At the same time that we are selling goods or making goods, or whatever we are doing, we can be working in harmony with this fundamental law of life. We can be assured that by this method, control is in our power.

I heard an address by the managing director of a certain firm who said in the course of his address that the emphasis in regard to facts used to be on the accuracy with which they were gathered, and the fairness and balanced judgment with which they were interpreted. Now, he said, we are coming to know that we can *make* facts. It seems to me that there is much food for thought in that sentence. We need not wait on events, we can create events.

I cannot do better than end with some words written by Wells long ago in the first chapter of "The New Machiavelli." "It is," he said, "the old appeal indeed for the unification of human effort and the ending of confusion. . . . The last written dedication of all those I burnt last night was to no single man, but to the socially constructive passion — in any man."

IX

THE PROS AND CONS OF FUNCTIONALIZATION

By

JOHN LEE, C.B.E.

REPRINTED BY PERMISSION OF MR. F. D. STUART, FROM THE REPORT OF
THE TWENTY-SEVENTH LECTURE CONFERENCE FOR WORKS
DIRECTORS, MANAGERS, FOREMEN AND FOREWOMEN,
HELD AT BALLIOL COLLEGE, OXFORD,
SEPTEMBER 27TH TO 30TH, 1928

&OS AND CONS OF FUNCTIONALIZATION

[handwritten in margin: Winter 1942-4, WWI little 1956, OX]

orting to reflect that one of the vastest pieces of industrial organization
f the world was associated with the beginnings of an undying literature.
f Solomon's temple called for a closeness of organization which amazes
t is examined. Solomon himself was the chief organizer, with a passion
association with Hiram of Tyre for the production of all sorts of ma-
l silver and cedar and purple, and for the purchase of the services of
n, including Huram-abi, the architect, was the beginning of a func-
for there were the skilled technicians, and side by side with them were
over 70,000 of the "strangers in the land" to bear burdens, and 80,000
e in the mountains, and 3,600 overseers, probably Israelites, as de-
honorable position. One would like to know more about this early
strial organization and by what means some of the tremendous stones
d conveyed, and how the great brass laver resting on twelve oxen,
on which they were wheeled from place to place, was brought to
the broad divisions show us the separation between artistic designing,
ion, the labor of transport and the labor of building with their parallel
supervision. Functional divisions, at least in their essential form, have
There is an admirable account in Mr. H. Stuart Jones' article on
" in "The Legacy of Rome" of the organization which "without
he Imperial household, became the Whitehall of Ancient Rome."
countant, the principal private secretary, the clerk of petitions, with
ions of function, and later on we find Hadrian breaking with "the
tizen must be equally qualified to render service in peace and war"
a purely civil service with functional divisions. So, also, we find
ctional divisions in the ecclesiastical orders, and throughout history we see recog-
nitions of the fact that organization always demands some functional differentiation.

As functional divisions are urged upon us today they come from that conception
of Scientific Management which believed that organization should be focussed upon
functional divisions. So it was that in Taylor's scheme there were to be eight foremen
each with his own function. This extreme doctrine has largely been surrendered, and
functional division takes a part which I think can best be called a co-ordinated part
in organization. What exactly that co-ordinated part is to be has not been thought
out. It seems to me to be quite fair to say that functional division of higher responsibilities has its kinship with that functional division of the work of production which
we call "Mass production." It comes from an emphasis upon Men in the bulk rather
than upon Men as individuals. In a sense it is a recognition of human limitation, but
I would prefer to describe it as a correlation of human capacities into an organic
whole. I take the following definition from a recent valuable book on Factory Organization: "By this plan, specific functions common to all or several departments
. . . are each placed in the hands of a man specifically qualified for his particular
function, and instead of giving attention to all the factors in *one* department, he gives

his attention to *one* factor in all departments." It means, obviously, that what ordinarily we have called "departments" are broken up, and there are fresh divisions on a functional basis culminating in the management. From the same admirable book we may sum up the advantages and disadvantages of functionalization before we come to our own analysis. There is no doubt a focussing of an expert efficiency which tends to raise the whole tone from the point of view of considered expertness. There is a basis for expansion which is not provided by the departmental system without vast change and the addition of departments. There is the presumption that men are better suited to the function to which they are allotted and that they will be for that reason more happy and confident in their work. Then there is the fact that it is a type of specialization which is in accord with the spirit of the age. So far for advantages. On the other hand, a precise delimitation of function is exceedingly difficult to fit in with an organization, and it does happen that a functional organization is very complex. It demands a sense of organization which conflicts with many natural human instincts and especially with the instinct of control, for to fit in a functional organization demands self-surrender. There is also a danger lest responsibility should be passed from function to function, since it is exceedingly difficult to divide and to define the functions with sufficient precision. Lastly there is the fear lest the functional division should not fit in with human qualities, so that capacities and inclinations may either overlap or find themselves lost between functions.

When we come to examine the position in our own way it is as well to remember that functional divisions of authority and of responsibility differ in degree rather than in kind. Put as we have put it above there would seem to be a fundamental difference between the departmental and the functional system, the former being sometimes called "geographical" or "territorial." It is very doubtful if there is today a purely "geographical" system of division in any industry. At any rate the accounting will be separate and will function for all the departments; so will the technical processes and at the other end the sales. Then it should be remembered that in life there is a considerable adoption of the functional system. The professions are functional and indeed as time goes on the functional side is emphasized, as can be seen in the medical profession, where it is now customary for two or three medical men to be associated together in serving a district, a remarkable change from the "geographical" or "territorial" to the "functional," and very considerably aided by the telephone and the motor-car. We may say, therefore, that in industry we are faced not so much by the crude issue between the functional and the territorial systems as by the more or less of the functional. Moreover, it will be as well for us to have in mind the danger which accrues from striving to build up a final organization at one stroke. "We shall be fortunate," says Mr. Stuart Jones, "if the builders of the new order bring to it the tact and patience of Augustus, and his infinite capacity for taking pains in framing provisional institutions so as to provide for orderly development." When we place a perfected departmental system side by side for purposes of comparison with a perfected functional system we are failing to recognize the fact that growth and development are of the essence of any human organization. The error which Taylor made in his eight functional foremen was to overlook the human need on the part of the workers for such definite direction as is incarnated in one person. It is true that to have a foreman who in turn appeals to eight functional chiefs is to make it but one remove; it is, however, just that one remove which makes all the difference. It was the intrusion of some of the departmental element which made the functional organization possible.

On this ground, therefore, I would hesitate to put into crude and rival divisions the pros and cons of the functional system. It will be wiser, I think, to take it for granted that the functional system is inevitable, just as mass-and-machine production was inevitable. But it is the work of human beings to safeguard humanity against many ills which seem to accompany movements apparently inevitable. A full-fledged functional system, vigorously introduced, is full of peril. In the first place it tends to dethrone the discipline of industry upon the human mind. It operates in this direction by its tendency to rob the industrial worker and his immediate director of the sense of a completed product resulting from their work. Put a little differently, it has in respect of direction precisely the demerit of mass production in workmanship. In the second place, though it would seem, on the face of it, to allot responsibilities according to particular capacities, it does leave gaps, and the more precise the functional division, the more likelihood there is of these gaps and of friction in respect of operations with regard to which it is doubtful whether they belong to this or to that function, or belong in a measure to more functions than one. This possibility of friction does much to counterbalance the increase of skill and of zeal and of happiness which follow from the allotment of responsibilities according to personal qualifications. In the third place there is a lack of elasticity; it follows in many cases that an increase of knowledge on the part of a functional director tends to bring him up against the hard walls which limit his functions. Lastly, there can be little doubt that to the really able functional director a long experience tends to irritation and to discontent; and discontent on the plane of leadership is a very grave evil. It is not always the case that the function fills all that he finds himself able to do. He peers over the walls, as into a Paradise, and he regards his reputation in one particular line as being almost a disaster to him. If only, he sighs, he could change his function for a while — but then it is of the very essence of the functional system that the functions are permanent or, at any rate, that they are not readily changeable.

So that what we stand for in constructive criticism of the functional system is to seek such an application of the system as will be least disadvantageous to human-kind. Manifestly, the continuous intensive development of industry and the increasing competition force upon us the adoption of every means to efficiency, and among those means the functional system of direction is inevitable. Where this system has been introduced to the best purpose the greatest care has been taken to procure co-ordination, sometimes by committees and sometimes by special co-ordinating functional directors. In its origin, however, as laid down by F. W. Taylor it was a much simpler matter than it has become, for it was "a recognition of qualitative differences, as to capacities required and the conditions of routine performance, between the function of execution in manipulating machine or tool and the function of planning and preparing work; and the grouping of operatives into two major divisions responsible respectively for these qualitatively different groups of functions." Thus the present claims for somewhat elaborate differentiation of function have grown from the fundamental differentiation into two, where probably all would be in agreement and where co-ordination was not so difficult. It is co-ordination which is the crux of the problem today. We may smile at the suggestion that a specially expert staff has been necessary in some cases to co-ordinate the precedent work of experts. It is clear, however, that functional development is only practicable, or at any rate is more likely to be successful, when it is firmly based upon a departmental division where co-ordination is secured to begin with. On this subject of organization we have much to learn, in general, from the Army, but in no particular is the lesson more valuable than in the means of weaving a functional system into a departmental system. Signals, communications, ordnance, aeroplanes, tanks — all of them highly technical modes of warfare — have successfully been brought into play, and they have their proper subordination to the general scheme while they have their full functional development. We may apply this lesson to industry in a spirit of paradox by saying that we shall get the best results from an adoption of the functional method where we do not attempt to substitute it at once and *in toto* for the departmental or geographical or territorial method. Probably much of the criticism which the functional principle has received has been due to this preliminary misunderstanding. It has been regarded as an alternative method of organization from top to bottom, and men trained by long years of experience and of habit to the other systems have found it difficult to adapt themselves to it. We should have made more progress if we had proceeded a little more slowly. We had forgotten that for the most part the organization under the old conditions was largely haphazard, and that we needed to teach the value of organization itself before introducing a principle which depends upon the sense of organization. The balance between functional direction and general direction has to be found in the particular industry, and it has to be found at various levels, and it is in the effort to discover this balance that we shall learn to develop the sense of organization and to find the true place for a functional system.

Then there is the question of the individual. Men and women who are conscious of their ability, who have the sense of responsible leadership, are bound to feel that the functional system robs them of scope. They have been accustomed to looking at the industry as a whole, at its processes as a whole, at its production as a whole. They find themselves not only focussed in their attention but actually robbed of other points of view. They feel that though all along they may have had a specialized functional interest, yet that it was accompanied by healthy marginal interests, and that these are ruthlessly cut off. Instinctively they regard themselves as sacrificed, under a functional system, to the success of that system. To these criticisms, weighty as they are, we have to make the reply that the functional system has some place in the adaptability of industry to be the chief force which is fashioning us in our time. Whether it be a tradition from the Individualism of last century or not, it is probable that our lack of social cohesion today is largely due to the fact that in our industrial enterprises we are not yet trained in social cohesion. It may be that the functional organization in future will play its part in welding us together more closely and more mutually. Plato told us, as St. Paul told us, that "there are diversities of natures amongst us which are adapted to different occupations," that "all things are produced more plentifully and easily and of a better quality when one man does one thing which is natural to him and is done at the right time and leaves other things." Possibly that referred rather to professionalism of calling than to functionalization as we understand it in the unit industry. Yet there is reason to suggest that just as this moderate functionalism was the basis of Plato's claim for a co-ordinated State, so the interweaving of functions and the close inter-dependence of human unit with human unit may come about from an acceptance of the functional system in industry in such a way that it may develop, but also that it may be co-ordinated. "To the Greek mind the city or state, convertible terms, was a community — an association of men — an ethical unity. It was this concept which dominated the social theory of Plato and Aristotle. Civic life was the normal life, and it was the relations which men sustained to each other and to the collective whole that constituted the problems of social philosophy."

They constitute also the fundamental problem of industrial administration. I have described functional organization as inevitable. I believe that it is inevitable if there is to be organized efficient production. But there is reason, at the same time, to be apprehensive if it is introduced as a completed whole without regard to its corollaries. So essential is co-ordination that I would plead for the continuance of the departmental organization as the basis and the introduction of the functional system, gradually, and only so far as the "sense of organization," to use words which Dr. Northcott uses in the book I have already quoted, justifies the venture. Nor is it certain that there are types of mind which suit the functional and others which suit the departmental. It may indeed prove to be wise, when we know something more about functional systems in practice, so to organize the functional tasks that men may pass from them to departmental tasks, or may pass from one functional task to another after a reasonable, probably rather a long, period. There may be an apparent loss at the time, but the widening and the freshening of outlook may prove to be an ample recompense. For it is not only that we are considering the influence of our method of industrial organization upon the men and women to whom we give the exercise of authority, but that we are remembering that this, in turn, will re-act and that the industry of tomorrow will gain. The precision of the detail which will be within the scope of the knowledge of the functional practitioner will be all the healthier when it is balanced by being transferred to the point of view of general management, or when, perhaps, it is correlated to the detail of the knowledge of another functional position. We have leaped rather too readily to the view that the functional positions are finally and permanently separated from each other and from the management. We have leaped far too hurriedly to the conclusion that the functional divisions, as we have made them to suit our industry, correspond to some basic psychological differences. It may be that the differences are not basic, and that a higher culture for industry is practicable by means of a functional system which has been weaved into a departmental organization. It may be that by some such means as these we can aid in the necessary task of co-ordination, and that we can use men, far more highly trained, and with actual experience in a few functional responsibilities, in the work of general direction, to the advantage of that direction.

Thus I am not at all ready to take up the cudgels either for or against the functional system. In the rush of enthusiasm in which it was introduced there were very real dangers, and these dangers were so evident that many were led rather hastily to scrap functionalization altogether. But it is clear that in some way or other we must provide for a close specialization and that where the same type of specialization is needed in various departments of an industry a functional allotment is inevitable. Not only is it specialization but it is particularization of a point of view. Wise management can see this coming, and set out to meet it without making a sudden change from departmental or territorial organization to purely functional organization. To go out and meet it is one thing, to provide for it, to test it within the range of its adoption so that its value for a wider range will be known — this seems to indicate the sound process. But it will depend upon the industry and it will depend upon the management. For we shall do well to ask ourselves how it comes about that in our industries, with all the opportunities which we have had for closer organization, in the main we have failed to procure any similitude of social cohesion. For this purpose there can be little doubt that functional organization is an effective means, since it demands personal skill and the frank recognition of the skill of others. In this way industry may yet take its place in the training of mankind.

Though I claim that functional direction is inevitable, just as more and more finely distributed mass production is inevitable, I do not think that, standing alone, these will be tolerable as the method of industry. The instinct of man will seek something which makes a wider demand upon his capacities. So if we are convinced that functional direction and machine-mass-production are essential to the successful conduct of industry and to the supply of an ever-increasing demand, we shall be bound to accompany both the direction and the work of production by other methods into which mankind can throw capacities and energies of a different kind. It is at this point that we can reach a summary judgment. Functionalization is an essential instrument in the conduct of industry, an essential element in organization. But it is an instrument in the hands of man, and an essential element in an organization which is to be subordinate to man. By what means mankind will be able to use functional direction in industry and yet keep himself free from its evils, if it should obtain the dominance, is not easy to say at this juncture. We have not yet gone far enough from the departmental or the territorial method to be able to conjecture what would be needed if functional organization became dominant; precisely in the same way we have not yet gone far enough in respect of mass or machine production to be able to estimate its appropriate limits. Nevertheless, we are able to peer into the future, and we can make something of a guess as to the direction in which correctives for functional organization, as for mass production, will be found. Clearly they will be of the nature of corporate efforts at an understanding of the full purpose of the industry; clearly, too, they will use some machinery of the corporate type for the focussing of a common attention upon the central purpose, accompanying it by manifold contributions from experience and knowledge. If it means therefore that functional organization makes this demand upon us, if it quickens our interest and warms our human associations, it may be that it will achieve far more than its votaries dared dream. It may lead the way to cheaper and better-organized production and thus to further triumphs of industry, but at the same time it may be the means of a revolt against the very narrowness of life, both in direction and in production, for which it may seem to have been responsible. Those who introduce functional direction with some such vision in their minds may be building far more securely than they know, and the structure after it is reared may be a true and real association, not merely in production but in that mutuality of endeavor which brings the best out of men and by that means builds for the generations which are to come. We know something of the legacy of Greece and of Rome and of the Middle Ages. It is clear that the legacy which we shall leave behind us is the legacy of industrial organization, far more inclusive in its scope than we yet realize. If we are to hand it on with due and appropriate and balanced and sensitive regard for the men and women who are to use it as a mighty instrument, we shall need to consider in what way it shall be constructed, not only to permit and to encourage each individual to do his best, but to permit and encourage the corporate whole to be more effective, by reason of the greater efficiency of the individual as individual and as part of the corporate whole. This is the task before us and we must watch all our experiments from this angle. It subtends more of human life than we suppose. It means that man is learning from industry in what manner he shall live, and that involves a recognition both of the corporate and of the individual aspects and of a *tertium quid*, the sacredness of the individual aspect as part of the corporate aspect.

A very effective parallel may be drawn between colonization and industry to illustrate this point. The task of British colonization today is infinitely more difficult and infinitely more complex than the colonization of ancient Rome. It is not because the distances which separate the Mother country from the colonies are immeasurably greater, but because the establishment of Britain's overseas must involve a nationhood of their own which yet shares in the nationhood of the home country and of the whole. Rome colonized the world and held her colonies in a firm grip. Today there must be something more than a strong grip from the center; there must be a radiant life pulsing through the whole. In industry the old departmental divisions will have many of the characteristics of the Roman colonies, and in so far as we use the functional system wisely it will seek the channels for a flow of life both outwards and inwards of which the purely departmental system did not prove itself capable. Yet in doing so we must remember that the functional system itself is an instrument only, and that it is not life but only a channel of life. This sums up the position which we shall claim for it. As yet no one can define the limits, but we can define the purpose. It may aid us to a far closer welding of the industrial structure, enabling all men's contributions more readily to be offered and more readily to be accepted. With this as our criterion we may well proceed, knowing that, as yet, we are in a very rudimentary stage in respect of knowing and understanding of what it is capable. But with an appropriate sense of balance, with a recognition of the sense of organization in which it can take its place, we can boldly adopt this and that experiment, provided that the sacredness of man is kept steadily before us, and that his culture and his development are definitely regarded as part of industrial culture and industrial development. Where functionalization unites the two it is a helpful ally; where it separates them it is an evil.

X

RELATIONSHIP IN ORGANIZATION

By

V. A. GRAICUNAS

Management Consultant, Paris

REPRINTED FROM THE BULLETIN OF THE INTERNATIONAL MANAGEMENT
INSTITUTE, MARCH, 1933, BY PERMISSION OF BARON HUGO VON
HAAN OF THE INTERNATIONAL LABOUR OFFICE, GENEVA

X

RELATIONSHIP IN ORGANIZATION

It has long been known empirically to students of organization that one of the surest sources of delay and confusion is to allow any superior to be directly responsible for the control of too many subordinates. Armies have observed this principle for centuries. "The average human brain finds its effective scope in handling from three to six other brains. If a man divides the whole of his work into two branches and delegates his responsibility, freely and properly, to two experienced heads of branches he will not have enough to do. The occasions when they would have to refer to him would be too few to keep him fully occupied. If he delegates to three heads he will be kept fairly busy, whilst six heads of branches will give most bosses a ten-hour day. . . . Of all the ways of waste there is none so vicious as that of your clever politician trying to run a business concern without having any notion of self-organization. One of them who took over Munitions for a time had so little idea of organizing his own energy that he nearly died of overwork *through holding up the work of others;* i.e., by delegating responsibility coupled with *direct access to himself* to seventeen subchiefs. . . . As to whether the groups are three, four, five or six it is useful to bear in mind a by-law; the smaller the responsibility of the group member, the larger may be the number of the group — and *vice versa.* . . . The nearer we approach the supreme head of the whole organization, the more we ought to work towards groups of three; the closer we get to the foot of the whole organization, the more we work towards groups of six." [1]

It is less well-known in business, though the subject has been mentioned occasionally in management literature. "At a dinner the other evening I heard the President of the General Electric Company asked how many people should report directly to the President of a large industrial company. He said that eight or nine were reporting at present, but that it was too many, and he was reorganizing his functions so that only four or five would report directly to himself; and I imagine that four or five is enough. Not that a chief executive should not have contact with others; but that is about as many general functions as should regularly and directly lead up to him." [2] But as this quotation indicates, the question is regarded as an open one. The principle is not accepted as final, a definite rule which should be followed by all those who seek to administer economically and effectively.

As long as this is so, wastes in organization arising from the multiplication of direct subordinates are likely to continue. Access to the highest possible superior offers opportunities for advancement and is itself in many cases a public acknowledgment of status. Personal ambition, therefore, exercises a constant pressure towards indefinite arrangements and away from clear-cut structure. Superiors who are themselves anxious to enhance their prestige and influence in an organization can do so most readily by increasing their area of control, adding sections and departments to their responsibilities with the least possible emphasis on the organization anomalies

[1] Sir Ian Hamilton, "The Soul and Body of an Army." Arnold, London, 1921, p. 229.
[2] H. P. Kendall, "The Problem of the Chief Executive," *Bulletin of the Taylor Society,* Vol. 7, No. 2, April, 1922.

thereby created. Strong personalities are sometimes unready to delegate and endeavor to exercise a direct personal supervision over far too many details. Considerations of a political character suggest that every kind of "interest" should be represented in contact with superior authority. Attempts to simplify situations where a superior has too many subordinates are almost invariably regarded as an attack upon his personal competence.

It is, therefore, of great importance for the art and science of organization that evidence of the validity of the principle as a matter of theory, should be added to the practical experience of those specially interested in organization. In fact, such theoretical evidence is overwhelming. It rests upon two simple considerations. The first is what is known by psychologists as "the span of attention." Generally speaking, in any department of activity the number of separate items to which the human brain can pay attention at the same time is strictly limited. In very exceptional cases, for instance, an individual can memorize groups of figures of more than six digits when read out and can repeat them accurately after a brief interval. But in the vast majority of cases the "span of attention" is limited to six digits. The same holds good of other intellectual activities.

It is, however, the second consideration which has caused the greatest confusion on this question. In almost every case the supervisor measures the burden of his responsibility by the number of direct single relationships between himself and those he supervises. But in addition there are direct group relationships and cross relationships. Thus, if Tom supervises two persons, Dick and Harry, he can speak to each of them individually or he can speak to them as a pair. The behavior of Dick in the presence of Harry or of Harry in the presence of Dick will vary from their behavior when with Tom alone. Further, what Dick thinks of Harry and what Harry thinks of Dick constitute two cross relationships which Tom must keep in mind in arranging any work over which they must collaborate in his absence. The presence of these relationships other than the single direct relationship is not always obvious. Yet the popular expression "he's no good in a crowd" refers to just such changes in human personality as the result of association. And they must constantly, and often simultaneously, constitute additional factors to be controlled.

Thus, even in this extremely simple unit of organization, Tom must hold four to six relationships within his span of attention:

Direct Single Relationships
　　Tom to Dick and Tom to Harry... 2
Direct Group Relationships
　　Tom to Dick with Harry and Tom to Harry with Dick..................... 2
Cross Relationships
　　Harry with Dick and Dick with Harry.................................. 2
　　　　　　　　　　　　　　　　　　　　　　　　　　　　　　　　　　　　　　　 ——
　　　Total Relationships.. 6

The number of direct and cross relationships will increase in mathematical relation as the number of subordinates assigned to Tom increases. The direct single relationships increase in the same proportion as the number of subordinates assigned. Each person added creates only one single direct relationship. Direct group relationships can be counted either once for each possible combination of subordinates, or once for each individual in each possible combination. Similarly cross relationships can be counted once as "unilateral" or twice as "bilateral." In any event the group and cross relationships increase more rapidly than the number of subordinates assigned, because each fresh individual adds as many more cross and direct group relationships as there are persons already in the group. Irrespective of the manner of counting, the number of relationships increases in exponential proportion.

The effect of these distinctions as brought out in the accompanying tables and chart, should be read as follows:

n — number of persons supervised;
a — number of direct single relationships;
b — number of cross relationships;
c — number of direct group relationships;
d — $a+b$;
e — $a+c$;
f — $a+b+c$,

computed on the maximum basis as indicated above. In the second table b', c', d', e', and f', indicate similar figures computed on the minimum basis.

Since it is not possible to assign comparable weights to these different varieties of relationship, it is probably safest to accept the most inclusive assumption as the standard by which to judge the relative complexity of supervision imposed by varying numbers of subordinates. This is represented by line f on the chart. Assuming that it is possible for one supervisor to watch a maximum of 12 cross and 28 direct group relationships, the conclusion follows that, in cases other than routine work, the rapid increase of cross and direct group relationships is the governing factor which actually limits the number of persons which can be effectually and efficiently supervised by one person. Hence the number of lateral divisions in each descending level of responsibility should be restricted to a maximum of five and, most probably, only four.

It is of interest also to note the possible number of different relationships in which the supervisor can stand to any immediate subordinate. On assumption f, for four subordinates there are eleven relationships with any individual, one direct single, three cross, and seven direct group. In a group of twelve, 2,059 per member. This single fact explains many notorious military disasters. Just why an executive already having four subordinates should hesitate before adding a fifth member to the group which he controls directly, becomes clear if it is realized that the addition not only brings twenty new relationships with him, but adds nine more relationships to each of his colleagues. The total is raised from 44 to 100 possible relationships for the unit, an increase in complexity of 127 per cent in return for a 20 per cent increase in working capacity.

The exception made in a preceding paragraph for cases of routine work, further emphasizes the importance of this principle. It explains at the same time Sir Ian Hamilton's by-law and certain cases where, in apparently successful organizations, larger numbers of subordinates report to a supervisor. It is obvious that, if it is cross and group relationships which introduce complexity into supervision, this factor will operate with much less force where the work done by each of various subordinates

Fig. 1. Direct and Cross Relationships

Table I Computed on Maximum Basis

relationship		formulae		1	2	3	4	5	6	7	8	9	10	11	12
direct single	$a =$	$= n$	$=$	1	2	3	4	5	6	7	8	9	10	11	12
cross	$b =$	$= n(n-1)$	$=$	0	2	6	12	20	30	42	56	72	90	110	132
direct group	$c =$	$= n\left(\dfrac{2^n}{2} - 1\right)$	$=$	0	2	9	28	75	186	441	1016	2295	5110	11253	24564
total direct single and cross	$d = a + b$	$= n^2$	$=$	1	4	9	16	25	36	49	64	81	100	121	144
total direct	$e = a + c$	$= n\dfrac{2^n}{2}$	$=$	1	4	12	32	80	192	448	1024	2304	5120	11264	24516
total direct and cross	$f = a + b + c$	$= n\left(\dfrac{2^n}{2} + n - 1\right)$	$=$	1	6	18	44	100	222	490	1080	2376	5210	11374	24708

Table II Computed on Minimum Basis

relationship		formulae		1	2	3	4	5	6	7	8	9	10	11	12
direct single	$a =$	$= n$	$=$	1	2	3	4	5	6	7	8	9	10	11	12
cross	$b' =$	$= \dfrac{n}{2}(n-1)$	$=$	0	1	3	6	10	15	21	28	36	45	55	66
direct group	$c' =$	$= 2^n - n - 1$	$=$	0	1	4	11	26	57	120	247	502	1013	2036	4083
total direct single and cross	$d' = a + b'$	$= \dfrac{n}{2}(n+1)$	$=$	1	3	6	10	15	21	28	36	45	55	66	78
total direct	$e' - a + c'$	$= 2^n - 1$	$=$	1	3	7	15	31	63	127	255	511	1023	2047	4095
total direct and cross	$f' = a + b' + c'$	$= 2^n + \dfrac{n}{2}(n-1) - 1 =$		1	4	10	21	41	78	148	283	547	1068	2102	4161

Fig. 2. Chart Showing Direct Group Relationships

Number of members per group

```
                              1  Subordinate
1
                                      A
                              2  Subordinates
1                                   A    B
2                                     AB
                              3  Subordinates
1                                 A    B    C
2                               AB  AC  BC
3                                    ABC
                              4  Subordinates
1                               A    B    C    D
2                         AB  AC  AD  BC  BD  CD
3                       ABC  ABD  ACD  BCD
4                              ABCD
                              5  Subordinates
1                             A    B    C    D    E
2                   AB  AC  AD  AE  BC  BD  BE  CD  CE  DE
3             ABC  ABD  ABE  ACD  ACE  ADE  BCD  BCE  BDE  CDE
4               ABCD  ABCE  ABDE  ACDE  BCDE
5                            ABCDE
                              6  Subordinates
1                           A    B    C    D    E    F
2               AB  AC  AD  AE  AF  BC  BD  BE  BF  CD  CE  CF  DE  DF  EF
3    ABC ABD ABE ABF ACD ACE ACF ADE ADF BCD BCE BCF BDE BDF BEF CDE CDF CEF DEF
4    ABCD ABCE ABCF ABDF ABEF ACDE ACDF ACEF ADEF BCDE BCDF BCEF BDEF CDEF
5            ABCDE ABCDF ABCEF ABDEF ACDEF BCDEF
6                          ABCDEF
                              7  Subordinates
1                         A    B    C    D    E    F    G
2          AB AC AD AE AF AG BC BD BE BF BG CD CE CF CG DE DF DG EF EG FG
3    ABC ABD ABE ABF ABG ACD ACE ACF ACG ADE ADF ADG AEF AEG AFG BCD BCE BCF
     BCG BDE BDF BDG BEF BEG BFG CDE CDF CDG CEF CEG CFG DEF DEG DFG EFG
4    ABCD ABCE ABCF ABCG ABDE ABDF ABDG ABEF ABEG ABFG ACDE ACDF ACDG ACEF
     ACEG ACFG ADEF ADEG ADFG AEFG BCDE BCDF BCDG BCEF BCEG BCFG BDEF BDEG
     BDFG BEFG CDEF CDEG CDFG CEFG DEFG
5    ABCDE ABCDF ABCDG ABCEF ABCEG ABCFG ABDEF ABDEG ABDFG ABEFG ACDEF ACDEG
     ACDFG ACEFG ADEFG BCDEF BCDEG BCDFG BCEFG BDEFG CDEFG
6          ABCDEF ABCDEG ABCDFG ABCEFG ABDEFG ACDEFG BCDEFG
7                        ABCDEFG
```

Note that for four subordinates it is quite easy to grasp and remember every combination of groups, but that from five on, this is no longer possible, because the various groups become a maze of confusion.

does not come into contact with that done by others. This is frequently the case at the lowest level of organization, each worker being given an assigned task involving little or no contact with colleagues. On the other hand, at the higher levels of organization where a large measure of responsibility and freedom is necessarily delegated to subordinates, themselves in charge of important divisions, the number and frequency of cross and group relationships is necessarily much increased.

But even at these higher levels, where immediate subordinates are doing work which does not impinge upon that of their colleagues larger numbers can be con-

Fig. 3.

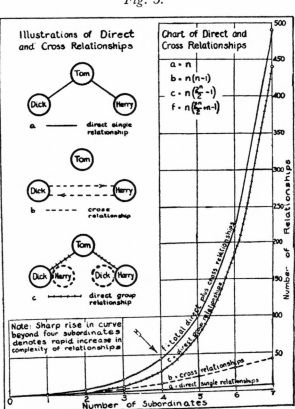

trolled. The General in command of a British infantry Division during the Great War had six subordinates reporting directly to him. Three of these were, however, in command of uniform infantry Brigades who had no regular cross relationships. Similar situations are found in business where a Head Office administers a number of subsidiary companies or branches widely separated geographically and having few relationships of a technical or functional character. But the general evolution of modern business tends towards an increasing degree of specialization. This enforces organization by function with a correspondingly greater demand for co-ordination, creating automatically a wider and wider range of group and cross relationships. The principle which has been discussed is, therefore, likely to become of greater rather than of less importance in all forms of organization.

XI

SCIENCE, VALUES AND PUBLIC ADMINISTRATION

By

LUTHER GULICK

SCIENCE, VALUES AND PUBLIC ADMINISTRATION

Administration has to do with getting things done; with the accomplishment of defined objectives. The science of administration is thus the system of knowledge whereby men may understand relationships, predict results, and influence outcomes in any situation where men are organized at work together for a common purpose. Public administration is that part of the science of administration which has to do with government, and thus concerns itself primarily with the executive branch, where the work of government is done, though there are obviously administrative problems also in connection with the legislative and the judicial branches. Public administration is thus a division of political science, and one of the social sciences.

At the present time administration is more an art than a science; in fact there are those who assert dogmatically that it can never be anything else. They draw no hope from the fact that metallurgy, for example, was completely an art several centuries before it became primarily a science and commenced its great forward strides after generations of intermittent advance and decline.

It is fashionable for physicists, chemists and biologists who have achieved remarkable control and great predictive accuracy in narrow areas to ridicule all the social scientists, particularly those in government, because of the small body of verified knowledge thus far accumulated and "laws" formulated outside of the field of the "exact sciences." It is even denied that there can be any "science" in social affairs. This naïve attitude is perhaps not to be wondered at in a group which has so recently arrived on the scene of man's intellectual theatre and has been permitted to play such a striking rôle for the past two centuries. Natural science, after all, has undertaken the comparatively simple and easy task of understanding the mechanistic and mathematical relationships of the physical world and has left to philosophy, ethics, religion, education, sociology, political science, and other social sciences the truly difficult and the truly important aspects of life and knowledge.

Social science rests at many points upon the physical sciences. Economics and politics, for example, are fundamentally conditioned by the discoveries of pure science and their technological application. The advance of certain of the exact sciences thus becomes of great concern and serves to condition and delay the advance of social science. The very fact that exact science has made a great forward surge in the past one hundred years, inevitably thrusts a whole new series of unsolved problems upon social science.

The social sciences are also mutually dependent. This is particularly true of political science because political science is not a unitary, but a co-ordinating science which deals on one side with man's political life, desires and behavior, and on the other with government and public administration in which must be utilized most if not all of the professions and sciences which man has developed.

The basic difference between the exact sciences and the social sciences, it has often been said, is that the social sciences must deal with values and ends. It is this which places them in a different category from the mechanistic sciences. It seems to the writer, however, that the importance of this element may be overemphasized, and that such overemphasis is certain to discourage the advance of social science as much as any other single factor. In many of the subsidiary but fundamental fields of social knowledge it is possible to put values and ends to one side, or to assume them as constants, just as is done in the pure sciences. For example, Gresham's law with regard to dear currency and cheap currency has validity entirely outside of any notion of what is "good" or "bad." Similarly Thorndike's studies in the age of learning, Boas' investigation of skulls and culture, Huntington's weather records, Buck's examination of public budget systems, Hurd's study of the movement of land values, King's analysis of income distribution, Mitchell's investigations of the price cycle do not depend for their validity upon the "good" or the "bad." Value finds its place in these studies not in the statement of variations and interrelationships, but in the social appraisal and application of the principles deduced. This does not mean that the social scientist will not be led on in his quest for truth by his individual value-interests, but it does mean that the results of his work, if scientifically done, may be used by others who have entirely different values in view. It would hardly be claimed that the structure of American democracy profited more from the thinking of the democrat Jackson than from that of the aristocrat Hamilton; nor that the concept of public and private law devised for the Roman Empire is of no value for a soviet republic.

It thus behooves the student of administration, along with other students of social science, to acquire the habit of separating (a) relationships and (b) value judgments as far as is possible in his work. In scientific literature, at least, he should endeavor to say: "Under conditions x, y and z conduct A will produce B; and conduct A¹ will produce C." He may have discovered this because he feels that B is desirable and C is undesirable, but if another student, or a statesman, confronts the same problem he may none the less be able to build upon and make use of the scientific work of the first student even though he has a reversed scale of values. Whenever a student of government says: "The mayor should now do A," this is to be interpreted:

1. Present conditions are xyz
2. Under conditions xyz, A gives B
3. B is good, therefore
4. Do A

If political scientists will make it a habit to split up every important "should" sentence in this way, they will not only make more useful to others the ideas which they develop, but may also introduce into their own work a new element of scientific validity. In other words, "should" is a word political scientists should not use in scientific discussion!

In the science of administration, whether public or private, the basic "good" is efficiency. The fundamental objective of the science of administration is the accomplishment of the work in hand with the least expenditure of man-power and materials. Efficiency is thus axiom number one in the value scale of administration. This brings administration into apparent conflict with certain elements of the value scale of politics, whether we use that term in its scientific or in its popular sense.* But both public

---

* See Frank W. Goodnow "Politics and Administration"; also "Politics and Administration" by the author in the Annals, September, 1933.

administration and politics are branches of political science, so that we are in the end compelled to mitigate the pure concept of efficiency in the light of the value scale of politics and the social order. There are, for example, highly inefficient arrangements like citizen boards and small local governments which *may* be necessary in a democracy as educational devices. It has been argued also that the spoils system, which destroys efficiency in administration, is needed to maintain the political party, that the political party is needed to maintain the structure of government, and that without the structure of government, administration itself will disappear. While this chain of causation has been disproved under certain conditions, it none the less illustrates the point that the principles of politics may seriously affect efficiency. Similarly in private business it is often true that the necessity for immediate profits growing from the system of private ownership may seriously interfere with the achievement of efficiency in practice. It does not seem to the writer, however, that these interferences with efficiency in any way eliminate efficiency as the fundamental value upon which the science of administration may be erected. They serve to condition and to complicate, but not to change the single ultimate test of value in administration.

In other words, the student of administration must take into account the conditions under which a given group of men are brought together to do a job. These conditions may include not only physical obstacles but also the democratic dogma, the fascist structure, a socialist economy, or the spoils system. But in any case the student of administration will not only explore relationships from the standpoint of efficiency within the framework afforded, but will consider also the effect of that framework upon efficiency itself wherever the opportunity is presented.

If it be true that the continual intrusion of varying scales of value has served to hinder the development of all of the social sciences, may it not be well to minimize this difficulty as is here suggested? This, it seems to the writer, is already possible in the study of public administration by regarding all value scales as environmental with the exception of one — efficiency. In this way it may be possible to approximate more nearly the impersonal valueless world in which exact science has advanced with such success.

But even so, great difficulties to scientific advance remain. If we may by various devices put fluctuating values to one side, and this is not as easy for other social sciences as it is for public administration, we are still confronted by two problems which the exact scientists have largely escaped. These are:

First, in dealing with human beings we encounter a rare dynamic element which is compounded in unknown proportions of predictable and of unpredictable, of rational and of emotional conduct, and

Second, we are not able, except in the rarest circumstances, to set up controlled experiments or to test theories over and over at will.

The human psyche is significant, not entirely because it is dynamic and in part unpredictable and irrational, but also because human beings are so extraordinarily rare. There are in one cubic centimeter of air 15,000,000,000 times as many molecules as there are individual humans on this earth. It is this scarcity of phenomena which makes the individual variations so difficult and important. If we had as many humans to deal with as the exact scientist has electrons, we might more easily discover the pattern of conduct and the normal probability curves of social life. And in political science, when we turn to aggregates of human beings, organized in nations, we are confronted by a situation of still greater scarcity. There is only one Soviet Union, one Great Britain, one United States of America. With this paucity of phenomena to observe, it would be a miracle indeed if scholars were able to see through to the underlying laws and set them forth, certain that every significant variation was covered. This immensely important problem of variation, which is at the center of social science, was not even suspected to exist in the constitution of matter until a very few years ago, and even now presents a theoretical rather than a practical problem to the physicist because he, amid the plethora of phenomena, may rely on solid averages as a starting point.

Social experiments, moreover, must be made by men on men. This greatly restricts the process of verification of hypotheses not only because of the value and dignity of human life, but also because human beings continually interfere with experiments involving themselves.

There is no easy escape for social science from these two limitations. The number of human beings, though increasing, cannot remotely approach the gigantic statistical arrays which confront the physical scientist even within the confines of the smallest particle of matter. Nor may we follow the biologists and develop extensive controlled experiments to which human beings will readily submit over and over for the sake of pure science. Nor may we hope to develop laboratories in which outside social conditions may be reproduced for purposes of experimentation, for after all these laboratories must contain active elements which behave just like human beings in a normal human setting — and this is precisely that which human beings cannot provide outside of themselves.

Should we look, then, to the invention of instruments as the open sesame of social science? Do we need for social science microscopes, or telescopes, or cathode-ray tubes — that is, instruments to extend our sensory equipment? Do we need thermometers, balances, barometers — that is, instruments with which to make more accurate measurements? Or should our search be directed primarily in some other direction?

Though the writer has been greatly intrigued by the search for new instruments, useful particularly in public administration, and has contributed to the invention or development of some,* it does not seem to him that the invention of instruments for the extension and refinement of the senses is the prime necessity at the present juncture. It is not mechanical instruments we need to enable us to see that which now escapes us. The great need is putting ourselves in a position to use the instruments which we already have.

What we require in the social sciences at the present time, it seems, is:

1. Analysis of phenomena from which we may derive standard nomenclature, measurable elements, and rational concepts;

2. The development of extensive scientific documentation based upon these analyses, and

3. The encouragment of imaginative approach to social phenomena, and the publication and circulation of hypotheses so that they may be scrutinized by others in the light of experience, now and in future years.

---

* The Merge-Calculator, the Proportional Representation Voting Machine, and various improvements in statistical machinery.

The analysis of phenomena, if it is to be of value in future years, or is to be added to the work of others and become part of a growing reservoir of knowledge, must be brought within a single system of definition and nomenclature. This is so obvious that it needs no further proof. It has been the device by which natural science has developed, and makes it possible for each scholar to stand on the shoulders of his predecessors, and not at ground level.

Definition requires careful analysis, analysis which must include the dynamic as well as the static facts. This will in itself show the way to the elements which can be measured, translated to mathematical terms, and thus brought into such form that they may be subjected to the most complete system of logic and inference which man has created. In the development of meaningful measurements, there may be room for new instruments. But, here again, instruments are not the first need. The first need is to discover and name the things that are to be measured. Surely we already have in the punch card, the instantaneous electrical transmission of information, automatic accounting, the electrical scoring of examinations and schedules, the perfected "straw vote," the photo-electric cell, the cinema, the decimal system of filing and classifying, and similar well-known devices, the basic instrumental equipment which is necessary for the advance of the social sciences. We have barely begun to use these devices. It will be observed that they are useful primarily in the summarization of experience for analysis. This is precisely the process which is needed because in the social sciences we start with the restless electron, and endeavor to build up the solid continuum.

The development of documentation is essential in the social sciences because it is the first step in accumulating sufficient data to submerge unimportant variables, and thus to furnish the basis of rational analysis. If we cannot have vast quantities of phenomena from which to work, we must at least accumulate those which we have from generation to generation so that scholars in considering the fate of mankind will not be confined to their own town and their own life span. The effort to "capture and record" administrative experience is surely fundamental. It is perhaps significant that modern science itself arose on the foundations of Greek analysis and documentation, and that science did not emerge even in civilizations further advanced than the Greek in some particulars, where such documentation was conspicuously absent.

And how may we encourage the imaginative approach, the formulation of generalizations, the statement of hypotheses, the building up and testing of theories? There is, of course, no simple answer. But three things are certain: first, we must subsidize social science research and philosophy through the universities and research institutes so that many men may be set free to study, think, and test out ideas; second, we must make it easy for those with ideas to secure their circulation among their fellows; and finally, we must contrive to give recognition to those who come forward with original and valid contributions. All of these factors played their part in the conquest of the natural world by exact science, and may be counted upon again to advance scientific knowledge and control in the world of human affairs.